Key Concepts in Classical Social Theory

D1352162

Recent volumes include:

Key Concepts in Tourist Studies
Melanie Smith, Nicola MacLeod and
Margaret Hart Robertson

Key Concepts in Social Gerontology
Judith Phillips, Kristine Ajrouch and
Sarah Hillcoat-Nallétamby

Key Concepts in Childhood Studies
Allison James and Adrian James

Key Concepts in Ethnography
Karen O'Reilly

Key Concepts in Sports Studies
Stephen Wagg

The SAGE Key Concepts series provides students with accessible and authoritative knowledge of the essential topics in a variety of disciplines. Cross-referenced throughout, the format encourages critical evaluation through understanding. Written by experienced and respected academics, the books are indispensable study aids and guides to comprehension.

ALEX LAW

Key Concepts in
Classical Social
Theory

Los Angeles | London | New Delhi
Singapore | Washington DC

SAGE Publications Ltd
1 Oliver's Yard
55 City Road
London EC1Y 1SP

SAGE Publications Inc.
2455 Teller Road
Thousand Oaks, California 91320

SAGE Publications India Pvt Ltd
B 1/I 1 Mohan Cooperative Industrial Area
Mathura Road
New Delhi 110 044

SAGE Publications Asia-Pacific Pte Ltd
33 Pekin Street #02-01
Far East Square
Singapore 048763

Library of Congress Control Number: 2010924368

British Library Cataloguing in Publication data

A catalogue record for this book is available from the British Library

ISBN 978-1-84787-601-0
ISBN 978-1-84787-602-7 (pbk)

Typeset by C&M Digitals (P) Ltd, Chennai, India
Printed in India at Replika Press Pvt Ltd
Printed on paper from sustainable resources

For Daniel

contents

contents

key concepts in
classical social theory

acknowledgements

This textbook owes a great deal to students on my classical social theory module over many years. Social theory can be daunting at the best of times and its study demands perseverance. In this I have been fortunate to work with a group of academics deeply committed to teaching social theory. At one time or another 'the classical social theory team' has benefited from the very different teaching styles of colleagues and friends, Norman Gabriel, Peter Kennedy, Wallace McNeish, Mick Smith and Hazel Work. Drawing on her vast teaching experiences, Jan Law has over the past few years brought classical social theory alive for our students in her own inimitable style. I personally don't know what I'd do without her.

Introduction: Classical Social Theory

Not many books begin with such gloomy material as 'Alienation' and end with 'Suicide'. Strictly speaking, neither does this one (it ends with the concept of *Verstehen*). The point is that any list of key concepts from classical social theory is necessarily selective. In the main, I focus on the key concepts that appear in the writings of Marx, Weber, Durkheim and Simmel, as well as a couple from outside this select group. These are essential to any understanding of how social theory emerged in its 'classical' phase.

Concepts group together like family relations. Some just seem to belong together like brother and sister. Key concepts tend to be strongly inter-related, especially within the particular theoretical traditions that they are associated with, such as Marxism, Weberianism, Durkheimianism, or Critical Theory. Towards the end of each concept a number of related concepts are listed to allow you to cross-reference 'the family' of concepts and get a sense of how they belong together in a larger theoretical framework.

Some concepts sit more uneasily together. They are the cranky uncles still causing a bad atmosphere at family reunions many years after some long-forgotten family quarrel. Classical social theorists were unable to agree between themselves on precisely which concepts and methods should be considered the most 'valid' or 'scientific'. Key concepts were, and still are, 'essentially contested concepts'. Each entry takes account of this mixed legacy.

Many key concepts are highly congenial, if a bit out of fashion, rather like an absent-minded grandparent. These concepts have perhaps not enjoyed the kind of predictive or logical success often claimed for the natural sciences. Nevertheless, our task is neither to dismiss nor to celebrate the aging concepts of classical social theorists but rather to learn what we can from them.

There also exists a range of more senior members of the extended conceptual family, such as conservativism, culture, evolution, history, individualism, nation, nature, science and society. Such concepts are a lot more general than the more limited areas of social theory demarcated by our key concepts.

Some of their assumptions rankle. Much to the distaste of our more sensitive language, they always spoke in terms of masculine nouns and pronouns – man, him or he – when they meant a typical human being.

WHY THESE CLASSICAL SOCIAL THEORISTS?

'Classical social theory' refers mainly to writings from 'the canon' of Marx, Weber and Durkheim. Sometimes Simmel is included, but more often he isn't. Selection for the classical social theory canon is partly a result of translation, partly textual interpretation, partly academic consensus, partly what is going on 'out there' in society itself. In 1920s America the canon included Simmel and Durkheim, but not Weber or Marx. Durkheim's place in the canon was assured by a conservative interpretation of his theory of moral solidarity as a normal function of an organic social order. Weber was taken up in the 1930s because he provided an alternative explanation of capitalism in terms of ethical values against Marx's explanation in terms of crude material conditions. As well as making a profound contribution to social theory, Weber's canonization was, in part, ideologically inspired against what were seen by ruling elites as the dangerous doctrines of Marxism. Marx was excluded from the canon at that time because his name was closely associated with a revolutionary movement that threatened the vested interests of capitalist society. Marx only joined 'the canon' of classical social theorists after the revolts of the 1960s (Bratton et al., 2009).

The classical social theory canon emerged rather slowly. For instance, Robert Nisbet's *The Sociological Tradition* in the mid-1960s covered a diverse range of social theorists, including Rousseau, Hegel, Comte, Austin, de Toqueville, Tonnies and Le Play, as well as today's canon (plus Simmel). The 'Marx, Weber, Durkheim' canon was arguably consolidated by a truly impressive work of theoretical exposition, Anthony Giddens' *Capitalism and Modern Social Theory*, which has never been out of print since it was first published in 1971.

Since then the canonical threesome have dominated classical social theory. As feminists and sociologists of ethnicity frequently point out, the three 'founding fathers' of social theory are all white men. A case has been made more recently for recognizing Charlotte Perkins Gilman (1860–1935) as a prominent female classical social theorist. Gilman was concerned to develop a socio-biological theory in order to explain and address gender inequalities. Socio-biological explanations of gender and 'race' are fiercely contested ideas today.

PRECURSORS OF CLASSICAL SOCIAL THEORY

Historically, classical social theory can be dated from around the 1840s, with Marx's early writings, to around the 1920s, by which time all of today's canonized theorists were dead. Of course, the major classical social theorists didn't just have a brainwave one day which then made them famous for all eternity. They all enjoyed intellectual precursors, whose legacy they built on through critique, revision and innovation.

All concepts have a history. Some concepts can be traced back to Ancient Greek philosophy, some to early religious thinking. The classical social theorists were influenced by the scientific revolution that the West passed through in the shape of figures like Copernicus (1473–1543), Galileo (1564–1642), Issac Newton (1642–1727) and Charles Darwin (1809–1882). This intellectual ferment flowed into the movement known as 'the Enlightenment' of the seventeenth and eighteenth centuries. From Edinburgh to Paris, Berlin to Naples, Amsterdam to Philadelphia, social and political thinkers tried to put reason in charge over irrational beliefs and superstitions.

By the time of classical social theory the ideas of the scientific revolution and the Enlightenment were being refashioned. New social and political doctrines mushroomed with the spread of democratic and revolutionary ideas that followed the French Revolution (1789-1799). Some classical social thinkers wanted to put the genie of modern ideas and practices back into the bottle of history. This has led certain critics to view classical social theory as essentially conservative in nature (Zeitlin, 1990). Or at least this was the case until 'the watershed' in social theory represented by Karl Marx (1818–1883) and his collaborator Friedrich Engels (1820–1895).

WHO ARE THE CLASSICAL SOCIAL THEORISTS?

Karl Marx

Karl Marx was raised in a middle-class, Jewish German household. He seemed to spend a lot of time drinking and sword-fencing while at university in the mid-1830s. After dabbling in Romantic poetry, dedicated to his future wife Jenny, he eventually wrote a doctoral thesis on some obscure aspects of Greek philosophy. Becoming more politically radical, Marx moved to Paris and was greatly influenced by the left-wing workers he met there. In the 1840s Marx wrote a series of (mostly unpublished) works, including the 'Paris Manuscripts' (1844) and the 'Theses on Feuerbach' (1845). He also met and collaborated with his lifelong supporter Friedrich Engels on *The German Ideology* (1845–6) and the (in)famous *Communist Manifesto* (1848).

After a stint in Belgium, Marx was forced to flee to London for political reasons. There he became involved with the International Workingmen's Association and ended up spending long periods between political activities studying in London's British Museum. Based on notes he took from a wide range of sources, he worked furiously through the night in his cramped home to write a large number of preliminary critical notes, known later as the *Grundrisse*, or 'Outlines' (1857–8).

Marx rarely produced finished versions of any of his ambitious studies. The exception to his legendary under-achievement is the first volume of *Capital* (1867), Marx's masterpiece of critical analysis of the relatively new capitalist society. Two other volumes of *Capital* were later edited and published by Engels only after Marx's death in 1888.

Where to look

A riveting and irreverent account of Marx's life and works is given by Francis Wheen in his *Karl Marx* (2000). More concisely, David McLellan cuts to the chase in his hugely informative and impossibly brief introduction, at a mere 80 pages, to *Marx* (1997). As a leading authority on Marx, David McLellan has also written a longer definitive account in *Karl Marx: A Biography* (2006). Werner Blumenberg's *Karl Marx: An Illustrated History* (1998) has plenty of pictures of the Marxes, their friends and associates, and the various places where they lived. Current debates over Marx's legacy can be found in a wide range of scholarly and political journals, including *New Left Review, Historical Materialism, Rethinking Marxism, Critique, Capital & Class, International Socialism* and *Monthly Review*.

Friedrich Engels

Engels not only supported Marx materially, politically and emotionally but was also a considerable social theorist in his own right. Before ever meeting Marx, Engels, the son of a wealthy factory owner, produced one of the great early sociological surveys, *The Condition of the Working Class in England* (1844). This book remains a powerful indictment from Engels' own personal observations, as well as official sources, of the mass human suffering in the heartlands of urban capitalism.

Despite producing a number of other studies of gender, housing, warfare, Darwinism, technology and colonialism, Engels was eclipsed by the grandeur and depth of Marx's vision. His reputation also suffered badly through an association with the discredited Communist regimes that appeared first in Russia in the 1930s. A much more sympathetic, if humanly flawed, Engels emerges in Tristan Hunt's enthralling (2009) biography *The Frock-Coated Communist*.

Where to look

Engels' own contribution is often subsumed under that of Marx. As well as Hunt's (2009) biography of Engels' life and work, Terrell Carver's

Engels: A Very Short Introduction (2003) outlines the main developments in his thought, while Pete Thomas discusses Engels' scientific method in *Marxism and Scientific Socialism* (2008).

Max Weber

Max Weber (1864–1920) came from a middle-class family in Germany and was surrounded from an early age by liberal intellectuals and businessmen. Weber was a precocious child. Much has been made of the role of an overbearing and religiously pious mother in his intellectual and emotional development. He married his distant cousin, Marianne Weber, who would play a central role in promoting Weber's intellectual importance after his death.

Like Marx, at university Weber got mixed up in male-only drinking fraternities and duelling societies. Unlike Marx, Weber was bitten by German nationalism, opposed the immigration of Polish labour, and served for a time with the German military. He also developed a rather ambiguous attitude to capitalism, the state, modernity and even Berlin, the city of his youth.

At the age of 26, Weber wrote his post-doctoral dissertation on 'The Agrarian History of Rome' (1891) and produced 'at lightning speed' a very lengthy official study of rural labour in east Prussia (1893). Weber soon became an established academic and campaigned for social and political reform from the top of the German political system.

With his father's death in 1898, Weber became even more neurotic. He suffered a nervous breakdown and for almost four years was unable to work. Weber's *Protestant Ethic and the Spirit of Capitalism* (1905) represented a spectacular return to the centre of intellectual life. Although unable to teach, Weber enjoyed another burst of intellectual ferment, writing a wide range of material that was collected and published posthumously by Marianne Weber as *Economy and Society*.

Where to look

Weber's troubled life and theoretical achievements are detailed in Joachim Radkau's monumental intellectual biography, *Max Weber* (2009). Dirk Kasler's *Max Weber: An Introduction to His Life and Work* (1988) considers the relationship between Weber's life and work. Reinhard Bendix's *Max Weber: An Intellectual Portrait* (1992) and Arthur Mitzman's *The Iron Cage: An Historical Interpretation of Max Weber* (1985) provide more detailed and equally fascinating accounts of the tensions in Weber's life, theory and politics. Frank Parkin has far less to say about Weber's psychological state of mind but is incisive on his social theory in an admirably short introduction to his *Max Weber* (2002). The continuing vitality of Weber scholarship can be gleaned from the specialist journal *Max Weber Studies* as well as *Journal of Classical Sociology* and mainstream sociology journals.

Emile Durkheim

Emile Durkheim (1858–1917) grew up in a Jewish family against a background of political turmoil. French society was rocked by a humiliating defeat in the Franco-Prussian war of 1870–71, which anti-Semites blamed on Jews. This was closely followed by the experiment in popular working-class democracy of the Paris Commune in 1871,which was crushed by the authorities with terrifying levels of violence and brutality.

Durkheim's family life was austere and modest. They particularly valued hard work, humility and merit. After repeated attempts to pass the entrance exams, Durkheim left the provinces to attend one of Paris's top schools, the *Ecole Normale Superieure*, to study for a teacher's degree in philosophy and a doctorate. There the serious Durkheim shone among a brilliant group of young intellectuals. He encountered the philosophy of Immanuel Kant (1724-1804) and the sociological writings of Auguste Comte (1798-1857). Combined, these influences later led him to work out a systematic form of 'sociological Kantianism'.

After a short spell as a school teacher he spent a year in Germany studying the university system, where he admired 'the hard working habits' of both students and teachers. Durkheim was mainly excited about German developments in the new subject of sociology.

Back in France, Durkheim was appointed the first ever lecturer in social science and education in 1887 at the University of Bordeaux. Durkheim approached his workload with methodical vigour, writing numerous articles, founding and editing perhaps the most influential social science journal ever, the *Annee sociologique*, and still managed to write three classic books: *The Division of Labour in Society* (1893), *The Rules of Sociological Method* (1895), and *Suicide* (1897). He also intervened as a public intellectual to defend civic republicanism against the anti-Semitism stirred up by 'the Dreyfus Affair' in 1898, when Captain Dreyfus, a Jew, was falsely accused by the authorities of treason.

In 1902 Durkheim was elevated to a post in education at the Sorbonne in Paris. Sociology had not yet been established as a respectable academic discipline. Durkheim saw it as his job to win recognition for sociology by placing it on a more systematic and less speculative footing than his predecessor Comte. He used his position to attract a group of talented 'young Durkheimians'. After encountering William Robertson Smith's

(2002[1894]) comparative history of religion Durkheim experienced a 'revelation', which culminated in perhaps his most brilliant study, *The Elementary Forms of Religious Life* (1912). Durkheim's health faltered from overwork and the severe grief he felt at the loss of his only son during the 1914–18 war, which he had supported as a patriotic duty 'against the German mentality'. In 1916 Durkheim died at the age of 59, with his grand ambition for sociology still incomplete.

Where to look

Durkheim has been well served by Steven Lukes' brilliant historical account of his life and work, *Emile Durkheim* (1992). There is no shortage of effective introductions to his work. Robert Alun Jones' *Emile Durkheim* (1986) examines carefully Durkheim's four major works. Kenneth Thompson's short introduction *Emile Durkheim* (2002) ranges a bit more widely over his life and politics. Anthony Giddens' *Durkheim* (1978) is concise and critical. Frank Parkin's short book *Durkheim* (1992) goes straight to the heart of the key issues raised by Durkheim's social theory: science, law, religion, socialism, and the state. Current Durkheim scholarship is ably represented by the journal *Durkheimian Studies* and more broadly across social theory journals.

Georg Simmel

Georg Simmel (1858–1918) has not always been, but is increasingly, recognized as a highly original voice among the classical social theorists. Simmel grew up in the centre of Berlin, then rapidly developing into a modern metropolitan city. His urban experience stimulated an individualistic intellectual outlook. He never fitted neatly into the mould of a specialized sociology defined by systematic scientific methods.

He came from a Jewish background but was baptized a Christian. Although widely recognized as a gifted intellectual and lecturer, Simmel continually met with anti-Semitic discrimination, which prevented him from securing an established academic position, despite the personal support of luminaries like Max Weber. He was supported financially by a friend of the family after his father died, allowing him to complete his studies and live as an independent scholar.

Simmel was nothing if not prolific. By the time of his death in 1918 he had published 25 books and around 300 articles, reviews and other pieces. His range of interests was wide and varied but never superficial or trivial. He studied psychology, philosophy, culture, music and history, and was awarded a doctorate in 1881 for a dissertation on Kant's philosophy. This allowed him to teach at the University of Berlin, but only on a freelance basis.

Simmel was often concerned with problems of social psychology and saw himself foremost as a philosopher rather than a professional sociologist. His first major work *On Social Differentiation* (1890) drew upon evolutionary ideas in social theory. An intense interest in social theory lasted about two decades, from the late 1880s to 1908. In that time he produced two further landmark studies in social theory: *The Philosophy of Money* (1900) and *Sociology: Inquiries Into the Construction of Social Forms* (1908).

His book on money is a quite brilliant analysis of its positive and negative effects on subjective experience, value and culture. His huge *Sociology* brought together Simmel's wider reflections on sociology over 20 years. While the book was well received, many criticized Simmel's lack of an overarching theoretical system. But this is exactly what Simmel argues in the book cannot be done since his object – society – no longer possesses inner cohesion or stability. While a number of scholars later detected certain underlying principles in his *Sociology* – form, reciprocity, distance, dualism, number, space, processes – Simmel himself never singled these out as holding everything else together.

Where to look

Unfortunately, Simmel has not been made the subject of an extended English language biography in the manner of McLellan on Marx, Lukes on Durkheim, or Radkau on Weber. The best, almost the only, coherent available introduction to Simmel's life and work remains David Frisby's lucid *Georg Simmel* (2002). A more specific consideration of Simmel's life and work is offered in Frisby's *Sociological Impressionism* (1992a). Simmel's monumental *Sociology* has only recently been fully translated into English (Simmel, 2009). Nicholas J. Spykman's *The Social Theory of Georg Simmel* (1925) was an early attempt to pull together the disparate threads of Simmel's life and work for an Anglophone readership and stood alone as an overview of Simmel until the 1980s. Ralph Leck's *Georg Simmel and Avant-Garde Sociology* (2000) situates Simmel within the contemporary cultural currents of modernism, while Gary Jaworski's *Georg Simmel and the American Prospect* (1997) discusses Simmel's reception in the United States. Simmel is regularly the subject of social theory journals such as *Theory, Culture & Society* and *Journal of Classical Sociology*.

WHERE TO GO NEXT

In this book I set out the main ideas associated with each key concept and the kind of problem it has tried to address. Wherever possible, I have closely followed the author's own words and tried to convey how vivid and fresh much of this writing still reads today. An all too brief discussion at the end of each entry points to some of the critical debates and developments in response to the concept.

My basic outline of each concept is intended to encourage you to read the original authors for yourself. At the end of each concept suggestions are made for further reading. The language used can sometimes seem a little strange at first. You may be put off by the reputation of classical thinkers as particularly 'difficult' to digest. In fact, if read with a little care and concentration the original works are often far more accessible and better written than some of the later books that comment on them.

Introductory readers and commentaries in classical social theory are often restricted to Marx, Weber and Durkheim. In this vein, Ian McIntosh's *Classical Sociological Theory* (1997) includes a number of the key original readings from the classical trio. A much wider compass is included by Craig Calhoun and colleagues, whose *Classical Sociological Theory* (2007) takes in writings by Rousseau, Kant and Smith in the seventeenth century through to Critical Theory and Structural-Functionalism from the 1930s and 1940s. Scott Applerouth and Laura Desfor Edles' *Sociological Theory in the Classical Era* (2009) provides both original readings and supporting commentaries.

In terms of secondary commentaries, Ken Morrison's *Marx, Durkheim, Weber* (2006) comprehensively outlines the main ideas. Covering similar ground, John Hughes, Peter Martin and W.W. Sharrock's *Understanding Classical Sociology* (1995) is a model of clarity. Of course, Giddens' *Capitalism and Modern Social Theory* (1971) set the bar here. John Bratton, David Denham and Linda Deutschmann have appropriated Giddens' title and his concern with the wider context of capitalism for social theory in their *Capitalism and Classical Social Theory* (2009). They also incorporate Simmel into the canon and bring out the relevance of classical social theory for capitalism today in an engaging way. In his *Classical Social Theory* (1997), Ian Craib has produced one of the most stimulating introductions to the ideas of our four main protagonists in a sweeping discussion of the core themes raised by their respective social theories.

Still more inclusive are the essays in Heine Anderson and Lars Bo Kaspersen's *Classical and Modern Social Theory* (2000). Bryan S. Turner's *Classical Sociology* (1999) also spreads the net of classical social theory more widely, although Weber is treated as the pivotal figure. George Ritzer and Douglas J. Goodman's *Classical Sociological Theory* (2007) extends the canon to include a number of female sociologists. Two ambitious recent attempts to escape from the canon are Alex Callinicos'

Social Theory (2007) and John Scott's *Social Theory* (2006). Callinicos sets the development of classical social theory within a long prehistory and its afterlife in more recent post-war social theory. Less chronologically, Scott ranges across the terrain of social theory according to shared themes in a highly stimulating manner not unlike Robert Nisbet's 'unit-ideas' of 'the sociological tradition' as he understood it in the mid-1960s. A healthy range of journals regularly discuss classical social theory including *European Journal of Social Theory, Theory, Culture & Society, Sociological Theory, Theoria* and *Journal of Classical Sociology*.

Alienation

The word 'alienation' implies a hostile force or impersonal environment against which we feel separated from or resentful towards. However, Marx's concept of alienation is not primarily a psychological one about personal feelings or cognitive dissonance. It is more concerned with the workings of unseen social forces that diminish what it is to be truly human. Alienation provides a key to much of Marx's substantive analysis of capitalism, class and commodities. Although he rarely used the actual term by then, it is woven throughout *Capital* (1867) and was a central idea in his preparatory notebooks known as the *Grundrisse* (1857–58).

ALIENATION IN 'EARLY MARX'

Marx developed the idea of alienation in a series of notes he produced in 1844 at the age of 26. These writings by the 'early Marx' were drafts of ideas never intended for publication. Marx saw the '1844 Manuscripts' (also called the 'Paris Manuscripts' or 'Economic and Philosophical Manuscripts') as part of a process of self-clarification, not as a final statement intended for a public readership. When they were first published in 1932 they were immediately hailed as an outstanding work of lasting insight into the human condition under capitalism.

Running through these early writings was the influence of the German philosopher Georg Hegel (1770–1831). Hegel was concerned with the way that 'self-alienation' is experienced as a circular process. First, consciousness alienates or objectifies itself in an external object. This is followed by a subsequent process of 'de-alienation', in which self-conscious agency returns to the subject once again. Marx accepted Hegel's point that human activity involves the loss and recovery of subjectivity. However, Marx rejected Hegel's notion that alienation is exclusively concerned with the loss and recovery of consciousness. For Marx, alienation involves an 'estrangement' from practical, sensuous, embodied activity, which both shapes and is shaped by consciousness.

Alienation for Marx refers to the separation of human capacities from their original source in creative, social individuals. A sustained capacity for practical problem-solving, Marx argued, is intrinsic to what it is to be truly human. Marx's concept of 'human nature' is not a fixed or essential nature but one that changes as the world around it changes. In some respects this separation of human powers has always accompanied the activity of human beings. All human societies must produce the basic preconditions for their own survival and reproduction, like shelter and food. It only becomes 'alienation' when both the *object* produced and the *means* of labour, the final product and the means of production, are systematically separated from the direct producer. This forcible separation of the products and the means of labour fully emerges only with the development of capitalism as a mode of production.

Marx's starting point was a terse critique of classical political economy, which assumed what it ought to be explaining. Marx accused the thinkers of classical political economy like Adam Smith of proceeding from the bald 'fact of private property' as naturally rooted in human selfishness. Marx (1844: 78) called this idea of natural human greed 'an imaginary original state of affairs'. The idea of natural property rights allowed the depredations of capitalism to be explained away by eternal human greed and selfishness instead of being the result of a concrete historical process.

Under capitalism, human beings not only produce objects as commodities. They also transform themselves into commodities. Human labour has less value than the object it creates. The devaluation of the human world 'progresses in direct proportion to the increase in value of the world of things' (1844: 78). Marx seeks to understand this inversion of value through 'the essential connection of private property, selfishness, the separation of labour, capital and landed property, of exchange and competition, of the value and the degradation of man, of monopoly and competition, etc. – the connection of all this with the money system.' Human devaluation has four intertwined aspects:

1 Humans become alienated from the *products* of their labour.
2 Humans become alienated from their own *work* activity.

3 Humans become alienated from their own *life* activity.
4 Humans become alienated from *each other*.

Alienation from products

First, wage labour produces objects that take on an alien existence separate from the direct producer. Marx argues that the final product 'congeals', 'objectifies' and 'realizes' the human labour undertaken to produce it. As commodities, 'congealed labour' is separated from the worker and sent to circulate in the market. In practice the worker suffers a three-fold 'loss' – a loss of reality, a loss of object, and a loss of selfhood: 'this realization of labour appears as loss of reality for the worker, objectification as loss of the object or slavery to it; appropriation as estrangement, as alienation' (1844: 78). The products of human labour enter an 'alien objective world' as independent entities. In *Capital*, Marx would later give a memorable account of this as 'commodity fetishism'. By alienating the product and placing it above labour, the worker is doubly deprived. Labour produces spectacular objects of consumption for those that can afford them – palaces, beauty, intelligence – but produces for themselves only slums, deformity, and stupidity.

Alienation from work

Second, this separation of labour from its product merely 'summarizes' the alienation inherent in the labour process. Carrying out work in return for wages under the control of others is not work carried out freely. It represents a form of 'compulsory, forced labour'. Without this compulsion work 'is avoided like the plague'. At work, the worker

> mortifies his body and ruins his mind. Thus the worker only feels a stranger. He is at home when he is not working, and when he works he is not at home. (1844: 80)

Paid work is not an *end* in itself but only a *means* – to earn money. Only through consuming food, drink, clothing or shelter outside of the workplace does the worker feel any sense of freedom. However, mere consumption without creative effort, Marx believed, reduces the worker to basic animal appetites rather than truly human subjectivity.

Alienation from nature

Third, labour is estranged from its own nature, or what Marx termed 'species-being'. 'Species-being' does not refer to some fixed properties that all individuals share in common like selfishness. Instead, beyond certain elementary functions like eating, sleeping, dying and so on, Marx suggests that human nature is rather malleable and open-ended, shaped by changing historical conditions. Conversely, historical conditions are produced by people themselves. Life activity always involves productive activity to procure socially the means of reproduction from nature.

Human society is not external to nature. It is always a distinct part of nature. As nature is turned into a mere *means* of production, so also the human part of nature becomes a mere means. Unlike animals, life activity for humans is *conscious* life activity, self-aware, reflexive and imaginative. Forcible separation from the work process and the end products doubly wounds Marx's sense of human nature.

Alienation from each other

Fourth, under the blows of self-alienation individuals become separated from each other. What is torment and misery for the worker turns into the satisfaction and pleasure of someone who is 'alien, hostile, powerful and independent' – the owner of the commodity. Marx arrives back at his point of departure: private property is the necessary result of alienated labour, not the other way round. Private property appears to be the *cause* of alienated labour but it is actually its *consequence*, just as the gods are originally not the cause but the effect of human mystification.

Only later, Marx argues, does private property appear as both the end product of alienated labour and the means by which labour alienates itself. Access to the necessities for both life and work is only possible through alienating oneself as a commodity producing other commodities in order to consume still other commodities. And so begins the cycle all over again. This vicious cycle of compulsion can only be broken by ending alienation itself, not simply by abolishing private property or wages. 'Wages are an immediate consequence of alienated labour and alienated labour is the immediate cause of private property' (Marx, 1844: 85).

CRITICAL DEVELOPMENTS

Marx's concept of alienation has been criticized on a number of counts. It has been contrasted to the supposedly more 'scientific' approach of the 'later Marx' in *Capital*, most famously by the French Marxist Louis Althusser (1918–1990). The younger Marx was too impressed by the ahistorical idea of a perfectible human nature while the later Marx was much more scientifically precise in analysing social structures, historical shifts, economics and the ideological superstructure. Because of its vagueness, some have likened the young Marx's concept of alienation to 'mere gibberish' (Wood, 2004: 6). A further criticism is that empirically the concept is out-dated and reflects the widespread destitution and poverty of labour in the nineteenth century. Today, it is often argued, many workers are affluent and work itself has been made more humane, creative and interesting.

On the other hand, thinkers like Herbert Marcuse (1941) and Henri Lefebvre (1972; 2009) revived the concept. Since the 1960s, Marx's concept of alienation has been seen as illuminating the experience of a society increasingly dominated by commodities and consumption. This condition is now global. Moreover, the extent to which work has been enhanced is a matter of considerable dispute. Harry Braverman (1974) noted how previously skilled work becomes degraded and simplified, as in more recent service sector jobs like call-centre operators. More fundamentally, alienated labour continues to be expressed in the form of money wages and accumulation.

RELATED CONCEPTS

Anomie; Capital; Commodity Fetishism; Division of Labour (Marx); Money

FURTHER READING

The obvious starting point is the short section 'Alienated labour' in Marx's '1844 Economic and Philosophical Manuscripts', available online in the Marx-Engels archive: www.marxists.org/archive/marx/index. The best introductory text on the place of alienation in Marx's system remains Henri Lefebvre's *The Sociology of Marx* (1972). An engaging account of the young Marx's discovery of the concept can be found in Francis Wheen's biography *Karl Marx* (2000).

Anomie

Anomie represents for Durkheim an enduring and deepening danger for modern society. Pessimistically, anomie expresses 'pathological' tendencies at the heart of the 'crisis' of modern society. Anomie refers to the unhappy, asocial condition generated by an absence of moral regulation. Life presents itself as offering limitless possibilities. Individuals become isolated and separated from the norms and rules that govern the social life of an integrated community. In this respect, anomie is often thought to be Durkheim's counterpart to Marx's notion of *alienation*. Durkheim criticizes individualism as 'the disease of the Western world'. Suspended from the community and its traditions, individuals are instead forced to endure a lonely, normless existence. Moral and emotional giddiness and anxiety result from an unrestricted freedom from traditional constraints.

ANOMIE AND CLASS

Anomie is fostered not by poverty but by improvements in the standard of living. Poverty imposes self-restraint and modesty on individuals while wealth unleashes insatiable demands. Wealth leads to the idea that individuals are self-sufficient and independent since objects come to be possessed by an individual with little inherent friction or difficulty. Therefore it is not the poor that are driven to despair or 'abnormal' rebellion but the wealthy:

> The less limited one feels, the more intolerable all limitation appears. Forcing us to constant discipline, [poverty] prepares us to accept collective discipline with equanimity, while wealth, exalting the individual, may always arouse the spirit of rebellion which is the very source of immorality. (Durkheim, 1952: 254)

Even if the distribution of wealth was more equal some form of moral discipline would still be necessary according to Durkheim. Because human beings are not restricted to their biological needs alone they can never be finally satisfied by material means. New needs are stimulated the moment an earlier need is satisfied: 'the more one has, the more one wants' (Durkheim, 1952: 248). Increased affluence becomes a 'constantly renewed torture'. Only the external moral regulation of society inhibits and limits the unquenchable thirst that individual egos have for self-gratification.

Durkheim's concept of anomie resembles Simmel's idea of alienation in a money economy. A feeling of futility pervades the overexcited desires and endless distractions of modern existence:

> Reality seems valueless by comparison with the dreams of fevered imaginations; reality is therefore abandoned, but so too is possibility abandoned when it in turn becomes reality. A thirst arises for novelties, unfamiliar pleasures, nameless sensations, all of which lose their savor once known.

anomie

Henceforth one has no strength to endure the least reverse. The whole fever subsides and the sterility of all the tumult is apparent, and it can be seen that all these new sensations in their infinite quantity cannot form a solid foundation of happiness to support one during days of trial. (Durkheim, 1952: 256)

Liberation from moral regulation in order to constantly pursue non-existent or transient goals is the mark of a profound dissatisfaction that pervades modern life.

Only socially imposed moral limits prevent this feeling from erupting into open warfare. In the name of the 'public interest', morally healthy societies for Durkheim are always moderate, calm, content, harmonious, happy and docile. Such a 'wholesome moral constitution' sets up a barrier to prevent social disintegration turning into all-out struggles between individuals and between classes. At one time religion served to pacify workers, teaching them 'contentment with their lot' because it was God's will and that 'just compensation' would come in the next world. It also controlled the appetite of the wealthy by reminding them that 'worldly interests are not man's entire lot, that they must be subordinate to other and higher interests, and that they should therefore not be pursued without rule or measure' (Durkheim, 1952: 255).

ANOMIC DYSFUNCTIONS

Anomie is manifested by what Durkheim calls the 'abnormal division of labour' in three ways. First, socio-economic functions become anomic during the dislocation produced by economic crises. Second, class conflict between capital and labour is anomic when large-scale industry separates the worker from the employer, narrow specialization increases, rebellion becomes more regular, and classes oppose each other violently as 'a permanent enemy': 'this state of permanent hostility is wholly special to the industrial world' (Durkheim, 1933: 356). Third, science becomes anomic when it is broken into a series of detailed specialisms divorced from any over-arching viewpoint.

In Durkheim's *Suicide* anomie is broken down further. First, 'acute economic anomie' is a result of extreme swings in the economy from boom to slump, which undermine 'normal' forms of regulation. Second, 'chronic economic anomie' refers to long-run processes of moral deregulation as industry and money become permanent ends in themselves. Third, 'acute domestic anomie' refers to the personal crisis triggered by the loss of a spouse. Fourth, 'chronic domestic anomie' refers to the more general 'antagonism of the sexes' within the increasingly deregulated confines of marriage.

Anomie is prevented when moral regulation is strengthened by frequent, regular and many-sided contact with other functions. This keeps individuals aware of their need for each other in society (Durkheim, 1933: 368). But with the development of national and world markets and a geographically dispersed international division of labour it is no longer possible to maintain direct interpersonal contact with other producers. The horizon of the economic world becomes, so to speak, limitless and incompletely understood. The result of these disproportions is periodic crises and the rapid restructuring of economic life.

Here Durkheim comes close to Marx's conception of *alienation*. The worker becomes a degraded appendage of the machine, forced to repeat the same monotonous movements, without interest or understanding: 'He is no longer a living cell of a living organism which unceasingly interacts with neighbouring cells, which influences them, responds to their actions, and transforms itself in relation to changing circumstances and needs' (Durkheim, in Giddens, 1972: 178).

Anomie is not for Durkheim, as alienation is for Marx, the 'normal' state of the division of labour. It only emerges in 'exceptional and abnormal circumstances'. Even a highly specialized division of labour does not necessarily produce anomic workers. The worker is 'not a machine who repeats his movements without knowing their meaning, but he knows that they tend, in some way, towards an end that he conceives more or less distinctly' (Durkheim, 1933: 372). So long as it facilitates a feeling of moral interdependence and social purpose, anomie is staved off.

CRITICAL DEVELOPMENTS

In post-war sociology a vast literature debated and analysed the nature and measure of anomie. In the process, Durkheim was depicted as a deeply conservative thinker, repelled by the decline of moral authority and sacred institutions. In part this was due to the reception of anomie in post-war America (Parsons, 1949). Everything judged 'deviant' could be explained in terms of anomie as the rejection of 'normal' consensual values in US society.

This failed to situate anomie within the historical transition from traditional to modern forms of solidarity. It also reversed the causal nexus that produces anomie for Durkheim: moral regulation becomes the *cause* not the *effect* of real changes in the division of labour. In contrast, Durkheim insists that a value consensus cannot logically precede the conditions that give rise to it. Moral regulation cannot simply be imposed to enforce social conformity but to provide answers to the changing needs of the social substratum.

Robert Merton (1968) gave an innovative twist to the concept of anomie as the incongruence that exists between unequal social structures and the universal value of social success. Anomie here refers to the dysfunctional strain between means and ends. Those with inadequate legitimate means to acquire social goods, such as the poor, will pursue deviant strategies, even if this means criminality. Excessive constraint on opportunity, as in the US, Merton believed, produces an anomic society. This is far from Durkheim's own concept of anomie as a product of unlimited possibilities for wealth acquisition and self-gratification.

Anomie is a deeply ambiguous concept (Levine, 1985: 63). Sometimes it refers to an absence of norms, sometimes their obsolescence, sometimes over-indulgent norms, sometimes their inconsistency. Sometimes anomie is pathological, sometimes it is normal. Sometimes Durkheim describes a situation where there are no intrinsic limits to individual aspirations and ambitions. Sometimes he emphasizes moral abnormalities; sometimes the need to restore strong moral norms to restrain an insatiable human nature. At other times, he refers to the limits that society imposes on aspirations which cannot be realized, emphasizing the strains and dissonances of unfulfilled goals leading to demands for social change.

As structural-functionalism declined in importance some return could be seen to Durkheim's original conception of anomie in theories of consumer society from the 1960s onwards and 'risk society' in the 1990s. As the rate of social, technological and cultural change speeded up under neoliberal capitalism, some detected a 'new Durkheimianism' of rampant anomie expressed in brutal individualism, insatiable greed, unlimited consumption, self-destructive addictions and 'anti-social behaviour'.

RELATED CONCEPTS

Alienation; Division of Labour in Society (Durkheim); Mechanical and Organic Solidarity; Normal and Pathological; Suicide

FURTHER READING

Anomie is introduced by Durkheim in the context of his *Division of Labour in Society* (1933) and his *Suicide* (1952). Summaries are available in Thompson (2002) and Jones (1986). An excellent discussion of ambiguous uses of anomie is given in Chapter 4 of Donald Levine's *The Flight From Ambiguity* (1985).

Base and Superstructure

Marx used the metaphor of 'base and superstructure' to characterize the relationship between the economic structure of society (the *base* or *infrastructure*) and political and legal institutions, ideologies, mass media and individual psychology (the *superstructure*). Neither the state nor the law nor the human mind can be understood as autonomous things in themselves. Instead each needs to be set within what Marx calls 'the material conditions of life' produced within 'civil society'. Political economy, the forerunner of sociology, provides the key to 'the anatomy of civil society', while civil society, in turn, is the basis of the state, law and psychology.

LEVELS OF ANALYSIS

Marx set out the 'guiding thread' of his studies in a highly schematic form in the Preface to his book *A Contribution to the Critique of Political Economy*:

> In the social production of their life, men enter into definite relations that are indispensable and independent of their will, relations of production which correspond to a definite stage of development of their material productive forces. The sum total of these relations of production constitutes the economic structure of society, the real foundation, on which rises a legal and political superstructure and to which correspond definite forms of social consciousness. The mode of production of material life conditions the social, political and intellectual life process in general. (1859: 4)

It is important to note that Marx is talking about the inter-relationship between three inter-related levels of analysis:

- the socio-economic relations in the productive 'base' of civil society
- the social institutions of the superstructure, government, law, religion, the military, education
- and a definite form of social consciousness in 'different and specifically formed feelings, illusions, modes of thought and views of life'. (1852: 173)

The crucial point is Marx's claim that one set of relations, the economic base, exercises a decisive influence over the 'superstructure' of institutions and ideologies. His argument is that the production of the material preconditions for human life – food, shelter, clothing and so on – takes analytical or logical priority over more secondary aspects of social life like politics, law, art or ideology.

Making general analytical connections between base and superstructure in no way relieves social science from the task of a careful empirical examination of complex social relations. The form taken by the superstructure can vary in numerous ways:

> This does not prevent the same economic basis – the same from the standpoint of its main conditions – due to innumerable different empirical circumstances, natural environment, racial relations, external historical influences, etc., from showing infinite variations and gradations in appearance, which can be ascertained only by analysis of the empirically given circumstances. (Marx, 1959: 791–2)

A METAPHOR OF CONSTRUCTION

Marx resorts to the metaphor of base and superstructure because he is making an analytical distinction about different kinds of social institutions. It is a metaphor taken from building construction rather than a description of reality. Like any building, the superstructure depends on the invisible foundation of its base if it is to support the visible edifice above ground level. In its strong sense, the metaphor suggests a one-way direction of causality: the economic base *causes* or *determines* the institutions of the state, culture, ideology, law or the individual personality. Taken in a weaker sense, one set of social relations (the base) merely 'conditions' or 'corresponds' to another (superstructure).

When the metaphorical aspect is ignored or taken literally, Marx's social theory is easily caricatured as a crude form of economic reductionism or determinism. The accent placed by both Marx and Engels on the indispensable role of human practice in social change, or 'praxis', somewhat blunts the charge of economic reductionism. However, neither really wavered from their founding claim that social being determines consciousness rather than the other way round.

CRITICAL DEVELOPMENTS

Later followers of Marx turned the base/superstructure metaphor into a rigid model that could be applied to almost any historical context or social institution. Here the institutional and ideological superstructure becomes a mere 'reflection' of the economic base; the superstructure is seen as dependent and pliable while the economic base is seen as fundamental and dominant.

After Marx's death, Engels was at pains to stress the complex interaction of many elements involved in social change. By concentrating their fire on adversaries who simply ignored or relegated the economic dimension, Engels (1890: 762) later explained that Marx and himself were 'ourselves partly to blame for the fact that younger people sometimes lay more stress on the economic side than is due to it' and criticized economic reductionism for 'the most amazing rubbish' produced by later 'Marxists'.

Amid the confusion and 'accidents' of historical change the economic structure, at best, provides a starting point for empirical analysis and political action. Engels could have had their present day critics in mind when he wrote:

> According to the materialist conception of history, the *ultimately* determining element in history is the production and reproduction of real life. More than this neither Marx nor I have ever asserted. Hence if somebody twists this into saying that the economic element is the *only* determining one, he transforms that proposition into a meaningless, abstract, senseless phrase. (1890: 760)

Notwithstanding Engels' disclaimer, the base/superstructure metaphor became a source of some embarrassment to later Marxists, especially those working on questions of the state, law, art and culture, and psychology.

For instance, the cultural theorist Raymond Williams (1980: 20) sought to replace 'the formula of base and superstructure with the more active idea of a field of mutually if also unevenly determining forces'. But Williams (1980: 36–7) also warned against dismissing the idea of base and superstructure in case the baby of material conditions gets thrown out with the dirty bathwater of economic reductionism when explaining cultural institutions and ideologies. Neither economic reductionism nor superstructural autonomy provide adequate alternatives to the necessity of concrete empirical analyses of social relations.

RELATED CONCEPTS

Class; Ideology; Historical Materialism; Social Forms and Sociation; Social Morphology

Marx's key statement of the base and superstructure metaphor is made in the Preface to his *A Contribution to the Critique of Political Economy*. Many critics have preferred to paint Marxism as having a crude mechanical view of base and super-structure. A more subtle statement of the concept can be found in Franz Jakubowski's (1990) *Ideology and Superstructure in Historical Materialism*.

Bureaucracy

For Max Weber bureaucracy is a, if not *the* only, defining feature of moder-nity. It represents the pure ideal-type of legal-rational authority. Bureaucracy is organized on a hierarchical and rational basis. Individuals and departments are coordinated through explicit rules and procedures, records and files, functions and positions, a transparent line of command, and entry qualifications. It represents the most efficient exercise of power in conditions of complex and large-scale populations. In its most perfected form, bureaucracy organizes the permanent staff of the modern state.

IDEAL-TYPE BUREAUCRACY

Weber (1978: 956–8) identifies six major characteristics of the ideal-type bureaucracy:

1 Official duties and functions are performed by accredited staff.
2 Offices are structured into a hierarchy of command and supervision from higher authority to lower functions.
3 'The bureau' or modern office is based on an accumulation of writ-ten documents and files, kept completely separate from private property.
4 Specialized office functions require personnel to acquire expert qualifi-cations and training.
5 'The bureau' demands that the official is fully dedicated to work-ing conscientiously at full capacity.
6 General office rules are comprehensive, stable and must be learned as the special technical competence of the official.

IDEAL-TYPE BUREAUCRAT

Weber (1978: 959ff.) gives a similarly formal account of the benefits and duties that go with 'the position of the official' or bureaucrat. Being a bureaucrat is a 'vocation'. This involves a demanding set of prescribed duties and training and an unswerving, methodical and impersonal loyalty to 'the office' in return for 'a secure existence'. Higher grades of officialdom demand 'social esteem' for their expertise in bureaucratic matters and qualifications. Unlike elected officials who are appointed or promoted 'from below', pure bureaucrats are appointed 'from above' by a superior authority. A legal right to 'tenure for life' allows them to discharge their duties free from personal interference and in strict accord with the rules. This independence is enhanced by a regular, albeit relatively modest, salary and pension. They also follow a fixed career structure that allows them to move up the hierarchy through examinations and qualifications.

BUREAUCRACY AND MODERNITY

Bureaucratic discipline and habits increasingly serve as modernity's organizing principle. George Orwell warned about the 'Big Brother' state in his novel *1984*, while the writer Franz Kafka, who had been subject to an early tirade against bureaucracy by Weber's brother Alfred, described a terrifying world of dehumanizing bureaucratic procedures. All functionaries have a common interest in protecting the bureaucratic machine. Bureaucrats strive for social closure by keeping expert knowledge an esoteric secret. Any idea of eliminating the bureaucracy Weber sees as 'more and more utopian'. Bureaucratic domination became an 'iron cage' with its own seemingly irresistible autonomous logic, making a revolution against bureaucracy 'technically more and more impossible'.

Bureaucratic continuity depends on a constant stream of revenue to pay for salaries, pensions, careers and offices. Modern public offices are paid out of general taxation, a revenue source which depends on a fully developed money economy. Modern states are wholly dependent on bureaucratic administration, although not all large states develop full-blown bureaucracies. Weber argued that more expansive states 'ruled by notables' like the Roman Empire and the British Empire developed relatively small bureaucracies because the state's area of responsibility at home was relatively small.

Modern bureaucracy has its origins in the state's need for standing armies and public finances, and the challenge of mass democracy. As warfare became increasingly organized and technological, it depended on a permanent apparatus. As society became more complex, state bureaucracies increasingly took responsibility for social welfare and the communications infrastructure.

Weber (1978: 983) claimed that mass democracy has a close affinity with bureaucratic impartiality. Mass democracy replaces rule by privileged 'notables' with rule by professional administrators, not only in the state but also in mass political parties and trade unions. Democracy should not be confused with the 'direct' rule of the electorate over the bureaucracy. While elected politicians come and go, bureaucracy is organized on a permanent basis.

TECHNICAL SUPERIORITY

Even more important for Weber is the superiority of the technical expertise invested in bureaucracy. In any case, bureaucracy can be put to non-democratic uses, as was graphically demonstrated in the bureaucratic states of Nazi Germany and Stalinist Russia in the decades following Weber's death. Weber focuses on the technical superiority of bureaucracy as the 'decisive reason' for its success over more personalized forms of organization.

> The fully developed bureaucratic mechanism compares with other organizations exactly as does the machine with non-mechanical modes of production. Precision, speed, unambiguity, knowledge of the files, continuity, discretion, unity, strict subordination, reduction of friction and of material and personal costs – these are raised to the optimum point in the strictly bureaucratic administration. (1978: 973)

Compared to 'administration by notables' or administration by 'collegiate bodies', with their interpersonal conflicts and rivalries, delays, lack of precision and compromises, bureaucracy functions efficiently and precisely 'according to *calculable rules*' and 'without regard for persons' (1978: 975). However, Weber also notes that the job security of bureaucrats can be harmful to technical efficiency, a charge that has become the common currency of critics of bureaucracy. 'Without regard for persons' has an ominous ring to it after the experience of bureaucratically-organized genocides in the twentieth century (Bauman, 1989).

Capitalism is eminently suited to the most 'dehumanized' forms of bureaucratic domination. Weber noted that the market also operates 'without regard for persons'. He adapted the principle of *sine ira ac studio* (without anger or bias) from the Roman historian Tacitus as the principle common to market indifference and bureaucratic impartiality, 'eliminating from official business love, hatred, and all the purely personal, irrational and emotional elements which escape calculation' (1978: 975). Similar rational principles of fixed trial procedures and a 'rational matter of factness' in decision making characterize the legal bureaucracy.

CRITICAL DEVELOPMENTS

By placing his analysis of bureaucracy at the centre of modernity Weber alighted on a phenomenon that became even more important as the twentieth century progressed. Bureaucracy became the dominant model for work organizations, sometimes known as 'Fordism' after the American car company. Historically, it underpinned repressive dictatorships in Nazi Germany and Stalinist-controlled Eastern Europe, as well as the welfare-warfare democracies of Western Europe.

Weber despaired over the irresistible march of the bureaucratic machine. His pessimism about bureaucratic domination resurfaced later in the Critical Theory of Horkheimer, Adorno and Marcuse and numerous theories about the 'bureaucratization of the world'. It also found an echo in the critique of disciplinary power in Michel Foucault's analysis of institutions like clinics, asylums, and prisons.

Weber's account of bureaucracy is limited by the one-dimensional nature of his ideal-type. No organization functions solely on the basis of written rules and codified duties. Strict rule-following may, in fact, prove to be an *inefficient* way to get work done. Rules are often broken, subverted or dodged by officials and workers. By the last quarter of the twentieth century, the classical ideal of bureaucracy had come under attack from neoliberal politicians and corporate managers who promoted more flexible and competitive 'post-bureaucratic' organizations. And far from being a bulwark against revolution, the thoroughly bureaucratic societies of the Stalinist regimes were overthrown by popular rebellions in 1989. Some have entered a spirited defence of bureaucracy as a necessary organizational structure (du Gay, 2000). Ultimately, Weber's ideal-type of bureaucracy must address his own question: technical efficiency for what?

bureaucracy

RELATED CONCEPTS

Division of Labour (Marx, Durkheim); Ideal-Types; Legitimate Domination; Modernity; Rationality and Rationalization

Weber's original account of bureaucracy in *Economy and Society* (1978) is a basic starting point. It is reproduced in Gerth and Mills, *From Max Weber* (1946), with a much shorter version in Whimster (2004). Paul du Gay's *In Praise of Bureaucracy* (2000) assesses the contemporary relevance of Weber's ideal-type. Zygmunt Bauman's *Modernity and the Holocaust* (1989) develops Weber's approach to dehumanized bureaucracy in a quite innovative fashion.

Capital

ACCUMULATION

At the heart of Marx's understanding of capitalism lies the competitive accumulation of capital. Like a miser, accumulating greater amounts of capital is the sole function of the capitalist:

> Accumulate, accumulate! That is Moses and the prophets! Therefore save, save, i.e. reconvert the greatest possible portion of surplus-value or surplus product into capital! Accumulation for the sake of accumulation, production for the sake of production. (Marx, 1976: 742)

But there is a great difference between the miser and the capitalist. Where the miser is a neurotic hoarder of money, the capitalist continually sends money back into circulation in the hope of increasing its size: 'while the miser is merely a capitalist gone mad, the capitalist is a rational miser' (Marx, 1976: 254). Capitalist rationality, like Weber's 'iron cage', is imposed on individual capitalists as a necessary compulsion: 'what appears in the miser as the mania of an individual is in the capitalist the effect of a social mechanism in which he is merely a cog' (Marx, 1976: 739).

Capital is 'a social mechanism'. No individual capitalist is able to exert overall control over the accumulation process. Both worker and capitalist are forced to submit to 'the dull compulsion' of the harsh laws of accumulation or else face ruin. In an endless cycle of accumulation, capitalism lurches from periods of frenzied growth, crisis, and the destruction of capitals, to stagnation, as happened for instance in the 'credit crunch' crisis of 2007 and 2008. But crisis is not all bad news.

Fewer capitals survive intact and become larger by taking over or merging with weaker ones. This prepares for a fresh cycle of accumulation to take place.

THE ELEMENTARY FORM OF CAPITAL

In the first volume of *Capital* Marx identified the commodity as the 'elementary form' of capital. In one respect the commodity seems like an obvious, self-evident place to start. In capitalism, life comes increasingly to depend on the production, distribution, sale and consumption of commodities. Capitalism is a system of generalized commodity production. The concept of capital outlined in *Capital* is a pure one, based on a closed model of society, moving from the simplest concept of the commodity towards the complex totality of capital's 'laws of motion'.

Other societies, like ancient Rome or feudal France, also produced commodities for sale. But prior to capitalism, commodity production did not dominate and structure all other social relations. Capital was not yet 'a social mechanism'. What was produced tended to be for the direct consumption of immediate social groups. Pre-capitalist commodity production was largely incidental to social life. In all previous societies the commodity form lacked the power to be generalized and impress itself throughout society.

In the opening passages of *Capital* Marx sets out the basic character of a simple commodity. A commodity is:

- a *useful* object that
- exists *independently* of both its producer and its ultimate purchaser
- that satisfies human *needs*
- but is wholly *indifferent* to these needs
- it can either be an object of *consumption* or a means of *production*
- it has two sides – subjective *use* value and objective *exchange* value
- its qualitative, subjective usefulness – or '*use-value*' – constitutes 'the material content' of wealth
- as 'the bearer' of quantitative, objective value – or '*exchange-value*' – it constitutes 'the abstract form' of wealth
- the exchange values of a particular commodity express something that all commodities share in *common*
- this common denominator is *abstract* human labour.

Commodities are thus double-sided, embodying both *use-value* and *exchange-value*. A thing can be useful without becoming a commodity, as when peasants pay rent directly to a feudal lord with corn that they themselves have produced or when a DIY enthusiast builds a garden shed. Only when things are forced to pass through the abstract medium of exchange – that is, money – does social reproduction come to depend on an indirect, impersonal but, at the same time, more fully *social* relationship between producer and consumer.

Marx depicts the cycle of capital accumulation by a simple formula – M-C-M^1. Here, money (M) is exchanged for a commodity (C) in order to later realize an increased amount of money (M^1). What makes this distinctively capitalist is that the commodity (C) is wage labour. Marx notes that previous modes of production operated the formula C-M-C. This was limited to a double transformation of the commodity (C), first into money (M) through a sale and, second, through using the money acquired to purchase and consume the use-value contained in a further commodity (C). Capitalism reverses this priority of use-value over exchange-value. *Capital*'s Chapter 4 on 'The general formula for capital' depicts the simple but unique law of motion of capital – M-C-M^1 – as one of adding value through the consumption of labour in the production process itself.

CENTRALIZATION AND CONCENTRATION OF CAPITAL

Capitalists find themselves in competition with each other in domestic and international markets. As they are driven to accumulate greater quantities of capital, smaller or weaker capitalists are put out of business. This leads to the *centralization* and *concentration* of capital. Centralization occurs when larger units grow at the expense of smaller ones; concentration grows directly out of production as an individual capitalist adds quantitatively to the stock of capital. A few individual capitals, say like Microsoft or the Royal Bank of Scotland, will grow to gigantic proportions, raising the stakes of economic crisis to new levels. If huge private businesses are threatened with bankruptcy the risk to social stability is also heightened.

LABOUR THEORY OF VALUE

On the surface it appears that profit is created from the sale of a product in the marketplace. However, Marx's *labour theory of value* holds that surplus value (potential profit) is created in the production process itself where labour is exploited at average levels of efficiency in society. Profit is the (all important) form through which the capitalist '*realizes*' surplus value. This process takes place under the pressure of market *competition* between capitalists. Competition forces each capitalist to reduce costs through both reinvesting in the most competitive methods of production, or what Marx called *'constant capital'* – buildings, machinery, tools, land – and reducing the cost of labour-power, or *'variable capital'*.

Constant capital is *'dead labour'*, work carried out by labour at an earlier stage in the accumulation process and now embodied in the means of production. Variable capital is *'living labour'* or 'labour-power', since what the capitalist purchases is the potential to consume labour rather than actual labour already performed, as would be the case when a peasant hands over some of their harvest to a landlord. Marx (1976: 342) uses the metaphors of living and dead labour to express the vampire-like nature of capitalist profit-making: 'Capital is dead labour which, vampire-like, lives only by sucking living labour, and lives the more, the more labour it sucks'.

It is a perennial problem of the production process to convert the potential of humans to labour into actual work done at the appropriate level and speed. Increasingly, labour is replaced by the use of technology in the labour process. As labour is displaced from the production process in greater numbers, a *'reserve army of labour'* is continually reproduced amongst the unemployed who find themselves unable to find a capitalist willing to buy their labour-power.

EXPLOITATION

In the *technical composition of capital*, the physical means of production (technology, buildings, infrastructure) increases disproportionately in relation to living labour-power (Marx, 1976: Ch. 25). Against individual workers production becomes more technologically intensive. The ratio of the *value* of constant to variable capital forms the *organic composition of capital*. The result is higher levels of productivity: fewer workers produce more commodities, cheapening the cost of commodities. The overall value of labour-power is also reduced since the cost of human reproduction becomes progressively cheaper.

Workers are not necessarily impoverished by their rising productivity. In *Capital* Marx points to the opposite process of rising employment, rising wages and rising consumption among workers, relative to the specific circumstances of the accumulation process. First, Marx (1976: 769) allows that wages may rise: 'A larger part of the worker's own surplus product, which is always increasing and is continually being transformed into additional capital, comes back to them in the shape of means of payment.' Second, this allows individual consumption to be expanded, 'so that [workers] can extend the circle of their enjoyments, make additions to their consumption fund of clothes, furniture, etc., and lay by a small reserve fund of money.'

Whether wages rise or fall, the essential relationship remains one of *exploitation* of labour-power by the structures of capital. Clearly, rising wages make a difference to the lives of individual workers. This does not in itself alter 'the golden chain' of exploitation: 'A rise in the price of labour, as a consequence of the accumulation of capital, only means in fact that the length and weight of the golden chain the wage-labourer has already forged for himself allow it to be loosened somewhat' (Marx, 1976: 769). Payment by wages (or salaries) always implies a certain amount of unpaid labour time to produce the surplus product, additional value, provided gratis and at no cost to capital.

Finally, capital is historical. Capitalism came into existence as a mode of production. Marx wagered that it would also disappear at some point in human history. It contains within itself both the germs of a different social order, which Marx called communist, and the seeds of its own destruction in its propensity to periodic crisis. But against his many critics that maintain otherwise, Marx did not envisage an automatic breakdown of capitalism. In his theory of crisis as an in-built tendency of capital, Marx tries to show how capital both embodies and overcomes previous historical developments.

CRITICAL DEVELOPMENTS

Entire libraries have been written about Marx's analysis of capital. Critical reviews by Werner Sombart and Eugen von Böhm-Bawerk appeared in the 1890s with the publication of Volume III of *Capital* (Marx, 1959). In the latter critique, fault is found with the formal logic in Marx's pure model of capital. What this tends to neglect is that Marx assumed for purposes of exposition that capitalism functions as a closed system. Later Marxists stressed that all sorts of countervailing tendencies work against the pure model being played out to some catastrophic collapse, not least the struggle between the classes itself.

Both Weber and Simmel attempted to build on what they saw as Marx's one-sided, economistic account of capitalism. In their different ways, they shared some of Marx's concerns about capitalism but sought to provide, as they saw it, a more rounded account of its origins, money, state bureaucracy and rationalization. Others associated with Critical Theory like Adorno, Horkheimer, Benjamin and Kracauer drew on German sociology and Marx to specify in various ways how capitalism's impersonal commodity culture reorganizes social experience and consciousness.

More orthodox Marxists tend to view much of this critique and extension of Marx's theory of capitalism as misguided, dealing merely with the superstructure divorced from its economic base. Others adapted Marx's economic sociology to explain contemporary capitalism. First, 'the regulation school' in France and elsewhere were concerned with the ways that different national economies were shaped through the intersection of what they called the 'regime of accumulation' and the 'mode of regulation' (Aglietta, 1979). Twentieth-century capitalism was organized around the mass production and mass consumption values of Fordism (after the American car manufacturer) as a regime of accumulation and the Keynesian-welfare state as a mode of regulation. By the 1970s, this began to be supplanted by neo-Fordism, a more flexible regime of accumulation alongside a neoliberal, market-oriented mode of regulation.

Second, theories of imperialism and 'the world-system' emphasize the international scale of capitalism and unequal geo-political positions of different nation-states. Marxist theories of imperialism by Lenin, Nikolai Bukharin and Rosa Luxemburg show how the global expansion of capital leads to inter-state competition, colonial conquest and world war. Taken as a whole, the world-system is divided into three unequal regions: core, periphery and semi-periphery (Wallerstein, 2004). Peripheral regions of the Developing World are exploited by the core for their raw materials and consciously held back in a state of underdevelopment. Where Marx defined capitalism as a system of class exploitation world-system theory transferred this to one of trans-national exploitation.

Where Marx pioneered a genuinely global-scale analysis of capital he anticipated debates about 'globalization' that have emerged since the 1980s (Robertson, 1992). Most other classical social theorists developed 'national sociologies', typically French or German, and considered 'society' in terms of discrete countries or nations or 'civil societies'. However, the concern of much classical social theory to compare different 'societies' or analyse processes supposedly universal to humanity means that the nationalization of social theory can also be over-stated.

With the reappearance of a financial crisis in 2008, many commentators went back to re-examine Marx's original insights in *Capital* (Harman, 2009). While Marx was voted the most influential thinker of all time, his greatest work *Capital* is not as widely read as this might suggest. It is not an alternative, more radical economic analysis but a historical sociology of capital. It was subtitled a '*Critique* of Political Economy' precisely because classical economics, like mainstream economics today, ignored the historical specificity of the social relations of capital.

RELATED CONCEPTS

Class; Division of Labour (Marx); Historical Materialism; Money; Primitive Accumulation; Protestant Ethic and the 'Spirit of Capitalism'

FURTHER READING

Marx's Volume 1 of *Capital* (1976) is not as difficult as is often made out. Accessibility has been helped greatly by introductions like Francis Wheen's short 'biography', *Marx's Das Kapital* (2006), Stephen Shapiro's *How to Read Marx's Capital* (2008) and David Harvey's *Limits to Capital* (2006). Chris Harman's *Zombie Capitalism* (2009) brings Marx's analysis of capitalism up to date.

Civil Society

It may seem obvious that social theory is concerned with the concept of 'society'. In fact, an interest in 'society' is not as central to contemporary social theory as might be expected (Frisby and Sayer, 1986; Outhwaite, 2006). This was not always the case. In earlier periods, social and political theorists tried to understand the transformation of 'civil society'. Adam Ferguson (1723–1816) developed an original historical analysis of civil society. For some, this represented a decisive turning point in the development of modern sociology (Swingewood, 1970). With his concept of civil society, Ferguson has been called the 'first real sociologist' (MacRae, 1969: 18). Michel Foucault (2008: 298) described Ferguson's *An Essay on the History of Civil Society* (1767) as 'the most fundamental, almost statutory text regarding the characterization of civil society'.

ADAM FERGUSON

Immediately Ferguson (1980: 2) rejects as 'fruitless inquiries' and 'wild suppositions' the idea that society developed out of people living in a 'state of nature'. Against such fictions, Ferguson appeals to the 'observable facts'. These are that human beings are just as likely to be the same today as they were back in the mists of time. The latest stage of society cannot therefore be more 'artificial' than the earliest stage, nor the earliest more 'natural' than the later. Primitive huts are not somehow more 'natural' than luxurious palaces.

Ferguson's concept of civil society has a number of inter-related elements. First, the need for society is a permanent feature of the human condition. Second, civil society is produced spontaneously rather than through some deliberate design or intention. Third, civil society circulates ambiguously between the affections of community and hostility towards outsiders. Fourth, civil society gives birth to the state and government. Fifth, civil society is continually transformed and moves through distinct stages of development. Sixth, the foundations of civil society are placed in jeopardy by capitalism.

A permanent civil society

Society is a permanent condition of humanity. People have always 'assembled in troops and companies'; fundamentally, 'mankind are to be taken in groups'; and 'society appears to be as old as the individual' (Ferguson, 1980: 3, 4, 6). Every person is formed by the common situation in which they find themselves, not by some exceptional individuality on their part. The history of the individual is 'but a detail' compared to the weight and significance of entire societies (Ferguson, 1980: 10). As far as human nature goes, all we can say is that humans, then as now, are predisposed toward social relations, friendship and antagonism, reason, and communication, not isolation. Human nature is social to the core; society is our natural state. It simply makes no sense to divide nature from culture.

A spontaneous civil society

Earlier thinkers like John Locke (1632–1704) equated civil society with a consciously organized political society. In contrast, Ferguson equates it with a spontaneous social order. Ferguson demonstrates the basic human need for civil society through a thought experiment:

> suppose, with a colony of children transplanted from the nursery, and left to form a society apart, untaught, and undisciplined, we should only have the same things repeated, which, in so many different parts of the earth, have been transacted already. The members of our little society would feed and sleep, would herd together and play, would have a language of their own, would quarrel and divide, would be to one another the most important objects of the scene, and, in the ardour of their friendships and competitions, would overlook personal danger, and suspend the care of their self-preservation. Has not the human race been planted like the colony in question? (1980: 4)

Society will always emerge spontaneously as people pursue their own ends. These ends are not only those of basic material security but also gregarious kinds of sociability: 'they are the most happy men, whose hearts are engaged to a community, in which they find every object of generosity or zeal, and a scope to the exercise of every talent, and of every virtuous disposition' (Ferguson, 1980: 58).

Inside and outside civil society

Civil society circulates ambiguously between association and dissociation. It is united against outsiders as well as by internal conditions of 'mutual support' (Ferguson, 1980: 17). A single civil society cannot encompass the whole of humanity but must be restricted to a more or less defined community. As Foucault (2008: 302) put it, 'Civil society is not humanitarian but communitarian'. Humanity divides into families, tribes, communities, parties, and nations.

Civil society is beset as much with opposition and acrimony as it is with cooperation and harmony. The internal bond is strengthened in the face of grave difficulties, say famine or war. National rivalries and preparations for war define civil society through constructing an external object against which it can set itself. People are quick to express anger against enemies that they only vaguely comprehend. They attribute to 'the enemy' all the lowest vices, cowardice, deceit, brutality and so on. What would be deemed unacceptable behaviour for individuals is celebrated when it is collectivized by nationalism and state policy.

Internally, civil society is not all harmony and love. It is also marked by hatred, animosity, quarrels, malice, repulsion and conflict: 'We are fond of distinctions; we place ourselves in opposition, and quarrel under the denomination of faction and party, without any material subject of controversy' (Ferguson, 1980: 21). People fight over the most trivial matters of honour as much as over actual material interests. Surprisingly, antagonism seems to strengthen civil society. Collective pleasure is taken in the use of reason, eloquence or physical force to subdue an opponent. Even sport and play take on violent qualities.

State and civil society

Individuals do not 'contract' with the state as an external body as liberal theory assumes. Rather, civil society itself generates state authority through its own internal dialectic of association and dissociation since 'some mode of subordination is as necessary to men as society itself' (Ferguson, 1980: 63). Political authority is established first in civil society – 'with the crowd … we follow a leader' – long before it is transformed into legal citizenship. 'In every society there is a casual subordination, independent of its formal establishment, and frequently adverse to its constitution' (1980: 133).

'Superior minds' and 'select councils' emerge in civil society *prior* to the formation of any political institution or government. Leaders seem to spontaneously appear in civil society, well suited to the 'mode of subordination' in politics and administration: 'Bring them together, each will find his place. They censure or applaud in a body; they consult and deliberate in more select parties' (1980: 63). Here the 'body' merely supports or rejects political leaders while 'select parties' make the decisions. Most people are indifferent to politics. They 'only pretend to employ their senses' but are generally content to leave things to politicians unless threatened by some dire emergency (1980: 67).

Historical change

Civil society is historically dynamic. It is not fixed in place like 'the good order of stones in a wall' (Ferguson, 1980: 68). As a spontaneous order based on internal reciprocity, civil society is like 'a passing stream not a stagnating pool' (1980: 7). It is not static but changeable. Civil society does not rest content with cultural and technical foundations inherited from the past. It seeks to improve gradually upon the collective stock of practical know-how. Ferguson (1980: 122) describes how successive individual improvements 'to remove inconveniences' are made without any overall or planned sense of their collective consequences.

For Ferguson, civil society passes through three stages: savagery, barbarism and civilization. The first two stages Ferguson calls 'rude nations' and the last 'polished nations'. At every stage human invention and industry is evident, as well as leisure and idleness.

'Savage nations' lack any conception of private property and meet their needs through hunting, fishing or fruit gathering. They are not arranged into classes and don't come under any political power or mode of subordination. 'Savage nations' display a 'love of justice and equality' and know of no external laws or police but still manage their domestic affairs in an orderly fashion. Ferguson saw in 'savage' qualities such as composure, honour, affection, candour, fortitude and order, virtues superior to 'polished nations', where ambition and vanity always chase after some personal distinction or privilege (1980: 95). In savage nations, force becomes a cult. Internally, domestic society is generous and faithful but externally, fierce and dangerous.

Only slowly do 'barbarous' habits and private property take hold. 'Barbarous nations' possess private property, cattle or crops, divide into rich and poor classes, and develop a mode of internal subordination. 'They know the relations of patron and client, of servant and master, and suffer themselves to be classed according to their measures of wealth' (1980: 81). Even within the same community people will quarrel, compete or steal from each other until brought to order by a despotic leader (1980: 97).

'Barbarous nations' enjoy a kind of political freedom through a mutual threat of force. Modern 'polished nations' suppress civil disorder

civil society

through laws that leave individuals unmolested to pursue personal advancement or commercial profits. Under an advanced division of labour, Ferguson worried that a specialization in military activities by professional armies would result in a despotic government and an endangered freedom.

Even though he characterized non-European societies as 'rude nations' and western ones as 'polished nations', Ferguson was immune to ideas about the innate superiority of one society over another. On many pages Ferguson challenges the conceits of his own society, for example: 'we are ourselves the supposed standards of politeness and civilization; and where our own features do not appear, we apprehend, that there is nothing which deserves to be known' (1980: 75).

Capitalism and civil society

Ferguson was very much a creature of his time and social position, viewing civil society as necessarily elitist, open only to a select few men who were not preoccupied with 'servile' daily problems of subsistence like women, labourers or beggars. But outside of commerce the modern bourgeois show no enthusiasm for public duty.

> It is here indeed, if ever, that man is sometimes found a detached and solitary being: he has found an object which sets him in competition with his fellow-creatures, and he deals with them as he does his cattle and his soil, for the sake of the profits they bring. (Ferguson, 1980: 19)

He pursues 'solitary pastimes' or cultivates 'a taste for gardening, building, drawing or music':

> With this aid, they endeavour to fill up the blanks of a listless life, and avoid the necessity of curing the languors by any positive service to their country or mankind. (Ferguson, 1980: 57)

While commercial society exacts its costs in alienation, inequality, corruption, passivity – which ultimately threaten the material and moral bases of civil society – the growing 'state of complication' it produces tends to drive all-round material 'improvement' and progress.

Civil society spontaneously checks the violent passions of naked self-interest. People are more than mere economic machines driven by appetite alone. They always seek the approval of their neighbours by being seen as virtuous. People gain fortitude from feelings of social solidarity. We consult, oppose, persuade and dissent far beyond what is always in our own narrow personal interest in safety and security. Commerce creates its own moral order. Through market interdependencies trust, industry, toleration and freedom are enlarged in practical and unplanned ways (Varty, 1997).

CRITICAL DEVELOPMENTS

Ferguson directly influenced Karl Marx and anticipated themes of social order and solidarity in Tönnies and Durkheim. His *Essay* informed the German philosopher G.W.F. Hegel's (1770–1831) critique of the liberal model of civil society. Despite this influence, Ferguson's pioneering work was generally forgotten within sociology until relatively recently (Swingewood, 1970).

He combined an analysis of the changing structure of civil society with ultimate questions about value – what kind of civil society is desirable. Working at a time before value became separated from facts in academic sociology, John Brewer (2007) locates Ferguson within a longer tradition of 'civic humanism'. This emphasizes a sense of public duty and civic virtue and is in tension with liberal ideas of being left alone and free from unwanted interference. Human flourishing is ultimately dependent on the sociability of and active participation in civil society (Hanley, 2009).

Ferguson rejected the rigid opposition between the state and civil society. Unlike earlier theories, for Ferguson the problem of political rule is already posed within civil society rather than imposed from outside. Foucault (2008) calls Ferguson's concept of civil society 'a new technology of government'. By this he means that government must satisfy civil society rather than the other way round: 'the rationality of the governed must serve as the regulating principle for the rationality of government' (Foucault, 2008: 312).

This raises the question of whether civil society needs an external form of government in the form of a state or whether civil society might become self-governing. Neo-liberal followers of Ferguson like Friedrich Hayek (1899–1992) claim that too much government chokes the personal freedom which only the spontaneous order of civil society can guarantee.

Marx built critically on Ferguson's (and Hegel's) analysis of civil society. He argued that political institutions should not be divorced from their origins in social relations. Political power for Marx was merely the official expression of the class antagonisms of civil society. Of later Marxists, Antonio Gramsci (1971) made the concept of civil society central to his understanding of revolutionary processes. Revolution was possible in a largely under-developed society like Russia in 1917 because it lacked a sturdy civil society to protect state power.

Current ideas of civil society propose it as an alternative to political conflict (Fine, 1997). Reduced to voluntary associations, clubs and groups, some find current usage of the concept of civil society a 'society-lite' alternative to more the more robust idea of the social facts found in Durkheim (Outhwaite, 2006). Civil society has become a highly flexible concept that can be turned to a wide range of purposes. It has been used to explain the overthrow of authoritarian states in Eastern Europe in 1989 as well as the decline of civic engagement in the United States.

Ferguson's original concept focused on the 'mode of subordination', not voluntary associations. After the civil war in Bosnia in the early 1990s the concept of civil society was used to distinguish different styles of nationalism. Nations based on the institutions of civil society are seen as tolerant 'civic nations', while those based not on civil society but on culture or blood are viewed as violently intolerant 'ethnic nations'. Although he used the term 'nation' rather loosely, Ferguson already detected the atavistic, destructive strains of nationalism, not as some ethnic 'essence' but lurking deep within civil society itself.

RELATED CONCEPTS

Division of Labour (Smith and Ferguson); *Gemeinschaft* and *Gesellschaft*; Mechanical and Organic Solidarity; Primitive Accumulation; Social Forms and Sociation

FURTHER READING

A number of versions of Ferguson's *Essay on the History of Civil Society* are readily available. Lisa Hill's book *The Passionate Society* (2006) considers the original context for the concept. William Outhwaite offers a brief overview of recent 'society-lite' ideas of civil society in *The Future of Society* (2006).

Class

Class is the basic concept that distinguishes Marxism from other traditions of social thought. Yet Marx had surprisingly very little to say about class as a formal concept. Beyond saying that classes have a determinate relationship to production as direct producers or non-producers, people cannot be 'classified' once and for all. Classes are formed out of an antagonistic relationship between different forms of property ownership that characterize a particular mode of production at a definite stage in its historical development. The main forms of ownership of the capitalist mode of production are labour-power, capital, and land. This structuring of antagonistic property interests cannot be isolated from the social and political activity of the mutually hostile classes. Class struggle gives a definite shape to the forms of organization, means of understanding and social interests known as 'class consciousness'.

WHAT IS CLASS?

In his major study *Capital*, Marx leaves discussion of classes until the final chapter of the final volume (III, 1959), where he asks: 'What constitutes a class?' He answers, 'the reply to this follows naturally from the reply to another question, namely: "What makes wage-labourers, capitalists and landlords constitute the three great social classes?"'

> The owners merely of labour-power, owners of capital, and landowners, whose respective sources of income are wages, profit and ground-rent, in other words, wage-labourers, capitalists and landowners, constitute the three big classes of modern society based upon the capitalist mode of production. (1959: 885)

Class seems to be based on income and wealth. However, Marx rejects wages, profit and ground rent as the basis for class. This would merely split society into an 'infinite fragmentation of interest and rank'. Landlords would not then belong to a single bourgeois class but would divide into separate classes as 'owners of vineyards, farm owners, owners of forests, mine owners and owners of fisheries'.

On the one hand, to ground class in a fixed essence like wealth or occupation fails to account for its historically specific existence. On the other hand, a purely descriptive stratification of class positions fails to account for the underlying nature of the social relation. Many Marxists, Weberians and other professional sociologists seek 'the essence' of class in formal categories of income, occupation or industry. The formal stratification of society into income or occupational 'classes' runs counter to Marx's emphasis on class as an exploitative social relation of production. While Marx recognizes that 'the stratification of classes does not appear in its pure form' and that 'middle and intermediate strata obliterate lines of demarcation everywhere' such brute facts are 'immaterial to our analysis' (1959: 885).

class

When Marx states that class is a social relation he does not mean that class exists primarily as an interpersonal relation between individuals. Class has less to do with how individuals personally interact than what *function* they fulfil within the overall social relations of production.

> It is not a matter of what this or that proletarian or even the whole proletariat *pictures* at present as its goal. It is a matter of *what the proletariat is in actuality* and what, in accordance with this *being*, it will historically be compelled to do. (1845: 134–5, italics in original)

Fundamentally, classes are 'historically compelled' to struggle with each other over conflicting interests.

CLASS ANTAGONISM

Marx and Engels famously set out the historical relation of classes early in *The Communist Manifesto* where they declared:

> The history of all hitherto existing society is the history of class struggles. Freeman and slave, patrician and plebeian, lord and serf, guild-master and journeyman, in a word, oppressor and oppressed, stood in constant opposition to one another, carried on an uninterrupted, now hidden now open fight, a fight that each time ended, either in a revolutionary reconstitution of society, or in the common ruin of the contending classes. (1998: 34–35)

In fact, none of these earlier modes of production were overthrown by the exploited class. It was not peasants that overthrew feudalism but the new, emerging 'middling sorts' of the capitalist class. Previous societies were divided hierarchically into complex gradations of rank, somewhat obscuring the division into fundamental classes: 'In ancient Rome we have patricians, knights, plebeians, slaves; in the Middle Ages, feudal lords, vassals, guild-masters, journeymen, apprentices, serf; in almost all of these classes, again, subordinate gradations' (Marx and Engels, 1998: 35).

BOURGEOIS AND PROLETARIANS

Modern society, Marx and Engels claim, simplifies class antagonisms, splitting society into 'two great hostile camps': bourgeois and proletarians. Engels later added a footnote to define what he took these terms to mean:

> By bourgeoisie is meant the class of modern capitalists, owners of the means of social production and employers of wage labour. By proletariat, the class of modern

wage labourers who, in having no means of production of their own, are reduced to selling their labour power in order to live. (Marx and Engels, 1998: 34)

Marx and Engels praise the bourgeois class for its revolutionary achievements: the overthrow of feudalism, the creation of a world market, technological dynamism, the ending of religious superstitions, urbanization, stimulating the creation of a world literature, all marvellous 'wonders far surpassing Egyptian pyramids, Roman aqueducts, and Gothic cathedrals' (1998: 38).

In the process, capital organizes the proletariat into a class as 'the conditions of life are more and more equalized, in proportion as machinery obliterates all distinctions of labour, and nearly everywhere reduces wages to the same low level' (1998: 45). This is a process known as 'proletarianization'. Increasingly, the lower strata of the middle class – shopkeepers, tradespeople and peasants – fall into the class of wage labourers as they are put out of business by the power of larger capitals. The proletariat develops just so long as it increases the amount of capital accumulated by the bourgeoisie. Wage labour is reduced to the status of a commodity, possessing only its labour power for sale, interchangeable with other commodities. Labour is alienated, a mere 'appendage of the machine', which controls the pace and skill of labour.

A CLASS IN 'RADICAL CHAINS'

Workers do not automatically move from being an objective 'class-*in*-itself' to become a subjective 'class-*for*-itself'. They need to overcome the market competition between individual labourers for jobs and wages. Workers can attain a self-conscious sense of their separate class interests – 'class consciousness' – only by means of a concerted ideological and political struggle. As the exploited class in society, it is bound in 'radical chains'. Its oppression and exploitation can be reversed only through self-emancipation. In freeing itself, the proletariat promises universal liberation for other oppressed groups and the overcoming of the artificial and distorting limits that capital places on the further development of the productive forces (Marx, 1843: 64). In this sense, Marx argued that the working class is compelled to become the 'universal class' of society.

CRITICAL DEVELOPMENTS

Marx and Engels' account of class has been the source of deep dispute in the social sciences. Many claim that Marx's class theory has been empirically refuted if not, indeed, completely falsified. First, the proletariat has not, except in exceptional historical situations, acted as a revolutionary class. Second, society has not become simplified into two giant hostile classes. In fact, as more white collar jobs exist in the economy it is doubtful if the term 'working class' refers to anything more than a significant minority of the labour force. Third, class politics appears to have declined as a form of collective identification and trade union membership has been on the wane for a couple of decades. Fourth, poverty and immiseration, while not completely disappearing, only marginally affect employed workers. Fifth, production is less important to the economy and politics today than consumption. Sixth, working-class or socialist movements have been devastated by political defeats, from the 1984–5 British miners' strike to the collapse of the Soviet Union.

This is a powerful charge sheet. However, the list of indictments cannot be taken as a decisive refutation of Marx's concept of class (Crompton, 2008). Marx's 'class model' has been revised to account for more recent empirical shifts in the class structure. Erik Olin Wright (1985) developed the concept of 'contradictory class locations' to account for the growth of what he called 'the new middle classes'. Others like Pierre Bourdieu (1984) shifted attention away from class at the point of economic production to the reproduction of class relations through cultural markers of distinction.

More often, however, class in Marx's sense is increasingly seen as irrelevant to much contemporary social theory. One expression of this is 'post-Marxism', which claims that class as the 'privileged' subject of social change is far too narrow to encapsulate a more complex economic, political and cultural environment. Michael Hardt and Antonio Negri's (2000) *Empire*, widely praised as 'the new *Communist Manifesto* for the twenty-first century', replaced the industrial proletariat with the self-governing 'multitude'. The multitude is characterized by dispersed networks of formerly marginal groups like the poor, houseworkers, immigrant workers or the unemployed and the 'immaterial labour' of service work.

Earlier Marxists – Lenin, Trotsky, Georg Lukacs, Antonio Gramsci, Karl Korsch, Walter Benjamin, through to recent figures such as Slavoj Žižek – have insisted that Marx's understanding of the working class is inseparable from his active, militant standpoint. The empirical class of wage labour must express its class essence as an active revolutionary alternative to what merely exists. This seems a long way from Weberian stratification and Marx's own determination to stick close to the empirical realities (and latent possibilities) of class society.

Class, Status and Party; Capital; Division of Labour (Marx); Mode of Production; Primitive Accumulation

FURTHER READING

Rosemary Crompton's *Class and Stratification* (2008) contains a brief account of Marx on class. Jon Gubby offers a defence of Marxist class theory in his paper 'A Marxist Critique of Weberian Class Analyses' (1997). Eric Olin Wright's *Classes* (1985) reformulates the whole Marxist concept of class.

Class, Status and Party

As part of his intellectual response to Karl Marx, Max Weber devised a sophisticated model of social stratification. Although Weber recognized Marx as 'a gifted writer', he claimed that Marx advanced 'pseudo-scientific' notions of class: 'The most classical expression of this pseudo-scientific use of concepts is the contention of a gifted writer that the individual may well mistake his own interests, but the "class" is "infallible" about its interests' (Runciman, 1978: 46–7). However, like Marx, Weber made only a few cursory statements about class as a separate but inter-related form of stratification, alongside 'status' and 'party'.

CLASS

Weber (Runciman, 1978: 43–4) defines class as a situation where:

- a large number of men have in common a specific causal factor influencing their chances in life, insofar as
- this factor has to do only with the possession of economic goods and the interests involved in earning a living, and furthermore
- the conditions of the market in commodities or labour.

Class situation depends on the probability of individuals using skills and resources to acquire goods, a position and 'inner satisfaction' under 'pure' competitive market conditions. In turn this always depends on the prior ownership and non-ownership of property.

Weber (1978: 302) distinguishes between property and services. Different types of *property* generate income while different kinds of *services* are sold in the market. 'A property class' is determined by the possession of property which generates an income. Ideally, property takes the form of people, land, mines, factories, ships, creditors, stocks and skills. Property attracts income in the form of rent from land to profits from mines and factories, shops, slaves and, ultimately, interest from money itself. Property-owners are not therefore a unified class but a heterogeneous, internally stratified class of landowners, financial speculators, rentiers, factory owners or entrepreneurs.

On the other hand, the 'propertyless' can only sell their 'services'. Again, this results in an internally diverse and divided class depending on the nature of the services that individuals offer for sale. 'A commercial class', including merchants, shipowners, industrial and agricultural owners, professionals and skilled workers, is determined by a relatively high market demand for its services. At the other extreme are routine labourers, defined by a low market demand for their services. In between are certain categories of public officials, professionals and skilled labour with only moderate marketability. This leads Weber to the rather extraordinary statement that slaves cannot be considered a class because they do not enter the market for either goods or services.

Alongside property and services, Weber's third criterion is socially mobile class situations, which results in his general category of 'social class'. Social mobility means that the shape of social class is constantly changing. Weber notes that the working class as a whole is becoming more 'semi-skilled' as work becomes automated, while both skilled workers and the petit bourgeoisie find upward mobility into white collar and technical work easiest. An educated few from petit bourgeois backgrounds will make it into the privileged strata of the higher ranks of banking, corporations and the civil service. All this potential for social mobility affects organized class conflict. Weber argues that class conflict depends on the relative social stability of large numbers of people, concentrated in large workplaces, with clearly-defined opponents and goals formulated by a sympathetic intelligentsia.

Weber emphasizes the internal stratification of classes and rejects the idea of class as a self-evident community of interest: 'a class itself is not a community, and it is misleading to treat classes as conceptually equivalent to communities' (Runciman, 1978: 46). A range of separate orders – political, economic, legal, social – intersect with each other to produce 'a community'. He also denies the force of Marxist concepts like 'class struggle' – about which 'there is not much to be said in a general way' (1978: 47) – and 'class interest':

> the concept of 'class interests' becomes ambiguous, indeed ceases to be in any meaningful way a clear empirical concept, as soon as it is taken to mean anything but the actual direction taken by the interests of a specific cross-section of those subject to a class situation, and following from the class situation with a specific probability. (1978: 47)

Individuals have different natural abilities, skills and qualifications rather than a universally shared class interest. Only if the contrast in life chances becomes stark through what is called 'relative deprivation', will the result be rational collective action rather than 'sporadic acts of irrational protest' (1978: 46).

STATUS

A 'purely' *economic* class situation is less significant for Weber than the 'purely' *social* situation of status groups. Status concerns the typical social estimate of honour or social standing of a group:

> we shall use the term 'status situation' to refer to all those typical components of people's destinies which are determined by a specific social evaluation of 'status', whether positive or negative, when that evaluation is based on some common characteristic shared by many people. (Runciman, 1978: 48)

Status groups depend on highly restricted and internally regulated forms of social intercourse. In extreme cases like the aristocracy it can lead to the closed world of intra-group marriage or become rigidly fixed into a closed, hierarchical caste system.

Status may overlap with class but it need not. Indeed, high economic power can contradict the low social status of financial speculators or bankers. Alternatively, status may be more equally distributed than class. Weber fancies that American businessmen and workers find themselves socially on the same footing once outside of their specifically economic settings. This status equality contrasts to the prestige, honour and snobbery that Weber knew well in Germany.

SOCIAL CLOSURE

Privileges are maintained through the exercise of 'social closure'. Social closure excludes 'outside' groups from access to honorific and material benefits by isolating certain scarce social and physical traits like family lineage or educational certificates as the criteria for membership. Social status involves a certain *style of life* demanded of every individual belonging to the group:

> For it is a consequence of the fact that it is lifestyle which determines social status that status groups are specifically responsible for all 'conventions': all 'stylisation' of ways of life, however expressed, either originates with a status group or is preserved by one. (Runciman, 1978: 52)

Status groups confer definite *honorific* benefits such as the right to consume food or wear clothing in certain ways. They may also confer *material* benefits such as appointments to certain economic positions.

STATUS AND CLASS

Status groups are usually but not always formed on the basis of class situations. Weber distinguishes this from the horizontal relationship among different ethnic groups. Oppressed groups like Jews may feel themselves to be special and possess high status despite the contempt of the dominant ethnic group. On the other hand, caste groups suffer the full force of ritualized relations of low-status inferiority.

At the privileged end of the status system, Weber notes, elite groups are prevented by convention from undertaking physical labour, including artistic labour, or paid employment. Here status and market principles may conflict with each other. In principle, a cash-oriented market rationality ought to be blind to status and social distinction.

> The ordering of society in terms of status means precisely the opposite: differentiation in terms of 'social standing' and lifestyles peculiar to particular status groups. As such it is fundamentally threatened when purely economic gain and purely economic power, completely naked and displaying the marks of its origin unconnected with status, can confer on everyone who has acquired it the same 'standing' which the interested status groups claim for themselves in virtue of their way of life. (Runciman, 1978: 53)

For these reasons the *nouveau riche* are treated with contempt by traditionally privileged status groups and excluded from their cultural orbit. Indeed, status claims may hold back or distort the development of the market, as when dealing in money is viewed as demeaning and socially inferior.

Power for Weber is not typically sought for economic gain as such but, rather, for the sake of the status that it brings. There are exceptions to this, Weber recognizes, such as the typical American 'boss' or the financial speculator who do actually desire 'pure' economic power. Generally, however, status is the primary source of power.

Classes properly belong to the economic order, while status groups are at home in the social order, although both mutually influence each other (Weber, 1978: 938). Status and class tend to blur into each other in the shape of 'occupational status groups'. In such cases entry into an occupation is dependent on evidence of a specific lifestyle. Generally, however, either class situation or status will predominate as the principle of stratification. Status predominates over class when social conditions are relatively stable and continuous, whereas class prevails over status during the upheaval and uncertainty released by technological change or economic crisis.

PARTY

Where class is determined by the economic order and status by the social order, 'party' is determined by the political order. Party in Weber's sense refers to a voluntary association of people who are pursuing some goal in common: 'in some way or other constituted as an association, that is, which possesses some form of rational organization and an apparatus of personnel which is ready to bring about the goals in question' (Runciman, 1978: 55).

By 'party' Weber did not simply mean political parties in a narrow sense, although his use of the term 'party' is suitably ambiguous. Party might refer to a political party, a campaign group, a social club, or a social movement. It could just as readily be applied to a factional struggle for control of the local bowling club as the struggle for seizing state power. Organized parties may, but equally may not, correspond with the class or status situation of its members. First, 'patronage parties' exist to secure positions of influence for their own people. Second, 'ideological parties' form around abstract principles and objective policies.

A party can employ different organizational means of securing power. Weber lists several types of party along the lines of his typology of legitimate domination. 'Legal parties' are rationally geared towards elections as the means to pursue their interests. 'Charismatic parties' emerge around the cult of a leader. 'Traditionalist parties' dispute or follow the traditional authority of a leader. 'Faith parties' struggle over doctrinal heresy. 'Appropriation parties' fight to control privileges and positions. Within parties, sub-parties may emerge on a temporary or more permanent basis.

For Weber, 'the crucial point' is that these depend on a voluntary adherence to the rules of the association. When it is no longer voluntary it ceases to be a party and becomes a closed group. The different organizational forms of party structure share in common a central group of leaders and staff, a more passive group of members or followers, and, finally, a much larger mass that forms their target audience. All parties depend on contributions to party funds and risk being 'bought off'. Parties resemble capitalist firms in that they try to control their market power by manipulating political choice.

LEADERSHIP AND VIOLENCE

Under legal-rational conditions the chief purpose of political parties is to bring forward leaders with a capacity for the judicious exercise of power. Elite political leadership requires qualities of forthrightness, responsibility and a sense of proportion. Leadership must exercise self-restraint in the use of violent means to realize 'good ends', but must also be prepared to use violence in a power struggle. It is necessary to face up to the fact, Weber argued, that the 'dubious means' of violence is the price that may sometimes have to be paid for elevated ends. Weber himself endorsed state violence in order to achieve the 'good end' of Germany's imperialist ambitions.

CRITICAL DEVELOPMENTS

In his demarcation of the class situation, Weber aggregates the common position of individuals engaged in market activity. In so doing he neglects the collective and exploitative relations of production within what Marx called 'the hidden abode' of the production process. Weber narrows class to market positions and effectively subordinates class to status as an explanatory concept. Unfortunately, his fragmentary comments on 'social class' do not lead to a fuller consideration of the possibilities of class as a collective formation. Party, on the other hand, seems little more than an ill-considered afterthought.

Weber's approach has informed most measures of classifying workers by loose occupational grouping. Systems of stratification based on market position view 'class' as a descriptive category, rather than primarily as an antagonistic social relation of production. Status informs claims that class is no longer salient now that consumption and identity appear to have lost their exclusive character. Often the working class is frozen in time, identified with the lifestyle and occupational positions of white, male manual workers from the middle four decades of the twentieth century.

Weber is rather cavalier in his assertion that any old trait will do for exclusionary status groups to succeed in effecting social closure.

Excluded groups have often already been marked out as inferior in terms of ethnicity, religion, sex or nationality. As Parkin comments:

> The communities singled out for exclusion – blacks, Catholics, Jews or other minorities – are typically those whose political and social rights have been deliberately curtailed by the forces of law and order. Such groups become the target for exclusionary practices precisely because their capacity to resist has been undermined by the state powers. (2002: 102)

Since Weber locates class in the economy and status in society, the role of the bureaucratic state in shaping stratification is surprisingly neglected.

RELATED CONCEPTS

Class; Ideal-Types; Legitimate Domination; Protestant Ethic and the 'Spirit of Capitalism'; Social Action

FURTHER READING

Chapter IV of Weber's *Economy and Society* (1978) contains the fragment on class, status and party. Edited versions are available in a number of collections such as Runciman (1978), Whimster (2004) and Gerth and Mills (1946). Chapter 4 of Parkin (2002) and Chapter 6 of Allen (2004) offer alternative interpretations.

Collective Effervescence

Durkheim coined the term 'collective effervescence' to indicate how communal gatherings intensify, electrify and enlarge religious experience. Bringing people together in close physical proximity 'generates a kind of electricity that quickly transports them to an extraordinary degree of exaltation' (Durkheim, 2001: 162). Collectively experienced euphoria helps to reaffirm social bonds:

> Within a crowd moved by a common passion, we become susceptible to feelings and actions of which we are incapable on our own. And when the crowd is dissolved, when we find ourselves alone again and fall back to our usual level, we can measure how far we were raised above ourselves. (2001: 157)

Collective effervescence allows society to recharge its batteries, to stay with Durkheim's electrical metaphor. Every society needs to reaffirm its moral unity through meetings, gatherings, rituals, ceremonies or assemblies.

Such moments of collective effervescence are only the most intense demonstration of a more general social condition. Individuals are elevated routinely when they feel sympathy and esteem coming from others. Confidence and security are derived from the warming currents of social solidarity in a shared language, norms and knowledge. Our 'moral harmony' with others nourishes and sustains an appetite for society.

SACRED EFFERVESCENCE

The 'moral consciousness' that derives from others in society was first given definite expression by effervescent religious practices. In Australian aboriginal society, when the clan or tribal group congregate everything is amplified and experienced more intensely. In the midst of this frenzy the religious ideal is constantly being reborn. Because, for Durkheim, the religious ideal is merely society's way of worshipping itself, it is really society that is reborn through collective effervescence.

It does this by dividing the world into two parts: a special world induced by *sacred* effervescent and an ordinary world of the *profane* mundane. Another aspect of this dual reality is that the sacred is intoxicating while the profane is sobering. In order to work followers up into states of delirium, prophets and saints display signs of excitability similar to drunkenness. Delirious feelings are projected onto sacred things known as 'totems'.

Collective effervescence leads to unpredictable and impetuous behaviour as people get carried away with themselves.

Feeling possessed and led by some external power that makes him think and act differently from normal times, he naturally feels he is no longer himself. He seems to have become a new being: the decorations he dons and the masks he uses to cover his face give material form to this internal transformation even more than they induce it. And as all his companions feel transfigured in the same way at the same moment, and translate their feeling through their shouts, gestures and posture, it is as though he really were transported into a special world entirely different from the ordinary, a setting populated by exceptionally intense forces that invade and transform him. (Durkheim, 2001: 163–4)

This ecstasy of collective experience seems to give permission for people to overthrow ordinary life. Moral norms, such as those that govern sexual conduct, are suspended. Rather than serving some narrow religious end, the sheer pleasure of effervescent play serves no external purpose. Religion incorporates the creative gestures of free play and the aesthetic pleasures of art as a release from the demands of profane existence.

SECULAR EFFERVESCENCE

Some of this surplus energy finds expression in the 'exuberant movements' of game-playing and sports. Durkheim even sees a similar intoxication going on in social theory:

> Social thought, because of its imperative authority, has a power that individual thought cannot have; by acting on our minds it makes us see things in whatever light it chooses; it adds to or subtracts from the real according to the circumstances. (2001: 173)

Collective effervescence occurs in specially consecrated events, not the routine absorption in crowds. More than merely passing phenomena, Durkheim might have been talking about a contemporary pop music festival:

> [A festival] always has the effect of bringing individuals together, setting the masses in motion, and so inducing the state of effervescence, sometimes even delirium, that is not unrelated to the religious state. Man is transported outside himself, distracted from his ordinary occupations and preoccupations. And we observe the same displays in both cases: cries, songs, music, violent movements, dances, the search for stimulants that increase vitality, and so on. It has often been observed that popular festivals lead to excess, blur the boundaries between licit and illicit. (2001: 285)

Social and political movements are also viewed by Durkheim as secularized religious movements. Every type of party, interest group and social movement feels the need to hold frequent meetings so that their members can renew their shared bonds through a 'collective demonstration' of their convictions. By bringing people closer together feelings that might fade away in the heart of individuals are reaffirmed through active contact with the group. At meetings, speeches are heightened and amplified by the contact that the speaker makes with the audience. Collective passions in turn encourage ever more audacious rhetoric by the speaker, who becomes the crowd personified.

During revolutionary periods of collective upheaval people enter into a phase of 'hyper-activity'. They come into more frequent and intense contact with each other and are transformed by the collective experience. Suddenly, anything seems possible.

> People live differently and more intensely than in normal times. The changes are not only those of nuance and degree; man himself becomes other. He is moved by passions so intense that they can only be assuaged by violence, extreme acts of superhuman heroism or bloody barbarism … Under the influence of general exaltation, the most mediocre and inoffensive burgher is transformed into a hero or an executioner. (Durkheim, 2001: 158)

In the French Revolution of 1789, the mass mobilizations were emboldened to take radical action by the intense emotions aroused by highly charged speeches.

PERMANENT EFFERVESCENCE

Durkheim felt that society's need for collective effervescence was a permanent one. People in society have a yearning to re-live great moments when a collective identity was strongly felt. Festivals and commemorations are invented for the purpose of stoking the memory of intense unity. Hence the French Revolution created a whole range of festivals to commemorate the purity of its republican principles even or especially after the revolutionary enthusiasm had ebbed away and disenchantment had set in. As Durkheim confidently predicted:

> A day will come when our societies will once again experience times of creative effervescence and new ideas will surge up, new formulas will arise to serve to guide humanity for a time. (2001: 323)

Because the energies consumed by popular enthusiasms cannot be sustained indefinitely they are transformed into forms of moral practice that are less emotionally demanding and sustainable. At least until the next outbreak of collective effervescence.

CRITICAL DEVELOPMENTS

Durkheim's stress on heightened collective practices represents a shift away from his earlier emphasis on the rational or functional basis of moral norms. Recent cultural sociology and social movement studies have found the concept attractive. What Maffesoli (1996) calls 'neo-tribes' are bound together by warm feelings of neighbourliness against the icy rationality of modern life. Similarly, 'rave culture' is seen as a 'new age' quasi-religious movement that connects people. Such neo-tribal effervescence 'demonstrates socio-cultural revitalization on a massive scale' (Olaveson, 2004: 86).

Limited to the spaces of consumer capitalism, neo-tribalism seems a rather thin version of what Durkheim meant by collective effervescence. First, Durkheim stressed the intense exaltation of collective effervescence; second, it supports rational thought rather than displaces it; third, Durkheim allowed for its negative and violent side; fourth, neo-tribalism is limited to local subcultures rather than society taken as a whole (Fish, 2005; Schilling and Mellor, 1998).

An account is needed of the dangers of more violent forms of effervescence, particularly in situations where fundamentalism, racism and nationalism arise from warm feelings of connectedness and homely neighbourliness. Durkheim, like Freud in *Totem and Taboo*, has a more ambivalent conception of collective effervescence (Shilling and Mellor, 1998). He recognized that unpredictable violence can result from the heady frenzy of collective effervescence.

As the division of labour limits or controls opportunities for collective effervescence a vital creative function is lost for periodically recharging the moral order. In its place, commercial substitutes are offered like the entertainment and sports industries. These may allow for commodified expressions of tribal belongingness but lack the kind of unifying moral order that Durkheim emphasized.

Collective effervescence is a particularly useful concept to account for the feelings and emotional impact of collective mobilization (Barker, 1999; Emirbayer, 1996; Traugott, 1984). For instance, during the revolutions of 1989 that shook many societies in Eastern Europe, a huge tidal wave of collective effervescence swept away entrenched political structures that just days before had seemed absolutely invincible (Tiryakian, 2009). By collectively taking high-risk action against authoritarian regimes, people suddenly felt energized and powerful. This focus on the affective and emotional dimensions of collective action has opened up a highly productive seam for the study of social movements, indicating some of the possibilities for Durkheim's concept today.

RELATED CONCEPTS

Collective Representations; Conscience Collective; Mechanical and Organic Solidarity; Sacred and Profane; Social Morphology; Totemism

FURTHER READING

Chapters 7 of Book II and Chapter 4 of Book III of Durkheim's *Elementary Forms of Religious Life* (2001) offer vibrant accounts of the collective effervescence. Both Jonathan Fish (2005) and Phillip Mellor (2004) offer a critical defence of Durkheim's original conception. Edward Tiryakian (2009) uses the concept to make sense of the Iranian and Nicaraguan revolutions of 1979, the Solidarity movement of 1980-1 in Poland and the 1989 revolutions across central and eastern Europe, while the leading social movements scholar Colin Barker (1999) integrates the concept within a Marxist framework of collective mobilization.

Collective Representations

In his later work, Durkheim more explicitly addressed the problem of collective meaning in society. His concept of *représentation collective*, or 'collective representations', refers to symbolic or intellectual ideas, although the French word *représentation* also connotes an idea of the accuracy of what is being depicted. As part of his effort to protect sociology from the charge of 'materialism', Durkheim asserted that social life is essentially a product of collective representations.

> In social life, everything consists of representations, ideas and sentiments, and there is nowhere better to observe the powerful effectiveness of representations. Only collective representations are much more powerful than individual ones: they have a power of their own, and relate to a distinctive science. (1908: 247)

Without concepts to represent thought, humans would cease to communicate as social beings (Durkheim, 2001: 334). The content of social life cannot be reduced directly to individual states of consciousness or material conditions. Collective representations 'make' society as a higher form of reality than immediate sense perception (Durkheim, 1983: 85). Emblematic symbols give material form to and help to inculcate intangible feelings of belonging. A piece of coloured cloth arranged in a certain pattern becomes a sacred national flag that individuals are prepared to kill and die for.

SOCIOLOGY OF KNOWLEDGE

All forms of knowledge depend on representations. Ideas, concepts and images are not free-floating, although they enjoy some autonomy from the intermediary role of the social substratum:

> In order for collective representations to become intelligible they must spring from something and, since they cannot constitute a circle closed in upon itself, the source from which they derive must be found outside them. (Durkheim, 1897: 171)

This is not to say that the truth of social life is made self-evident by its representations. As far as Durkheim is concerned, 'profound causes' operate deep below the level of individual consciousness. Such causal depths make the actual meaning of symbols difficult to comprehend from outside their social context.

Durkheim assumes that social morphology determines collective representations. For instance, tribes that organize a camp in a circle also conceive space as circular. Social organization is the model for spatial organization (Durkheim, 2001: 14, 17; Durkheim and Mauss, 1963). But for Durkheim collective representations are not related to social morphology in the same way that the ideological superstructure is related to the economic base for Marxism. In a specific rejection of historical materialism Durkheim states:

> But collective consciousness is something different from a mere epiphenomenon of its morphological base, just as individual consciousness is something different from a simple efflorescence of the nervous system. (2001: 319)

Durkheim attempts to steer between two alternative approaches to representations. On the one hand is the idea from empiricism that representations emerge out of sensory perception and personal experience. On the other hand is the idea derived from Kant that representations are innate and logically prior to human experience and perception, which they help to organize. In the case of empiricism, it is difficult to see how empirical perception, which changes from moment to moment, is able to spontaneously organize this stream into stable and rational representations. Durkheim is more sympathetic to Kant's rationalism than empiricism. But if Kant's categories are pre-given and fixed by a mysterious innate human ability, then why do representations vary so much across human history and cultures?

Although Durkheim generally accepts the Kantian critique of empiricism, neither of these solutions are adequate to the collective character of representation. Collective representations express the various concepts, images and objects through which society thinks itself into existence. External symbols allow the closed-off worlds of individual representations to communicate with each other.

> Solely because society exists, there also exists – *outside* of individual sensations and images – a whole system of representations that enjoy marvellous properties. *Through* them, men understand one another, intellects can intermingle. These intellects have a kind of force, a moral ascendancy by virtue of which they affect particular minds. (Durkheim, 2001: 332, my emphases)

Derived from religion, concepts become fixed and crystallized at a certain moment in their development. Because they express the way that society as a whole imagines the objects of experience, collective representations are more stable than individual representations.

Durkheim builds up a hierarchical model of collective representation, ascending from concepts to categories to total classification. First, *concepts* are directly derived from the regularity and stability of impersonal social life. Hence they seem immutable and universal. Second, *categories* refer to those more general concepts like time and space that play a leading role in knowledge by encompassing and subordinating other concepts. They both derive from society and provide 'the permanent frameworks of mental life' (2001: 336). Third, *classification* schemes arrange things in order according to their resemblance to each other in some respect. Classification, or class, is the highest, most abstract category since it operates beyond perception at the level of the whole or the totality and encompasses all other concepts and categories (2001: 337)

INDIVIDUAL AND COLLECTIVE REPRESENTATION

Since Aristotle it has been understood that primary categories – time, space, number, cause, substance, personality and so on – provide 'the armature of intelligence' essential to any meaningful human existence (Durkheim, 2001: 11). Representations do not inhere in time and space as such. Time is not an unending flow as philosophers believe but a social institution, an abstract, impersonal framework that divides and measures a temporal sequence into hours, days, weeks, months, seasons, years. Space is not an unending expanse but is always subject to representations that divide, coordinate and measure – left–right, up–down, length–width, above–below, north–south and so on.

Only the most general representations can convey the sense of society as an impersonal 'consciousness of consciousness' (2001: 339).

Collective representations are the product of a vast cooperative effort that extends not only through space but over time; their creation has involved a multitude of different minds associating, mingling, combining their ideas and feelings – the accumulation of generations of experience and knowledge. A very special intellectuality, infinitely richer and more complex than that of the individual, is concentrated in them. (2001: 18)

This has a generic quality since society thinks about itself only in its broadest, most permanent features. Representations reach towards the totality of experience accumulated in the enduring, impersonal stock of collective knowledge.

Durkheim (1895: 41) insists that collective representations are different in kind from individual representations: 'Myths, popular legends, religious conceptions of every kind, moral beliefs, etc., express a different reality from individual reality'. As contact between different groups develops, the collective horizon is enlarged and the idea grows of a much larger whole beyond the immediate group. Classifications are continually revised. Categories become more universal and abstract, releasing them from a direct social determination. Hence, 'logical organization is differentiated from social organization and becomes autonomous' (Durkheim, 2001: 341).

Representations become 'social products of the second degree'. Because they are collective they must 'correspond to the nature of things'.

If these concepts involve artifice simply because they are constructed, it is an artifice that ever more closely approximates nature. Just because ideas of time, space, genus, cause, and personality are constructed from social elements, we must not, therefore, conclude that they have no objective value. On the contrary, their social origins suggest that they have some basis in the nature of things. (2001: 20)

This gives them an aura of objective authority (2001: 333). Society refines and modifies the crude subjective material of rudimentary concepts over historical time until they come closer to the thing represented. This social inheritance guarantees against collective representations being entirely illusory. That logical thought has social origins in no way degrades it or reduces it to the contingency of its immediate context. Society exercises considerable powers of collective creativity far exceeding those of any individual genius, who at any rate is always formed within society.

Collective representations provide society with some degree of logical control over its judgements but in a different way from the *conscience collective.* First, collective representations unify the diversity of complex differentiated societies whereas only a singular *conscience collective* is necessary for moral control in simple undifferentiated societies. Second, meaning is often unconscious in collective representations in stark contrast to the high level of conscious meaning demanded by the *conscience collective* (Durkheim, 1974: 21). Third, Durkheim indicated that the *conscience collective* expresses ideals to which reality ought to aspire whereas collective representations express the existing reality in concepts, categories and classes (Gane, 1992). The *conscience collective* is an ideal of moral value while collective representations are abstract symbols of social reality.

RELIGIOUS REPRESENTATIONS

Durkheim's original model for collective representations is religious belief. Religion represents 'the pre-eminent form and abbreviated expression of the whole of collective life' (Durkheim, 2001: 314). Reality, ideal and base, sacred and profane, is refracted through religious beliefs.

> Religious representations are collective representations that express collective realities; rituals are ways of acting that are generated only within assembled groups and are meant to stimulate and sustain the mental states in these groups. (2001: 11)

Durkheim regards as axiomatic the idea that religious beliefs, bizarre and other-worldly as they often seem to the rational mind, contain a kernel of truth. Religion superimposes onto reality the concept of the sacred as an ideal answer to profane imperfections. This ideal conjures up abstractions about reality and allows society to make collective sense of its own existence. Because of this, religious ideals outlast religious institutions.

Counter-intuitively, Durkheim argues that even science has its origin in religion. Reason is rooted in faith, logic in mystery. In religion, gods are conceived and represented as abstract powers rather than experienced first hand. Early religion was a cosmology which raised questions about the origins, workings and purpose of the world, encompassing what would later develop into science and philosophy.

> Religion endeavours to translate these realities into an intelligible language that is not different in kind from the language employed by science; both involve connecting things to one another, establishing internal relations between them, classifying them, and systematizing them. (2001: 324)

Science is merely a more rigorous form of religious thought, which it progressively supplants. Science has a privileged status today because people have a faith in it that is not essentially different from religious faith. Science takes over 'the practical truth' of religion's logic of division and classification but rejects its dogmatic speculations about the divinely-ordained nature of things.

CRITICAL DEVELOPMENTS

Durkheim's concept of collective representations indicates a shift in focus away from a positivist concern with the 'brute facts'. However, collective representation is not necessarily intended as the key concept to replace Durkheim's earlier emphasis on social facts and social morphology. Marcel Mauss wanted to retain an idea of the material aspects of collective representations: 'It forces one to seek or see the acts beneath the representations, and the representations beneath the acts and the groups underlying both' (Mauss, 1927: 68). Mauss compared collective representations to 'the social physiology' of structures in motion, complementing the social morphology of the fixed material substratum.

Representations seem to be both socially determined and autonomous. The 'how' of representing as a process gets tangled-up with the 'what' of the object being represented. Society creates representations and representations create society. For some, Durkheim's concept of collective representations ultimately relies on assumptions about psychological underpinnings (Lukes, 1982:18). In his work on collective memory, the Durkhemian Maurice Halbwachs (1992) tried to build a bridge between Durkheim and psychology. More recently, 'postmodern' takes on Durkheim have focused more on representations of reality rather than external reality itself (Meštrović, 1993: 45). Yet this seems to contradict Durkheim's own claim that representations exist as an external reality *outside* of individual sensations and images.

RELATED CONCEPTS

Base and Superstructure; Conscience Collective; Ideal-Types; Sacred and Profane; Social Facts; Totemism

FURTHER READING

The most developed study of collective representations by Durkheim is *The Elementary Forms of Religious Life* (2001). Short excerpts can be found in Mustafa

Emirbayer's collection, *Émile Durkheim: Sociologist of Modernity* (2003). W.S.F. Pickering's edited collection *Durkheim and Representations* (2000) brings together a range of fascinating essays by leading contemporary Durkheimian scholars.

Commodity Fetishism

Section 4 of the first chapter of Marx's *Capital* (1976) is called 'The fetishism of the commodity and its secret'. There Marx resorts to fantastical imagery and language to capture the mysterious qualities of the commodity behind its more obvious, surface appearance. When the commodity appears to be something autonomous in its own right, a social relation between human beings assumes 'the fantastic form of a relation between things ... I call this the fetishism which attaches itself to the products of labour as soon as they are produced as commodities, and is therefore inseparable from the production of commodities' (1976: 165). Commodity production is the organizing principle of capitalism as a mode of production.

THE MYSTERY OF THE COMMODITY

If looked at purely from the point of view of its usefulness, there is nothing particularly strange or mysterious about a commodity. All the materials and human labour in the production of, say, a table, result in wood shaped in a certain way to perform the essential functions of things we call tables. But as soon as the table is let loose on the world as a commodity it takes on another life beyond its own physical existence.

> A commodity appears at first sight an extremely obvious, trivial thing. But its analysis brings out that it is a very strange thing, abounding in metaphysical subtleties and theological niceties. (Marx, 1976: 163)

Marx states this as a surreal riddle: 'It not only stands with its feet on the ground, but, in relation to all other commodities, it stands on its head, and evolves out of its wooden brain grotesque ideas, far more wonderful than if it were to begin dancing of its own free will'. At another point Marx even gets the commodity to speak up for itself:

If commodities could speak, they would say this: our use-value may interest men, but it does not belong to us as objects. What does belong to us as
objects, however, is our value. Our own intercourse as commodities proves
this. We relate to each other merely as exchange-values. (1976: 176–7)

What are we to make of Marx's uncanny imagery of the supernatural
qualities of the commodity? The commodity is more than its material form
and function:

it also reflects the social relation of the producers to the sum total of labour
as a social relation between objects, a relation which exists apart from and
outside the producers. (1976: 164–5)

Because commodity production is premised on impersonal, abstract
exchange relations, its origin in exploited labour is concealed. In the
relationship of things (goods) to other things (money), commodities
encapsulate the 'phantom-like objectivity' of 'abstract human labour'.

DECIPHERING THE SOCIAL HIEROGLYPH

The value of capital acts like 'a social hieroglyphic'. It becomes naturalized
and immutable, standing above society and outside of history. This has an
important methodological lesson for Marx, since the dominant social science
of his day – political economy – became fixated on the chimera of free-
floating commodities:

It is however precisely this finished form of the world of commodities – the
money form – which conceals the social character of private labour and the
social relations between the individual workers, by making those relations
appear as relations between material objects, instead of revealing them
plainly. (1976: 168–9)

Commodity fetishism thus forms the objective structure of alienation
specific to capitalist society. As an objective force structuring reality,
commodity fetishism is closely connected to the subjective consciousness of a reality that has become reified and opaque. Marx famously
claimed that if the appearance and reality of the world coincided
exactly, then there would be no need for scientific understanding.
Knowledge of a society dominated by the commodity fetish is difficult
to acquire since the categories developed by classical economics to
understand it merely re-describe the deceptive outer appearances of the
commodity world.

THE CAPITAL FETISH

Marx also identifies a similar fetish inside the labour process itself, a 'capital fetish'. Capital is 'mystified' in the form of buildings, tools, technology and materials. These confront and dominate the worker 'as something *alien, objective, ready-made*, existing without their intervention, and frequently hostile to them'. Labour power takes the form of a commodity of a special kind; a commodity begetting commodities, set in motion by still other commodities. 'Capital *employs* labour', Marx states, as 'the personification of things and the reification of persons':

> In this process, then, the *social* characteristics of their labour come to confront the workers so to speak in a *capitalized* form; thus machinery is an instance of the way in which the visible products of labour take on the appearance of its masters. The same transformation may be observed in the forces of nature and science, the products of the general development of history in its abstract quintessence. They too confront the workers as the *powers* of capital. They become separated effectively from the skill and knowledge of the individual worker; and even though ultimately they are themselves the products of labour, they appear as an *integral* part of capital wherever they intervene in the labour process. (1976: 1054–5)

It seems as if profit is shared between the three actors involved in its production – capital, land and labour. Capital takes its share in the form of profit from investment as dividends or interest; landowners in the form of rent from private ownership of the earth; labour in the form of wages from the sale of its ability to work. But these morally just claims on the surplus product are about as equivalent to each other, Marx says, as 'lawyer's fees, red beets and music'.

By naturalizing themselves as self-evident substances, interest, rent and wages are made independent of their concrete, historically determined social origin. Business profits at least maintain a connection to the source of profit in a way that neither interest nor rent can: 'If capital originally appeared on the surface of circulation as a fetishism of capital, as value-creating value, so now it appears again in the form of interest-bearing capital, as in its most estranged and characteristic form' (Marx, 1959: 829).

> In capital-profit, or still better capital-interest, land-rent, labour wages, in this economic trinity represented as the connection between the component parts of value and wealth in general and its sources, we have the complete mystification of the capitalist mode of production, the conversion of social relations into things, the direct coalescence of the material production relations with their historical and social determination. It is an

enchanted, perverted, topsy-turvy world, in which Monsieur le Capital and Madame la Terre do their ghost-walking as social characters and at the same time as mere things. (1959: 830)

Interest, rent and wages are 'a distorted form' of the distribution of socially produced value. Only the specific social form of exchange relations – the 'enchanted, perverted, topsy-turvy world' – transforms them each into the respective forms of payment that they wrest from the total social product.

Fetishized commodity production presupposes a world of equal exchange values, where two things quite unlike each other are exchanged through the medium of a third thing, money, the abstract agent of equality. Value may be socially produced, but as it takes on an independent power it covers up the tracks of its origins in the social relations of production.

CRITICAL DEVELOPMENTS

Marx's analysis of commodity fetishism posed a central dilemma for later Marxists. If commodity fetishism exerts such awesome power to reify the structures of reality and consciousness – to become 'a second nature' – then how could this condition ever be transformed?

An outstanding attempt to address this within the Marxist tradition was made by Georg Lukacs (1923). Lukacs links 'reified consciousness' to Weber and Simmel's analysis of rationalization, bureaucracy, calculability and precision in modernity. In so doing he explicates how specialization and the division of labour compel the structures of reification to sink ever deeper into human consciousness. Lukacs subjects both rational, formalistic theory and the 'authentic immediacy' of positivism and empiricism to sustained critique. Such contemplative knowledge about the world, unmediated by practice, corresponds to the commodity structure. Sight is lost of the social whole, which is increasingly irrational and destructive. Though initiated by human labour, the exchange logic of commodity fetishism has placed the entire process beyond human control.

This is not the traditional problem for Marxism of ideological 'false consciousness' but the deep structuring of the phenomenal world by commodity exchange. For Lukacs, the proletariat alone can understand its class position and break through the shell of reification. Outside of collective action, the proletariat is fated to remain dominated by commodity fetishism and the capital fetish. Even if Marx's diagnosis of commodity fetishism gets behind surface appearances, Lukacs' prognosis of proletarian self-emancipation has failed to materialize. Such, perhaps, is the obstinacy of the commodity fetish.

RELATED CONCEPTS

Alienation; Capital; Fashion; Mode of Production; Modernity; Money; Social Facts

FURTHER READING

Chapter 1 of *Capital* (1976) introduces the idea of commodity fetishism. Stephen Shapiro's *How to Read Marx's Capital* (2008) gives an accessible overview. Ben Fine's *The World of Consumption* (2002) brings the idea of commodity fetishism into the economic sociology of the present day.

Conscience Collective

Durkheim (1933: 79) defines the '*conscience collective*' as 'the totality of beliefs and sentiments common to the average citizens of the same society [that] forms a determinate system which has a life of its own'. Although sometimes translated into English as 'collective conscience' or 'common consciousness', the original French term '*conscience collective*' has become established in Anglophone sociology. Yet this doesn't entirely resolve the translation problems. The French word '*conscience*' embodies both the English terms 'conscience', as in a moral or religious conscience, and 'consciousness', as in a self-aware state of mind (Lukes, 1992: 4). A further ambiguity was noted by Durkheim between the terms 'social' and 'collective'. If these are considered 'synonymous', then the term '*conscience collective*' would simply refer to 'the total social conscience'. But Durkheim restricts the term to 'the totality of social similarities' typical of mechanical solidarity.

A MECHANICAL CONSCIENCE

Conscience collective is strongly related to and helps support his concept of mechanical solidarity. The main point is that it has a separate, independent existence beyond individual consciences but yet it reaches through each of them into all parts of society.

It is the same in the North and in the South, in great cities and in small, in different professions. Moreover, it does not change with each generation, but, on the contrary, it connects successive generations with one another. (Durkheim, 1933: 80)

As a continuing legacy of past generations, the authority of the *conscience collective* derives largely from 'the authority of tradition' (1933: 291).

At the level of a single individual, all sorts of social principles and traditions coalesce. Individuals have at least two consciences. The first refers to that of the individual personality and the second to the collective morality of society. In reality, these are always linked because 'we take part in several groups and there are in us several collective consciences' (1933: 105 n.44). The *conscience collective* coheres around a single substratum (1933: 106). Durkheim's concept of the *conscience collective* can therefore ambiguously slide between the two meanings depending on whether he wishes to emphasize collective morality or individual psychology.

The *conscience collective* varies according to the 'social density' produced by volume, intensity and the rules of conduct. In mechanical solidarity the *conscience collective* is widespread and engulfs individual conscience; its average intensity is keenly felt as a collective imperative; and the rules of conduct are detailed and well defined. The more defined collective beliefs and practices are, the less scope that there is for individual deviation. The *conscience collective* forces everything into a 'uniform mould' of a consensus where 'all consciences vibrate in unison' (1933: 152). The *conscience collective* is supplemented by repressive sanctions. Conversely, the less harsh the rules of conduct, the more they will be subverted or challenged and the *conscience collective* progressively weakened as a moral obligation.

As the division of labour in society advances, the average volume, intensity and detailed rules of the *conscience collective* decline. As the *conscience collective* becomes more general, abstract and indeterminate, spaces are left for the increased development of individual differences. As rules become more abstract and general, and individual reflection becomes more widespread, the less that the *conscience collective* exerts a hold on society. Volume, intensity and explicit rules do not grow at the same rate for the collective as they do for the individual. In organic solidarity, the cult of the individual becomes a kind of collective religious object.

It is, indeed, remarkable that the only collective sentiments that have become more intense are those which have for their object, not social affairs, but the individual. (1933: 167)

CRITICAL DEVELOPMENTS

Durkheim used the concept of the *conscience collective* sparingly in his later work. This was due, first, to his claim that the *conscience collective* was being eclipsed by the division of labour as a force for social solidarity and, second, that the term was too sweeping, static and all-embracing to capture the specific dynamics of belief and morality (Lukes, 1992). Instead, in his later work he began to make use of the concept 'collective representations' and gave belief systems more autonomy from the material substratum than he allowed for the *conscience collective*.

Sometimes Durkheim (1933: 129–30, 172–3, 407) refers to the common conscience in organized societies as beliefs widely held throughout society. Sometimes he focuses on the level of the group, such as occupational groups. Here it is unclear if Durkheim means that because the group is functional for integrating the social whole, then its typical belief system also contributes to overall social integration.

Adorno (2000; see also Hagens, 2006) argues that the *conscience collective* is made into 'a mysterious being' that miraculously fills the gaps in individual motivation left by Durkheim's radical divorce of social facts from individual psychology. Durkheim, Adorno further charges, confuses the objectivity of social life with the objectivity of the *conscience collective*. Morality is effectively placed beyond the reach of individuals. Collective beliefs may be profoundly mistaken about the actual nature of a society founded on power and domination rather than consensus and mutuality. Such beliefs may not be 'moral' at all but merely a way of legitimating powerful institutions. For Adorno the *conscience collective* therefore has no intrinsic normative status in the form of an obligation or duty, as Durkheim assumes.

Durkheim mistakenly conflates the institutionalized *conscience collective* as obligatory because it somehow corresponds to the objective material structures of the substratum. While Durkheim allows for some moderate conflict, equilibrium and cohesion predominate. Wider political and social conflicts and the possibility of more truthful collective representations are generally cast as illegitimate, anomic or simply deluded about society's essentially integrated character.

Collective Effervescence; Collective Representations; Division of Labour in Society (Durkheim); Mechanical and Organic Solidarity; Normal and Pathological; Social Facts

FURTHER READING

Durkheim outlines the concept throughout *The Division of Labour in Society* (1933), especially Book 1 Chapter 2. Useful commentaries include Lukes (1992), Jones (1986), and Parkin (1992).

Division of Labour (Smith and Ferguson)

The idea of the 'division of labour' has been around for a long time, at least since Plato and Aristotle. It informed the proto-sociology of the fourteenth-century Muslim scholar Ibn Khaldun (Baali, 1988). As a concept, the *division of labour* signifies two things simultaneously – division *and* labour. *Division* implies fragmentation, partition and separation, while *labour* implies polar opposites of collaboration, integration, solidarity, association and cooperation. It refers both to the *division* or separation of tasks and the *combination* of the divided elements. A more accurate concept might therefore be 'the division and combination of labour'.

The prominence of the concept in sociology rests primarily with the work of four major social theorists: Adam Ferguson, Adam Smith, Karl Marx and Emile Durkheim. Adam Ferguson (1723–1816) and Adam Smith (1723–1790) made the idea central to modern social theory. In his world-renowned book, *An Inquiry into the Nature and Causes of the Wealth of Nations* (1776), Smith emphasized the key role of the division of labour in material improvement and social cohesion. In contrast to Smith, Ferguson in his pioneering work of historical sociology, *An Essay on the History of Civil Society* (1767), emphasized the human cost of the division of labour.

HOW THE PIN TRANSFORMED SOCIETY

The concept of the division of labour is the very first thing that Smith discusses in the *Wealth of Nations*. By the mid-eighteenth century, the new industrial system in England had dispersed and broken up trades and production into more and more specialized activities, bringing social relations into what Ferguson (1980: 182) called a 'state of complication'.

This complicated 'social division of labour' between separate branches of industry was not unrelated to more basic subdivisions within the workplace. Smith (1952: 37) reasoned that 'what takes place among the labourers in a particular workhouse takes place, for the same reason, among those of a great society'. To make his point about the wider social division of labour, Smith gives his famous example of the manufacture of pins. After all, what could be more basic than making a humble pin?

> One man draws out the wire, another straights it, a third cuts it, a fourth points it, a fifth grinds it at the top for receiving the head; to make the head requires two or three distinct operations; to put it on, is a peculiar business, to whiten it is another; it is even a trade itself to put them into the paper; and the important business of making a pin is, in this manner, divided into about eighteen distinct operations, which, in some [factories], are all performed by distinct hands, though in others the same man will sometimes perform two or three of them. (1952: 3)

For Smith the advantage of this over other forms of production lies in the increased 'productive power of labour'. Whereas in the past it would take one worker a full day to make just one pin, with the tasks divided up between ten people Smith calculated that they could make 48,000 pins a day, or 4,800 for each worker! This represents a remarkable gain in labour's productivity through the division of simple tasks.

While Smith concedes that not all types of labour can be divided to the same degree as pin manufacture, he identified a new, general principle of social organization. First, workers become more expert and efficient if individual tasks are divided and simplified. Second, time is saved by removing the need for individual workers to change tools or position for each and every stage of production. Third, as tasks become simpler they can be more easily performed by machinery.

A necessary precondition for the division of labour is the accumulation of a stock of materials and tools:

> The quantity of materials which the same number of people can work up, increases in a great proportion as labour comes to be more and more

subdivided; and as the operations of each workman are gradually reduced to a greater degree of simplicity, a variety of new machines come to be invented for facilitating and abridging those operations. (Smith, 1952: 117)

One 'natural effect of improvement' is that less labour is needed for each unit of output, cheapening the cost of manufactured goods. Outside the workplace, according to Smith, even the 'lowest ranks' of society can enjoy the 'universal opulence' of national wealth. Ferguson (1980: 181) makes the related point that consumers now demand high-quality goods perfected by specialization.

EXCHANGE AND THE DIVISION OF LABOUR

Why did this occur? For Smith and Ferguson there is something inherent in human nature, perhaps our ability to reason and speak, that gives people a natural 'propensity' to exchange one thing for another. This basic 'propensity to exchange' integrates human diversity into ever more complex divisions of labour, 'like the parts of an engine' as Ferguson (1980: 182) put it.

In 'civilized society' people are unable to meet all their own needs. They get what they want by appealing to the self-interest of other individuals. In one of the most famous statements in social philosophy, Smith reasons:

Give me that which I want, and you shall have this which you want, is the meaning of every such offer; and it is in this manner that we obtain from one another the far greater part of those good offices which we stand in need of. It is not from the benevolence of the butcher, the brewer, or the baker that we expect our dinner, but from their regard to their own interest. We address ourselves not to their humanity but to their self-love, and never talk to them of our own necessities but of their advantages. (1952: 7)

If exchange produces the division of labour, which in turn produces greater social wealth, then 'opulence' can be best secured by a market society.

Markets develop where transport and communication make multiple exchanges easier. Free movement of goods and people encourages individuals to exchange their surplus product for the produce of other people's labour. From this, the division of labour gives rise to the money economy. Scattered, small-scale communities will be more impoverished than large-scale urban societies since, without exchange and specialization, 'every farmer must be butcher, baker and brewer for his own family' (1952: 8).

SOCIAL CONSEQUENCES

Smith emphasized the positive advantages of the division of labour for creating a more prosperous, cohesive society through higher levels of productivity. But his account was no simplistic apology for the new capitalist society. At many points, Smith condemns the negative effects of the division of labour on a 'mutilated and deformed' human nature:

> His dexterity at his own particular trade seems, in this manner, to be acquired at the expense of his intellectual, social, and martial virtues. But in every improved and civilised society this is the state into which the labouring poor, that is, the great body of the people must necessarily fall, unless government takes some pains to prevent it. (1952: 341)

Social inequalities do not arise from nature but instead reflect habit, custom and education. Smith's example of the difference between the philosopher and the street porter highlights the role of the division of labour in the separation of intellectual and manual abilities:

> These varied occupations present an almost infinite variety of objects to the contemplation of those few, who, being attached to no particular occupation themselves, have leisure and inclination to examine the occupations of other people. The contemplation of so great a variety of objects necessarily exercises their minds in endless comparisons and combinations, and renders their understandings, in an extraordinary degree, both acute and comprehensive. (1952: 341)

This has sometimes been characterized as the difference between Smith writing as an economist, praising productivity gains, and Smith writing as a sociologist, criticizing human stultification (Rosenberg, 1965). But these two processes are connected. As the intellect of individual workers is degraded so the overall intellect of society increases. Monotony in production is related to diversity in consumption. 'In a civilised state ... though there is little variety in the occupations of the greater part of individuals, there is an almost infinite variety in those of the whole society' (Smith, 1952: 341).

Smith, like Durkheim, tended to see the division of labour as helping to integrate society. However, Ferguson (1980: 183–7), like Marx, viewed the division of labour as socially disintegrative and 'alienating' (Hill, 2008): 'In every commercial state, notwithstanding any pretension to equal rights, the exaltation of a few must depress the many'. Some social positions allow for 'the enlargement of thought' while others are made inferior and ignorant:

'the genius of the master' compares to the imbecility of the worker; the 'wide comprehension' of the statesman compares to the ignorance of his 'tools'; the general has a wide knowledge of war while the soldier is limited to obeying simple commands. Workplace monotony destroys human creativity but increases precision and repetition:

> ignorance is the mother of industry as well as superstition. Reflection and fancy are subject to err; but a habit of moving the hand, or the foot, is independent of either. (Ferguson, 1980: 182)

Although painted as a forerunner to Marx, Ferguson's sympathies are clearly with the ruling elite's capacity for preserving the virtues of civility against 'rude society'. He generally accepts that one class must submit to a specialized occupation of one-sided, simple, soul-destroying labour (Brewer, 1989; Hill, 2006).

CRITICAL DEVELOPMENTS

By the 1760s and 1770s, then, Ferguson and Smith recognized that it is no longer individuals that embody technological and intellectual innovation. Knowledge is a product of society, accumulated through and expressed by the social division of labour. They did not manage to clearly separate the social division of labour from the technical division of labour as Marx was to do. Marx learned from Smith and especially Ferguson, that science develops as a productive force in the service of capital, distinct from and in opposition to labour.

It is one of the few concepts from social theory that has had a profound effect on the natural sciences in the shape of evolutionary theory (Limoges, 1994). The favour was returned when the concept was absorbed into evolutionary sociology by Herbert Spencer (1820–1903). For Spencer a social organism and an individual organism were similar insofar as they formed 'a living whole' of mutually interdependent parts. Society evolved from simple homogeneity to complex differentiation. The division of labour in society is as 'rigorous' as that of physiology. If one part stops working it causes all the other organs to fail, as when iron-workers depend on coal being produced by miners or clothes manufacturers depend on textile producers (Spencer, 1971: 111–12).

Spencer's biological division of labour stressed internal differentiation, mutuality, inter-dependence, function, growth and structural wholes. Society was seen a self-regulating system, about which little could be done to ameliorate the condition of the poor, justifying free markets and the principle of natural selection through 'the survival of the fittest'.

Alienation; Bureaucracy; Civil Society; Division of Labour (Marx); Division of Labour in Society (Durkheim); Modernity

FURTHER READING

Both Ferguson and Smith's seminal contributions are widely available. John D. Brewer's essay 'Conjunctural history, sociology and social change' (1989) sets Ferguson in a sociological context. More wide-ranging are James Buchan's engaging little book *Adam Smith and the Pursuit of Perfect Liberty* (2006) and Lisa Hill's scholarly study *The Passionate Society* (2006).

Division of Labour (Marx)

For Marx the division of labour is 'the category of all categories'. Marx typically developed his concepts by studying and then critiquing the ideas of the most advanced thinkers of his day. His conceptual reconstruction of the division of labour had five main phases. First, he examined the origins of the division of labour. Second, Marx emphasized how the division of labour is re-combined to produce 'a collective worker' or 'social labour' embodied in knowledge, technology and science. Third, from Adam Ferguson, Marx learns that the material progress brought about by the division of labour is bought at the cost of social alienation. Fourth, Marx revises Adam Smith by shifting the emphasis from the division of labour in society to the division of labour in production. Fifth, the division of alienated labour can be abolished under changed social conditions.

HETEROGENEOUS AND ORGANIC LABOUR

First, Marx criticized the circularity of Smith's argument that market exchange *causes* the division of labour. For exchange to be possible,

72

key concepts in classical social theory

independent occupations must already exist. Exchange merely brings independent trades into a new, inter-dependent relationship (Marx, 1976: 472). Whereas Smith gave a pseudo-naturalistic explanation about a human 'propensity' to exchange, Marx and Engels locate the emergence of specialization in the domestic division of labour:

> which was originally nothing but the division of labour in the sexual act, then the division of labour that develops spontaneously or 'naturally' by virtue of natural dispositions (e.g. physical strength), needs, accidents, etc. etc. Division of labour only becomes truly such from the moment when a division of material and mental labour appears. (1845–6: 158–9)

From this 'natural' source, the division of labour is extended gradually, first, with the increase of population and contact with other groups into a 'tribal' division of labour, which essentially reproduces 'the slavery latent in the family'. Engels later corrected Marx's claim, using the latest anthropological evidence that the family actually developed out of the tribe (Marx, 1976: 471: n. 26). Next, the 'ancient' division of labour united several tribes in a city, giving rise to multiple divisions of labour between the main classes, town and country, state and society, and industry and trade. Subsequently, the 'feudal' division of labour was restricted by divisions within and between town and country, 'princes, nobility, clergy and peasant in the country and soon also the rabble of casual labourers in the towns'. By Smith's own time, competition had developed *within* towns and nations, as well as *between* towns and nations competing for trade.

Out of 'simple cooperation', the 'classic' form of the division of labour developed. This happened in two ways. Marx (1976: 461) calls these 'heterogeneous' and 'organic' manufacture. In 'heterogeneous' manufacture, independent crafts are brought together by an employer, ending their spatial separation. In examples like watch production or coat manufacture formerly independent heterogeneous crafts are brought together and 'socialized'. In 'organic' manufacture, the skills of a single craft are progressively subdivided. For example, pin production is broken down into an 'organic' series of inter-dependent stages. Either way, the result is a more systematic division of labour.

SOCIAL LABOUR

Second, in Smith's day the *division* of total labour predominated, as in his example of pin production, with its emphasis on individual 'dexterity'. By Marx's time, the social *combination* of individual labour predominated. The social division of labour, for Marx, is a 'manifold whole' of differentiated forms of specialized labour. This is premised on the assumption that other members of society are also occupied in similarly one-sided but qualitatively different types of labour.

'Social labour' or the 'collective worker' becomes embodied in what Marx called the *'animated monster'* of machinery and capital's use of science. Tools and knowledge passed down by human culture for centuries are taken out of human hands, simplified, and powered by machinery. Marx (1976: 460–1) drew explicitly on Darwin's theory of biological evolution to note how the differentiation and simplification of specialized labour is one of the material preconditions for the development of machinery. Machinery combines simple tools. Any individual imperfections of the detail worker are ironed out by 'the whole mechanism' which compels the worker to labour methodically like a machine (1976: 469).

SOCIAL ALIENATION

Third, social labour forms a totality but one whose individual component parts are alien to each other. The division of labour is not necessarily a universal force for social cohesion and improvement as Smith (and later Durkheim) assumes (unlike Ferguson). It reflects the particular interest of capital. Its overall effect is a forced combination by capital of individually monotonous labour. Repetitive, mindless labour destroys the human need for regular changes in life activity. Marx emphasizes, following Adam Ferguson, that this is not the product of free, self-conscious cooperation. It is an alien power, reducing labour to a 'pure detail', totally dependent on the division of labour.

Neither does the division of labour enhance workers' skills or the quality of finished products. Unlike ancient Greeks like Xenophon or Plato, as a modern economist Smith was mainly concerned with the *quantity* rather than *quality* of labour. Where the modern worker is indifferent to work, earlier crafts were fully immersed in a diverse range of skills, lending their work an 'artistic' character. They therefore had a material interest in limiting any further subdivision of labour. Smith neglects how mediaeval resistance by craft guilds to the spread of the division of labour nurtured the artistic quality of work.

TECHNICAL DIVISION OF LABOUR

Fourth, Smith and his forerunners confused the *'social* division of labour' with what Marx calls the *'technical* division of labour'. On the one hand, the social division of labour is coordinated blindly by the market exchange of commodities between manufacturers. On the other hand, the technical division of labour is internally coordinated within the workplace by an organized social and technical hierarchy. In the latter case, the individual within production becomes one-sided and degraded. In the former case, individual wants are stimulated as many-sided, thanks to world trade and colonialism and the cheapening of commodities. Initially, the technical division of labour derives from the social division of labour. It subsequently reacts back on the social division of labour, breaking up unified trades into independent manufacturers of parts rather than finished products.

Marx adds that 'anarchy' in the social division of labour and 'despotism' in the technical division of labour mutually condition each other. In the workplace, ownership is concentrated in a single authority, the capitalist, who dominates the dependent parts, labour. In society, ownership is dispersed among many independent capitalists, who respond only to the anarchy of competition. In production, everything is planned and calculated; in society, things are left to chance. Marx reserves particular invective for the contradictory principles of bourgeois society:

> The same bourgeois consciousness which celebrates division of labour in the workshop, the lifelong annexation of the worker to a partial operation, and his complete subjection to capital, as an organization of labour that increases its productive power, denounces with equal vigour every conscious attempt to control and regulate the process of production socially, as an inroad upon such sacred things as the rights of property, freedom and the self-determining 'genius' of the individual capitalist. It is very characteristic that the enthusiastic apologists of the factory system have nothing more damning to urge against a general organization of labour in society, than it would turn the whole of society into an immense factory. (1976: 477)

ABOLITION OF THE DIVISION OF LABOUR

Fifth, far from turning society into a huge factory, Marx famously argued that the division of labour could be overcome and abolished. At the moment, everyone is restricted to specialize in some 'exclusive sphere of activity': as 'a hunter, a fisherman, herdsman, or a critical critic'. With the abolition of the division of labour everything becomes possible:

> where nobody has one exclusive sphere of activity but each can become accomplished in any branch he wishes, society regulates the general production and thus makes it possible for me to do one thing today and

another tomorrow, to hunt in the morning, fish in the afternoon, rear cattle in the evening, criticise after dinner, just as I have a mind, without ever becoming hunter, fisherman, herdsman or critic. (Marx and Engels, 1845-6: 160)

This is often interpreted as utopian day-dreaming, something wholly out of character for Marx. However, Marx's reasoning is more logical (Weiss, 1976). So long as humans meet their needs through some form of production, the antithesis between work and life can never be completely overcome. However, essential work could be subordinated to a more rounded, cultivated life. If the division of labour simplifies and replaces labour by machinery, time spent doing monotonous work can be drastically reduced and more fairly distributed, leaving individuals free to follow whatever they have 'a mind' to.

CRITICAL DEVELOPMENTS

Harry Braverman (1974) resurrected Marx's emphasis on the technical division of labour by demonstrating that many skilled jobs, including white collar work, have been repeatedly subdivided and simplified, from the 'time and motion' studies of 'scientific management' to the Fordist assembly line through to 'service work'. Marx and Engels' emphasis on the domestic division of labour has been critically appropriated by feminist thinkers through concepts of the 'sexual division of labour', the 'gender division of labour' and the 'household division of labour' to describe gender divisions of domestic and public work (Shelton and John, 1996).

The concept has been taken up by geographers as 'the spatial division of labour' to describe the uneven geographical distribution of jobs, sectors and industries (Massey, 1984). The reorganization of production on a global scale by multinational firms and the rise of newly-industrializing nations since the 1970s led to the idea of 'the new international division of labour'. We can see today's call centre functions as following a similar process of deskilling, simplification, specialization and technical controls over the speed and quality of work once under the control of more skilled clerical labour. That deskilling and the alienated division of labour have not been overcome indicates that the power of capital to continually re-divide labour remains a fundamental feature of contemporary society.

RELATED CONCEPTS

Alienation; Capital; Civil Society; Class; Division of Labour (Smith and Ferguson); Primitive Accumulation

FURTHER READING

Chapter 14 of *Capital Volume 1* (1976) summarizes Marx's ideas on the division of labour. Helpful primers can also be consulted, like Chris Arthur's *Marx's Capital* (1992) and Stephen Shapiro's *How to Read Marx's Capital* (2008). A brilliant account of how Marx's thinking developed is given by Rob Beamish in *Marx, Method and the Division of Labor* (1992).

Division of Labour in Society (Durkheim)

What holds modern society together and binds individuals to it? How can the individual appear autonomous and free but depend utterly on society? Durkheim points to the division of labour for an answer. Durkheim rejected pessimistic views of the division of labour as leading inexorably to fragmentation and social disintegration. He also resists some of the more sweeping, trans-historical accounts of the division of labour, arguing that it only fulfils the needs that it itself creates, 'or heals the wounds which it inflicts'. Its true function is to create a feeling of social solidarity, which Durkheim views as inherently moral. Everywhere, people are compelled to specialize at the same time as they are asked to follow the same ideals.

A DIVISION OF SOCIAL LABOUR

Durkheim notes earlier concerns with the division of labour going back to Aristotle, and attributes the first theory of it to Adam Smith. He follows Herbert Spencer's evolutionary model, rising from simple to more complex forms of specialization (Corning, 1982). Durkheim repeatedly emphasizes Spencer's Darwinian struggle for survival. Durkheim credits Comte with the first strictly sociological account of the division of labour. The central hypothesis guiding Durkheim's study is Comte's argument that the continual subdivision of labour 'especially constitutes social solidarity and becomes the elementary cause of the extension and growing complication of the social organism' (Durkheim: 1933: 63).

This focus shifted the problem of the *social* division of labour away from the end goal of the *economic* division of labour in higher productivity, cheaper goods, or more profit. Durkheim sees the social *function* of the division of labour in terms of moral regulation and social integration rather than economic utility.

> We are thus led to consider the division of labour in a new light. In this instance, the economic services that it can render are picayune [trivial] compared to the moral effect that it produces, and its true function is to create in two or more persons a feeling of solidarity. (1933: 56)

The 'categorical imperative' of the modern division of labour is: 'Make yourself usefully fulfil a determinate function' (1933: 43).

By disregarding or downgrading the specifically economic rationale for the division of labour behind a moral one, Durkheim challenges Smith's idea that social cohesion results from the blind drive of individual self-interest. Social unity is not brought about by self-interested individuals exchanging contracts in the market. Rather, exchange itself depends on common beliefs that constitute the moral unity of society. Society always precedes self-interested individuals in Durkheim's sociology.

This does not mean that Durkheim logically deduces the division of labour from some abstract moral principle. A rigorous science is necessary, not to abandon ethics as such, but to improve society without recourse to 'destructive and revolutionary' doctrines. What is happening in society is analogous to the more general pattern in nature. In biology, the specialization of an organism corresponds to a higher stage of development (1933: 41). Durkheim compares specialization to a form of 'evolution [that] is realizing itself with unpremeditated spontaneity' (1933: 39). Later, Durkheim's naturalism would seem rather naïve and lacking support in empirical observation.

CRIME AND THE DIVISION OF LABOUR

In the case of society, it is exceedingly difficult to measure with absolute certainty the moral function of the division of labour or to establish if it is essential to social cohesion or is of merely secondary importance. This is why Durkheim uses law as a proxy measure of immorality. Law is a stable index of moral solidarity. It sanctions various degrees of punishment for different violations of moral norms. Because it stands above society, superior to it, punishment is inflicted on behalf of society: 'Crime brings together upright consciences and concentrates them' (Durkheim, 1933: 102). Crime offends against the necessary illusion that society is united. Because it makes social solidarity appear more fragile, the unanimity of public opinion is demanded.

There are two kinds of legal sanction: 'repressive' and 'restitutive'. Repressive sanctions inflict 'damage' or suffering on the transgressor, such as imprisonment or some other penalty established by criminal law. Restitutive sanctions are not punitive but aim to restore the relationships temporarily disrupted from their normal state, as in civil, commercial or procedural law. Repressive law rests on the *conscience collective* while restitutive law is only weakly integrated into society (1933: 69–70). Restitutive law corresponds to individuals spontaneously exchanging contracts in the market and functions in the division of labour.

In restitutive law, the moral obligation is first spelled out and the sanction follows from it. In repressive law, the sanction is spelled out but the moral obligation is not explicitly stated. This occurs because it is already implicit in what everyone knows: repressive law does not demand respect for life but punishes the murderer. Repressive law has little to do in reality with justice, deterrence or the rehabilitation of offenders and everything to do with the need to expiate the offence committed against common morality. An act offends against the average morality not because it is criminal; rather, it is criminal because it offends morality (1933: 81).

A MORAL DIVISION OF LABOUR?

What Durkheim's discussion of law and criminological types leads to is the decline of the *conscience collective* and the rise of the personal conscience of separate individuals. A whole series of repressive laws, especially over sexual relations, family and religion, gradually disappear. Society becomes organized around functional occupations as a result of the division of labour. Traditions based on family, heredity and place of origin no longer have the same binding effect on individuals.

Well-defined religious obligations broke down gradually as scientific, political and economic practices began to carve out independent spaces for themselves. This 'law of regression' indicates the failing vitality and declining coverage of collective beliefs at the same time as the level of functional inter-dependence of the division of labour rises. Society begins to lose a common structure that would unify such practices.

> Functional diversity induces a moral diversity that nothing can prevent, and it is inevitable that one should grow as the other does. We know, moreover, why these two phenomena develop in parallel fashion. Collective sentiments become more and more impotent in holding together the centrifugal tendencies

that the division of labour is said to engender, for these tendencies increase as labour is more divided, and, at the same time, collective sentiments are weakened. (Durkheim, 1933: 361).

As the division of labour stimulates further social differentiation, moral solidarity becomes more abstract, rational and diffuse. It exercises less direct restraint over individuals, who are free to pursue their own development.

Rational individual consciences, expressed through inter-dependent functional specialization and many-sided sociability, 'normally' produce much stronger bonds of social solidarity than the inflexible *conscience collective*. Society is coordinated by contract exchange, not moral bonds. But advanced organized societies are not entirely devoid of moral bonds. It is not enough that there are rules; they also have to be perceived as just and right (1933: 407). Social solidarity always has to have a normative dimension in order to get individuals to identify strongly with its commands. In its integrative function of creating order, harmony and cohesion the division of labour possesses a definite if more diffuse moral character.

Complex societies are integrated by four types of moral solidarity: an ideology of individualism, an obligation to specialize, a sense of justice, and the morality of specialized occupations. First, individualism and the 'cult of personal dignity' becomes a new religion for society (1933: 172). But since it does not venerate society, individualism cannot become a true source of moral integration. Second, individuals are morally as well as materially obliged to specialize in particular functions as essential to the greater whole. Third, the modern sense of justice demands a level-playing field of equal opportunities and is offended by inherited material privileges and advantages. Finally, occupational groups produce similar kinds of individuals in a modern form of mechanical solidarity. Occupational cooperation is freely-chosen, Durkheim (1933: 227) assumes, giving rise to 'permanent' duties and mutual obligations. Durkheim made concrete proposals for occupational guilds to assume political and welfare functions hoping that occupational solidarity would mitigate the worst effects of individualism and anomie arising from an 'abnormal division of labour'.

CRITICAL DEVELOPMENTS

Published in 1893, Durkheim's first book, *The Division of Labour in Society* (1933), is considered a classic of social theory. Durkheim challenged the economic orthodoxies of his day, so much so that he struggled to get a teaching post in Paris (Lukes, 1992). His pre-eminent position on the division of labour was ensured by Talcott Parsons' (1949) elevation of norms and values as social causes over Spencer's (1971) utilitarian account of rational interests. But the book initially suffered from a poor reputation and was later criticized for making faulty assumptions about 'primitive man'. Durkheim himself had second thoughts, which he tried to refine in later studies.

First, Durkheim tends to treat moral solidarity as unified and fails to account for conflict and contradiction between certain moral principles and laws, which leads to a view of the state as a collective expression of consensus (Jones, 1986: 57). Second, he forces repressive law and restitutive law to reflect different social substrata, neglecting evidence that contradicts his model. Third, Durkheim committed what philosophers call 'the fallacy of misplaced concreteness' by attributing causal power to 'moral facts', which were really his own theoretical constructions rather than a description of social reality. Fourth, nowhere does he explicitly define what he means by 'division of labour'. It is associated variously with differentiation, occupations, specialization, organization and functions. Finally, Durkheim is too optimistic that the division of labour will evolve to become 'normal' at some unspecified point in the future. That Durkheim began to address some of these shortcomings in later work is a recognition that theoretical concepts can only develop through informed critique.

RELATED CONCEPTS

Anomie; Conscience Collective; Division of Labour (Smith and Ferguson); *Gemeinschaft* and *Gesellschaft*; Mechanical and Organic Solidarity; Social Morphology

FURTHER READING

Clearly, *The Division of Labour in Society* (1933) is where Durkheim develops his argument. Better first to read a shorter summary of the work in introductory texts such as Jones (1986: Ch. 2) or Thompson (2002: Ch. 3.4). Lukes (1992: Ch. 7) gives a vivid account of the development of Durkheim's concept in a biographical context.

division of labour in society (Durkheim)

Fashion is one of the most familiar aspects of modernity. It is also one of the most deceptive. Behind the more obvious features of fashion lies a series of sociological ambiguities and paradoxes. These ambiguities were identified at the start of the twentieth century by Georg Simmel (1997) in a number of essays on fashion, adornment and style. For Simmel, fashion is one of the most characteristic features of modernity (Frisby, 1985). Because it represents a passing fragment of everyday experience, fashion expresses underlying connections that normally go unnoticed.

IMITATION AND DIFFERENCE

Fashion marks what Simmel sees as the essential duality of human nature. People's dispositions are structured by similarity and difference, identity with a group and differentiation from a group in the 'calm devotion to people and things just as much as energetic self-assertion against them both' (Simmel, 1997: 187). Fashion allows individuals to simultaneously stand out from the crowd but also to conform to whatever styles and tastes are general.

On one side, Simmel suggests that individuals have a natural propensity to *imitate* each other. Through imitation the individual adapts to the social group. On the other side, individuals *differentiate* themselves from the crowd. They break away from what is already given towards something new and different. Fashion is a battleground between these two tendencies. Imitation of a general fashion allows similarities with the group to be established; a conspicuous change in fashion indicates difference and distinction.

A willingness to follow social conventions like fashion allows individuals a greater sense of freedom. Simmel (1997: 200) sees fashion as a 'social form of marvellous expediency' where people can turn towards society in their outward appearance and at the same time deepen the more fundamental freedom of inner life. The outward display of what is publicly acceptable in terms of fashion allows an individual to reserve for themselves what is truly personal and private. Like everyday pleasantries and conventions, following the fashion of the day becomes a fitting disguise to protect the inner life of the individual.

key concepts in classical social theory

FASHION CONSCIOUSNESS

There is no inherently aesthetic reason why certain styles become fashionable. Almost anything will do the job. While we have a functional need to be clothed, this tells us nothing about the actual styles we wear, why fashion dictates long or short hair, coloured or black coats, lapels or ties of a certain width, and so on. From this criteria fashion seems completely arbitrary: 'Judging from the ugly and repugnant things that are sometimes modern, it would seem as though fashion were desirous of exhibiting its power by getting us to adopt the most atrocious things for its sake alone' (Simmel, 1997: 190).

This relative sense of distance as glamour and elegance is illustrated by body adornments (1997: 208). The intimacy of the tattoo is perceived as crude while impersonal jewellery appears elegant. Between these extremes stand clothes, neither subjective like a tattoo nor objective like jewellery. New clothes seem more objective in their formal 'untouchable coolness' since they have not yet been modified by the body of the wearer over time. Old clothes are more informal, progressively personalized by repeated wearing, losing the general objectivity of distance and impersonality.

An excessive fixation with fashion reflects an individualism emptied of personality and experience. The common currency of fashion is typically exaggerated by extreme fashion consciousness.

> If pointed shoes are in style, then he wears shoes that resemble spear tips;
> if pointed collars are in style, then he wears collars that reach up to his ears;
> if it is fashionable to attend scholarly lectures, then he is never seen anywhere else, and so on. (Simmel, 1997: 194)

Fashion makes up for an individual's lack of importance since it enables them to join a group renowned in terms of fashion alone. Unremarkable but chic individuals become the personification of something far wider.

MONEY AND DISTRACTION

Fashion and money have a special affinity with each other (Simmel, 1900). An economy based on money is indifferent to all distinctions. Simmel (1900: 457–463) indicates how a worker in a shoe factory is a different kind of producer than a shoemaker 'fashioning' customized shoes. Fashionable products can be purchased by those in possession of money with relatively little cultural resistance. Capitalism cheapens the cost of fashion because of its rapid turnover of fashion products.

As an ambiguous mix of destruction and construction, fashion is always doomed to extinction. Obsolescence is built in to the fashion product and fashion's 'impatient tempo' speeds up the number of distractions on offer for the modern consumer. As it grows and becomes general, one part of a social group will tire of today's fashion and look for some new way to display their difference and distinctiveness. Rapid changes in fashion reflect a culture that demands differentiation and demarcation.

ANTI-FASHION AS A LIFESTYLE

Life becomes a 'style', a lifestyle, concerned with the display and visibility of fashionable taste. Lifestyle represents an aesthetic attempt to resolve the modern tension between objective and subjective cultures. Personal security comes from the authority of objective culture: 'Stylized expression, form of life, taste – all these are limitations and ways of creating a distance, in which the exaggerated subjectivism of the times finds a counterweight and a concealment' (Simmel, 1997: 216). Simmel discusses how changing fashions in 'modern furniture' express a 'false individualism' by trying to turn functional domestic objects into unique works of art.

The deliberate opposition to fashion through the ostentatious anti-fashion of outdated clothes merely inverts the fetishism of the fashionable. Anti-fashion equally demands attention for a spurious individualism. As such anti-fashion merely confirms in a negative way the power of fashion in modernity:

> The deliberately unmodern person accepts its forms just as much as the slave to fashion, except that the unmodern person embodies it in a category: in that of negation, rather than in exaggeration. (1997: 195)

Simmel speculates that such individuals reject modernity precisely because their sense of individuality is so weakly developed that they fear that it will be swallowed up by contact with 'the forms, tastes and customs of the general public' (1997: 196). A more rounded personality submits readily to such general trends because it is reassured of its own voluntary agency in the matter.

CLASS DISTINCTION AND FASHION

Similarly dressed people tend to have the same point of social origin.

> Thus, on the one hand, fashion signifies a union with those of the same status, the uniformity of a social circle characterized by it, and, in so doing,

the closure of this group against those standing in a lower position which the higher group characterizes as not belonging to it. (Simmel, 1997: 189)

The very highest social classes are reluctant to encourage rapid change, which they consider 'suspicious and dangerous' since they have nothing to gain and much to lose from any transformation. In contrast, fashion is a special field of activity for the bourgeoisie – 'the real seat of fashion':

> A class which is inherently much more variable, so much more restless in its rhythms than the lowest classes with their silently unconscious conservatism, and the highest classes with their consciously desired conservatism, is the totally appropriate location for a form of life in which the moment of an element's triumph marks the beginning of its decline. (1997: 202)

As soon as the lower classes imitate some fashion it is quickly abandoned by the higher classes. Since modernity allows increased social mobility and contact between the classes, 'the more frantic becomes the hunt for imitation from below and the flight towards novelty above' (1997: 190).

WOMEN AND YOUTH

Women adhere strongly to fashion because of their unequal position within society. Fashion compensates women with a certain individualization within culturally acceptable limits. On the one hand, the imitation of general forms of fashion allows women to drift with broad social currents without suffering personally for their choices. On the other hand, a limited individualism is permitted through fashion's 'ornamentation of the personality'. Fashion gives women a safety valve through which they can assert a form of individuality denied to them in other social situations. Having less need for visible markers of distinction, men seem generally indifferent towards fashion.

Extreme fashion consciousness is found in ambiguous, insecure groups like youth and the *demimonde*. Young people differentiate themselves from peers and other age groups and identify singularly with their own group, often defined exclusively in terms of the latest fashion. In the nineteenth century the *demimonde*, literally the 'half-world' of 'kept women', the mistresses of upper class men, were treated as pariahs and outcasts from society. Women of the *demimonde* detested the hypocrisy of respectable society and, with a stream of disposable money, they adopted evermore extravagant fashions. Simmel sees the cultural rebellion of outlandish *demimonde* fashion as 'an aesthetic form of the destructive urge' (1997: 198).

CYCLES OF FASHION

Fashion's time cycle is ambiguous. Like the commodity more generally, fashion forms a paradox: it is the monotonous return of the ever-same in the guise of the diverse ever-new. Retro-fashion has been around a long time. As Simmel argued a century ago:

> As soon as an earlier fashion has been partially expunged from memory there is no reason why it should not be allowed to return to favour and why the charm of difference, which constitutes its very essence, should not be exercised against that very fashion which derived its attraction when it came onto the scene from its contrast to the style now being revived. (1997: 204)

Fashion locks people further into modernity's sense of the permanent present. In this 'permanency within change', 'change itself does not change' (1997: 204). Fashion always sits on the dividing-line of past and future, intensifying the present moment. At the point of purchase the fashionable product seems immortal, 'as though it wished to live forever', even though every individual fashion is transitory (1997: 203). It represents a break with the past and all that went before. Yet something will come along shortly to displace what is so much in demand at this precise moment.

CRITICAL DEVELOPMENTS

Around the same time that Simmel developed his analysis of fashion, Thorstein Veblen wrote his classic study *The Theory of the Leisure Class* (1899). His concept of fashion parallels Simmel's in certain respects. The leisure class are wealthy enough to spend all their time engaged in non-productive consumption. Memorably, Veblen argued that fashion is the most immediate way for the upper class to conspicuously display a life of wasted effort through, first, its expense, second, its impractical design and futile ornamentation, and third, its novelty and constant turnover.

Veblen also differs from Simmel in a number of ways. Where Simmel sees the content of fashion as wholly arbitrary Veblen attempts to dissect its aesthetic element. Each new fashion is initially felt to be more beautiful than the previous one but is subject to an 'aesthetic nausea' over time as its inherent ugliness and uselessness eventually become apparent. In turn, the new aesthetic standard will itself succumb to odious disenchantment. While both identify wealthier classes as the seat of fashion, Simmel pays more attention to the ambiguities involved for the bourgeoisie, while Veblen tends to read off more directly from the conspicuous consumption needs of his ill-defined 'leisure class'.

key concepts in classical social theory

Simmel's insights were rarely applied to the explosion in studies of youth fashions since the 1960s. Instead, 'subculture theory' tried to read from the contents of fashion of youth styles, from mods to punks to rave, different ways in which fashion subverted dominant cultures and norms. Further critical engagement with Simmel's pioneering theory of fashion would arguably extend the contemporary sociology of youth subcultures, lifestyle and fashion.

RELATED CONCEPTS

Commodity Fetishism; Metropolis; Modernity; Money; Social Forms and Sociation; Social Space

FURTHER READING

Michael Carter discusses Simmel and Veblen, and more recent thinking about fashion, in his book *Fashion Classics from Carlyle to Barthes* (2003). Simmel's essay on 'The philosophy of fashion' as well as 'Adornment' and 'The problem of style' can be found in *Simmel on Culture* (1997).

Gemeinschaft and Gesellschaft

Many classical social theorists wanted to understand the nature of the transition to modernity that they were living through. Typically this was done through the construction of a conceptual dichotomy. Adam Ferguson contrasted 'rude' nations to 'polished' civil society; Henry Maine identified a shift from status to contract; for Marx it was a transition from one mode of production, feudalism, to another, capitalism; Herbert Spencer (1971) compared a pre-modern 'militant society' to a modern 'industrial society'; for Durkheim, it was a shift from mechanical solidarity to organic solidarity. The transition to modernity was often seen as a mixed blessing, bringing with it positive developments in material progress but at the cost of negative effects for social solidarity.

This nostalgia for a lost world was given eloquent expression by Ferdinand Tönnies (1855–1936) in his famous dichotomy of *Gemeinschaft* and *Gesellschaft* (2002), translated into English as 'community' (*Gemeinschaft*) and 'association' or 'society' (*Gesellschaft*). All social relationships are seen by Tönnies as the outcome of 'the will' of individuals to associate with each other. Either people associate with each other purely for the sake of it, for instance as friends or neighbours, or they associate for some other reason external to the relationship itself, for instance in an economic role. Two fundamental principles underpin social relationships – share or trade.

'NATURAL WILL' AND 'RATIONAL WILL'

One kind of will, *Wesenwille* or 'natural will', is affective and expresses a whole way of life. Three forms of natural will – pleasure, custom and commemoration – broadly correspond to three levels of *Gemeinschaft* – kinship, neighbourhood and friendship (2002: 42–4). The other kind of will, *Kurwille* or 'rational will', instrumentally separates means from ends in a fragmented series of exchanges. Three forms of rational will – aspiration, calculation and intellect – underpin the political, economic and scientific institutions peculiar to *Gesellschaft*.

Natural will gives rise to the affective bonds of community; rational will results in the impersonal bonds of society. On the one hand, *Gemeinschaft* develops spontaneously out of the natural will of human sympathy into strong feelings of solidarity and belonging. On the other hand, *Gesellschaft* is constructed artificially by a rational will for a predetermined end based on intellectual calculations about efficient means. Tönnies argues that businessmen, scientists, politicians, the dominant class, men and the elderly tend to be characterized by rational will; peasants, artists, working class, women and youth by natural will.

ORGANIC AND MECHANICAL

Published six years before *The Division of Labour in Society* (1893), Tönnies' *Gemeinschaft and Gesellschaft* inverts Durkheim's later metaphors of mechanical and organic solidarity. *Gesellschaft* operates like a mechanical system, characterized by large-scale urban life, trade, money and rational calculation, while *Gemeinschaft* operates like an organism, characterized by small-scale, stable institutions of family and the village, founded on common feelings of belonging and obligation.

Under *Gemeinschaft* people treat each other as whole human beings, they reciprocate tasks and share a strong collective identity of family, community

key concepts in classical social theory

and religion. Since everyone knows their place in the community the social order is highly stable. In *Gemeinschaft* people are 'essentially united in spite of all separating factors, whereas in *Gesellschaft* they are essentially separated in spite of all uniting factors' (2002: 65). *Gemeinschaft* grows out of the intimacy and physical proximity of the family as an ideal model for community. It expresses the natural will in 'feminine' qualities of unconditional affection, intuition and creativity.

This is transformed in *Gesellschaft*. Individuals become mere parts of a mechanical system and perform roles only to the extent that they offer some personal advantage. Social relations become more unequal, anonymous and alienated. Legal contracts and market exchange produce a shallow moral order that masks widespread social antagonisms and egoistic competition. Labour and capital, rich and poor constantly engage in class conflict, not only over the distribution of economic resources but also over conflicting moral wills.

Gesellschaft is forged by large-scale trade carried out by a commercial class with weak roots in any local or national community as they scour the globe instrumentally in an international search for profitable opportunities. Communities lose much of their local distinctiveness as individuals become organized into 'masses'. In a society dependent on market contracts, large commercial and industrial cities develop. Here traditional roles and values lose their power to reproduce the affectual bonds of community. Money and calculation acquire a decisive importance. Society becomes more individualist, impersonal and anonymous. Isolated, self-interested individualism weakens the affective bonds of social solidarity.

Echoing Marx, for Tönnies production presupposes cooperation in the labour process, while trade presupposes competition in the marketplace. Nevertheless, the dominance of the rational will affects every type of social relation and social group. Abstract rationality transforms relations at work as well as in the market, simplifying and reducing more rounded skills and occupations. Science replaces religion as the carrier of moral authority and formal laws replace customary obligations. Social life is increasingly regulated by an autonomous bureaucratic state apparatus.

TYPOLOGY AND REALITY

Tönnies regarded these two concepts as ideal-types rather than empirical facts about the world. They are not meant to represent distinct stages in the historical development of modernity but are diverging tendencies that might be found to different degrees in any society. Life cannot be based entirely on one type to the exclusion of the other. Neither rationality nor emotions wholly dominate social relationships.

Generally, however, Tönnies sees in mechanical *Gesellschaft* something of a turn for the worst. *Gemeinschaft* has all the positive moral values – love, loyalty, honour, friendship – which *Gesellschaft* singularly lacks (Nisbet, 1993: 76). Influenced by Thomas Hobbes' image of society as a 'war of all against all', a society dominated by exchange relations expresses the alienation of individuals from each other, a lack of solidarity and a mutual hostility bubbling just below the surface. Hence the 'supreme rule' of society is politeness:

> It consists of an exchange of words and courtesies in which everyone seems to be present for the good of everyone else and everyone seems to consider everyone else as his equal, whereas in reality everyone is thinking of himself and trying to bring to the fore his importance and advantages in competition with the others. (Tönnies, 2002: 78)

Even politeness and common decency are merely strategic disguises that individuals wear as they compete with one another. People are restrained only because they fear retaliation.

CRITICAL DEVELOPMENTS

Among Tönnies' achievements is to provide a strictly sociological explanation for the rise of capitalism and the modern state (Nisbet, 1993: 78). Weber (1978: 4) thought that Tönnies' book was a fundamental contribution to sociology, essential background for his own studies. In contrast, Durkheim in his critical review found it 'very laborious'. It should be noted, however, that Durkheim accepted much of Tönnies' conceptual division of society into two essential types and that *Gemeinschaft* came first historically (Cahnman, 1973: 240). Durkheim objected to the characterization of *Gesellschaft* as superficial and transitory, held together only by the external force of the state. In reply, Tönnies accused Durkheim of confusion and misunderstanding since the state itself was a spontaneous product of *Gesellschaft* (Cahnman, 1973: 250).

In America the Chicago School of Sociology gave *Gemeinschaft* and *Gesellschaft* a spatial emphasis as part of their understanding of the rural-urban dichotomy. In Germany the Nazi regime used a bastardized version of Tönnies' idea of *Gemeinschaft* to hark back to the '*Volksgemeinschaft*' of an uncorrupted, racially pure community. As a vocal anti-Nazi, Tönnies was no idle daydreamer longing for the return of a homey *Gemeinschaft*. Tönnies was dubbed 'the strike professor' because he looked to the labour movement for the recovery of a 'common life'.

Somewhat pessimistic, he nevertheless defended urban life and industrial production against Germany's growing band of reactionary ruralists and refused to abandon the necessity for rationality against illusions about harmonious communities and 'culture'.

Despite later denials that he had invented a formula along the lines of 'Gemeinschaft = good, Gesellschaft = bad', Tönnies' concepts were ambiguous enough to be interpreted or caricatured in precisely that manner. In his own writings, Gemeinschaft ambiguously represents an authentic form of social solidarity while Gesellschaft is seen as artificial, transitory and superficial. Society is reduced to economic relations of exchange and compared negatively to a romantic idea of small-scale, face-to-face communities. In society people seem devoid of mutual human feeling. Within the private sphere everyone can do whatever they like, but are unable to do anything outside of it. In this sense, the romantic idea of community (Gemeinschaft) signalled a backlash against 'society' in social theory.

RELATED CONCEPTS

Civil Society; Conscience Collective; Ideal-Type; Mechanical and Organic Solidarity; Modernity; Rationality and Rationalization

FURTHER READING

An accessible short introduction to the conceptual pair is Jorn Falk's chapter on Tönnies in Heine Andersen and Lars Bo Kaspersen's textbook *Classical and Modern Social Theory* (2000). Tönnies' masterpiece *Community and Society* (2002) is readily available in a number of versions. Arthur Mitzman's *Sociology and Estrangement* (1987) expertly places Tönnies in the historical context of German intellectual life.

Historical Materialism

Individuals reproduce themselves by developing social institutions, tribes, communes, cities, classes or families. They cannot live in 'dot-like isolation' (Marx, 1973: 485). 'Historical materialism', the name given to the methodological approach developed by Marx, recognizes the essentially social character of life. Its central postulates can be stated succinctly.

'Materialism' refers to the following premises:

- social being determines consciousness
- human beings necessarily act collectively in society to establish the means of their own physical and social reproduction
- physical and social reproduction are mutually dependent on each other
- in the course of its reproduction societies develop distinctive structures of cooperation and competition known as modes of production
- beyond a minimal level of subsistence societies divide into antagonistic classes.

'Historical' refers to additional premises:

- there is a tendency for the productive forces of society to grow over time
- human beings make their own history within pre-given social conditions
- societies develop inner contradictions which are resolved either by revolutionary transformation or social implosion.

MARX'S METHODOLOGY

It seemed essential for Marx to clarify his methodological principles in order to develop the scientific study of the new capitalist society that had only begun to emerge. By the late 1840s the 'new social science' of the 'critical-utopian socialists' Claude Henri Saint-Simon, Charles Fourier and Robert Owen proposed fantastic schemes and plans for the alleviation of suffering among the proletariat. For Marx and Engels (1998: 75) such schemes demonstrated a 'fanatical and superstitious belief in the miraculous effects of their social science'.

Marx and Engels sought to understand the definite social relations of a particular social structure: capitalism. Historical materialism provides a 'guiding thread' for a detailed empirical investigation into changing social relations.

> The premises from which we begin are not arbitrary ones, not dogmas, but real premises from which abstraction can only be made in the imagination. They are the real individuals, their activity and the material conditions under which they live, both those which they find already

existing and those produced by their activity. These premises can thus be verified in a purely empirical way. (1845–6: 149)

These 'real individuals' are not conceived by Marx and Engels 'in any fantastic isolation and rigidity' but must be studied in their practical interrelated development by the 'positive science' of empirical observation. 'Empirical observation must in each separate instance bring out empirically, and without any mystification and speculation, the connection of the social and political structure with production' (1845–6: 154). From this, historical materialism would later veer off in a positivist direction.

'THE FIRST HISTORICAL ACT'

Individual human beings are subject to the necessity of producing their own material existence:

> life involves before everything else eating and drinking, a habitation, clothing and many other things. The first historical act is thus the production of the means to satisfy these needs, the production of material life itself. (Marx and Engels, 1845–6: 156)

Satisfaction of basic material needs creates 'new needs'. These give rise to more or less stable institutions of social and physical reproduction, above all the family, and the social cooperation expressed in productive forces. From this emerges the division of labour, the separation of town and country, production and trade, mental and manual labour, the state and civil society.

Marx and Engels deny that historical materialism depends on 'deductive proofs' about society. There can be no 'recipe or schema ... for neatly trimming the epochs of history' (1845–6: 155). History is made actively by human beings but in definite material conditions. These cannot simply be leapt over by a sheer force of will or by redefining reality with a few choice phrases.

> Men make their own history, but not of their own free will; not under circumstances they themselves have chosen, but under the given and inherited circumstances with which they are directly confronted. (Marx, 1852: 146).

Making history involves the 'practical-sensuous activity' of embodied people. Marx wants to bring into the closest relationship both the active interpersonal side of social relations and the impersonal side of the productive forces. Social relations are transformed historically because the development of the productive forces makes further changes possible.

ABSTRACTION AND OBSERVATION

We can look over Marx's (1973) shoulder as he developed his ideas in the series of notebooks he prepared during the winter of 1857–8, published a century later as the *Grundrisse*. In these densely-argued sketches Marx attempted to lay the ghost of German Idealist philosophy in the work of G.W.F. Hegel (1770–1831). Hegel argued that the senses can only ascertain an 'Idea' of the external world through the appearance of phenomena rather than its real essence. As Marx stated in *Capital*:

> For Hegel, the process of thinking, which he even transforms into an independent subject, under the name of 'the Idea', is the creator of the real world, and the real world is only the external appearance of the idea. With me the reverse is true: the ideal is nothing but the material world reflected in the mind of man, and translated into forms of thought. (1976: 102)

Marx refuses to lapse into a naïve empiricism which takes at face value sensory data from self-evident observations. Abstract concepts retain their importance for Marx:

> the method of rising from the abstract to the concrete is only the way in which thought appropriates the concrete, reproduces it as the concrete in the mind ... The concrete is concrete because it is the concentrations of many determinations, hence unity of the diverse. It appears in the process of thinking, therefore, as a process of concentration, as a result, not as a point of departure, even though it is the point of departure in reality and hence the point of departure for observation and conception. (1973: 101)

It is worth reading Marx carefully here. Abstract concepts form 'the point of departure' while an understanding of complex empirical reality is 'the result'. Historical materialism does not simply reflect empirical data. Because it exists as a many-sided concentration of elements – a 'unity of the diverse' – the explanation and exposition of concrete reality first isolates the core abstractions through 'the working up of observation and conception into concepts'. The more complex that society becomes, the more general becomes conceptual abstraction.

To understand capital as a general abstraction – 'the starting-point as well as the finishing-point' – is to establish the order of things within bourgeois society itself. This is why his major work is called *Capital* rather than *Capitalism*. Marx's point is not to provide a narrative history of all the empirical evidence or historical events that led up to capitalism as a concrete society. Perhaps surprisingly, the point of historical materialism 'is *not* the historic position of the economic relations in the succession of different forms of society' but instead the inner-relationship of the categories of bourgeois society 'which is precisely the opposite of that which seems to be their natural order or which correspond to historical development' (1973: 107).

Historical materialism is retroactive in the sense that later developments are the key to understanding earlier ones. Just as 'human anatomy contains a key to the anatomy of the ape', so 'bourgeois society supplies the key to the ancient'. This retroactive principle is qualified by Marx's (1973: 105) warning against 'those economists who smudge over all historical differences and see bourgeois relations in all forms of society'.

LOGICAL METHOD

The problem of untangling the concrete 'unity of the diverse' all the while demonstrating the 'inner connection' between things through abstract concepts greatly exercised Marx. After all, for historical materialism 'the subject, society, must always be kept in mind as the supposition' (1973: 102). But this does not resolve the logical articulation of abstract theory. Marx (1973: 100–1) outlines the logic of historical materialism.

First, it seems to be correct to begin with 'the real and the concrete', with the population, 'which is the foundation and subject of the entire social act of production'. However, this approach, which is close to Durkheim's social morphology, is mistaken since 'population' is an empty abstraction if classes are left out. But, second, even 'classes' are 'an empty phrase' unless specific categories of wage labour and capital are defined. And these categories presuppose even more basic ones like money, exchange, the division of labour, prices and value. To begin with 'population' would therefore create 'a chaotic conception of the whole'. Finally, Marx specifies 'the scientifically correct procedure' of starting from the simplest, most basic concepts and working backwards to 'the population', which is no longer 'a chaotic conception of a whole' but is conceived as 'a rich totality of many determinations and relations'.

This rationale for 'the scientifically correct procedure' led Marx to a more detailed exposition of the logical order for demonstrating 'inner connections'. Here Marx ascends from simple abstractions to the complexity of empirical reality in its totality:

> The order obviously has to be 1. the general, abstract determinants which obtain in more or less all forms of society, but in the above-explained sense. 2.

The categories which make up the inner structure of bourgeois society and on which the fundamental classes rest. Capital, wage labour, landed property. Their interrelation. Town and country. The three great social classes. Exchange between them. Circulation. Credit system (private). 3. Concentration of bourgeois society in the form of the state. Viewed in relation to itself. The 'unproductive' classes. Taxes. State debt. Public credit. The population. The colonies. Emigration. 4. The international relation of production. International exchange. Export and import. Rate of exchange. 5. The world market and crises. (1973: 108)

When it came to actually writing *Capital*, Marx began Chapter 1 with the 'elementary form' of the commodity, which is 'more or less' present in all societies (1). He then finds the 'inner structure' of specifically bourgeois society in the dominance of exchange value over use value (2). From there *Capital* attempts to build towards more precise determinations, from the division of labour, classes, circulation, money and so on, all the way through to the world market and global crises (2–5).

CRITICAL DEVELOPMENTS

Rather than progressing as the social science of 'a rich totality of many determinations and relations', historical materialism underwent two different kinds of simplification. One kind of simplification was the descent of thought into what was termed 'dialectical materialism' in societies governed by the Stalinist state model. It claimed that Marxism was a science which had identified all the inevitable laws of social development. Partly these positivist laws of social development had their roots in an earlier generation of Marxists, principally Karl Kautsky (1854–1938) and Georgi V. Plekhanov (1856–1918) (who coined the term 'dialectical materialism'). This was reformulated as a 'law of causality' in the 1920s by Nikolai Bukharin (1888–1938) in his textbook, *Historical Materialism: A System of Sociology* (1921).

Bukharin's positivist 'law of causality' was critiqued during the interwar years by Antonio Gramsci (1891–1937), Georg Lukacs (1885–1971) and Karl Korsch (1886–1961). Against Bukharin these critics emphasized the active side of historical materialism. Here, a second simplification validates historical materialism through political activity or 'praxis'. In his major work *History and Class Consciousness* (1923) Lukacs claimed that historical materialism could be falsified empirically yet 'the method' would still retain its validity. What counted for Lukacs was that scientific enquiry was informed dialectically by revolutionary practice.

Influenced by Lukacs, Walter Benjamin (1940) gave historical materialism a more idiosyncratic, messianic twist in a brilliant series of theses 'On the concept of history'. Benjamin (1940: 394) rejected positivist notions of inevitable 'progress' as a mechanical, puppet-like version of 'historical materialism' and insisted instead that 'the subject of historical knowledge is the struggling, oppressed class itself'. Later Marxists like Henri Lefebvre (1972, 2009) qualified this by referring to Marx's own dictum that careful empirical analysis remains essential to historical materialism if it is to avoid becoming an arbitrary judgement on concrete reality.

Largely ignoring this, 'analytical Marxists' (Elster, 1985) attempted to ground historical materialism in the formal logic of the rational action of ideal-typical individuals. Historical materialism also came under critique from postmodernists for its pretension to advance 'a grand narrative' account of large-scale social transformation. Both critiques were met by sophisticated counter-critiques, building on the central corpus of historical materialism (see Callinicos, 1989, 2004).

RELATED CONCEPTS

Base and Superstructure; Capital; Class; Division of Labour (Marx); Mode of Production; Primitive Accumulation

FURTHER READING

Marx's methodological statements are scattered throughout his writings. Both Henri Lefebvre's *The Sociology of Marx* (1972) and *Dialectical Materialism* (2009) are more faithful than most to Marx's own method. A useful outline is provided in Part 2 of Allen Wood's *Karl Marx* (2004). Alex Callinicos' *Making History* (2004) is an ambitious attempt to reformulate historical materialism in light of the experience of the past century and recent developments in social theory.

Ideal-Types

By 'ideal-type' Max Weber did not mean 'ideal' in the sense of something good that ought to exist. Weber's notion of 'ideal' is that of a 'pure' analytical model of the 'typical' features of a phenomenon abstracted from reality.

> It is formed by a one-sided *accentuation* of one or *several* perspectives and through the synthesis of a variety of diffuse, discrete, individual phenomena, present sometimes more, sometimes less, sometimes not at all; subsumed by such one-sided emphatic viewpoints so that they form into a uniform construction in *thought*. In its conceptual purity this construction can never be found in reality, it is a *utopia*. (Weber, 2004: 387–8)

Ideal-type abstraction is in no sense arbitrary but rationally distils empirical complexity into a logical essence. A process of exaggerated simplification isolates the typical characteristics of social action and points towards their existence in empirical reality. Weber claimed that the concept of ideal-types only made explicit what many social scientists had already done but had not consciously formulated.

Weber is clear about what an ideal-type is *not*. First, as a logical construct the ideal-type does not *describe* empirical reality. Rather, it clarifies our conceptual understanding of what to look for in empirical data. Second, the ideal-type does not directly provide a *hypothesis* about reality. As a regulative principle it indirectly helps social scientists to construct research questions and hypotheses about social reality. Third, as a one-sided exaggeration the ideal-type does not provide an account of some '*average*' level of social reality.

Scientific truth for Weber consists of 'concepts and judgements that are not empirical reality nor represent such reality, but which allow it to be *ordered in thought* in a valid manner' (2004: 402). Scientific validity cannot be deduced from empirical data: the known facts need to be interpreted from known concepts. By bringing it into a rational relationship with empirical data the ideal-type can be tested, verified and revised further. A carefully constructed ideal-type does not need to be verified positively by the 'facts'. Indeed, a deviation from the empirical evidence may help clarify the content of an ideal-type.

HEURISTIC VALUE

Ideal-types are not an end in themselves, they serve as a heuristic *means*: 'The construction of abstract ideal types is not an aim, but a means' (Weber, 2004: 389). Weber cautioned against empirical knowledge becoming 'the servant' of ideal-type theoretical constructs rather than vice versa. This can happen when the theorist treats empirical or historical data as mere illustrations of the ideal-type or, 'far worse', confuses the distinction between the ideal type and empirical data by integrating them into a 'genetic classification' scheme, which confuses the abstract logic of concepts with empirical causal relations. Weber thought that what was valid in Marxist theory was its heuristic value as an ideal-type. But Weber also thought that Marxism confused 'pure mental constructs' with real laws and that empirical data were forced to fit the abstract model of capitalism.

For Weber the relationship of the ideal-type to empirical data about reality is always an indirect one, a 'heuristic' device that directs and guides empirical analysis and research. Ideal-types provide a solution to the methodological problem of how to arrive at objective knowledge of subjective motivations. Hence the subjective motivations of both Calvin's doctrine of predestination and Benjamin Franklin's 'spirit of capitalism' broadly correspond to ideal-types of rationality.

No sphere of social action, regardless of how society judges it morally, is exempt from the reach of ideal-types. As Weber puts it, 'There are ideal-types of brothels as well as religions'. Weber gives the example of constructing capitalism as an ideal-type. First, out of the confused variety of large-scale industry certain features may be abstracted. Second, from this a characteristically capitalist culture can be identified around the governing principle of the investment of private capital. Finally, we arrive at the isolation and accentuation of those unique aspects of capitalist culture related to and dependent on private capital in a self-contained, logical ideal construct. This gives us the abstract 'idea' of capitalist culture rather than the thing itself.

IDEAL-TYPE HISTORY

There is no access to history without the help of concepts. Historians are sometimes thought to be in the business of re-arranging concrete events into a pre-conceptual narrative. However, they are forced to borrow ideal-type concepts like 'individualism', 'imperialism', or feudalism'. While these may remain ambiguous in the hands of the historian, the social scientist is required to systematically define and clarify their conceptual apparatus.

Ideal-types can be used comparatively to understand historical shifts, such as the shift from industry based on handicraft production to industry based on capitalist production. An ideal-type may be used to test the hypothesis that mediaeval society was based on strict 'handicraft' forms of economic organization. If the historical evidence suggests otherwise and the ideal-type diverges from reality, then the hypothesis will prove that mediaeval society was *not* strictly a handicraft society. Moreover, the heuristic value of the mediaeval ideal-type will lead to a more precise understanding of the role of non-handicraft activities in the mediaeval economy.

CRITICAL DEVELOPMENTS

Ideal-types have been judged by some to be too ambiguous, confusing or abstract. In this sense Weber failed to serve his stated aim of formulating substantive hypotheses from an ideal-type as an aid to generalization (Runciman, 1978: 3). Weber tended to conflate different kinds of ideal types, sometimes dealing with specific historical periods while elsewhere undertaking trans-historical analysis. Sometimes ideal-types are concerned with the subjective motivation of social action and sometimes with the objective structures that are the result of social action. In his own substantive studies, Weber forgot his own austere instruction to distinguish between conceptual definitions, essential characteristics, descriptive classifications, and testable hypotheses.

Some Marxists accepted Weber's argument that historical materialism also traded in ideal-types. Georg Lukacs (1923) criticized Weber's argument for developing rather sterile formal categories at the expense of a causal explanation of historically specific social relations and structures. Ideal-types have been applied to numerous social and historical phenomena. The historian of the ancient world, Moses Finley (1983), found an ideal-type approach particularly useful to formulate hypotheses about the nature of the ancient city.

Others like Alfred Schütz attempted to shore-up Weber's methodology by more systematically elucidating the relationship between the objectivity of ideal-types and the subjective meaning of social action. For Schütz (1970: 273) ideal-types are 'constructs of the second degree, constructs of constructs made by actors on the social scene'. These second-order constructs are pure inventions of the social scientist, whose starting point is the 'fictitious consciousness' of an imaginary 'puppet'. Schütz attempted to strengthen the scientific basis of Weber's ideal-types by two governing postulates: the postulate of logical consistency and the postulate of adequacy. While much sociology today accepts the heuristic value of ideal-types in principle it lacks Weber's (and Schütz's) vaulting ambition for an objective science of subjective meaning.

RELATED CONCEPTS

Bureaucracy; Class, Status and Party; Legitimate Domination; Protestant Ethic and the 'Spirit of Capitalism'; Rationality and Rationalization; Social Action; *Verstehen*

FURTHER READING

Weber discusses ideal-types in 'Objectivity in Social Science and Social Policy' in Sam Whimster's *The Essential Weber* (2004). A concise summary is provided by Frank Parkin's, *Max Weber* (2002). For a more wide-ranging discussion see Sven Eliaeson's *Max Weber's Methodologies: Interpretation and Critique* (2002).

Ideology

In the nineteenth century the concept of 'ideology' came to refer to a systematically false set of ideas. The term was advanced first by Destutt de Tracy in 1796 but the pejorative sense of ideology was stated most famously by Marx and Engels in *The German Ideology* (1845–6). They took the concept of ideology to critique the failures, as they saw it, of other thinkers who, wittingly or unwittingly, justified dominant ideas about the social order (Eagleton, 2007; Meszaros, 2005). For Marx and Engels, the ruling ideas are merely an ideal expression of real material conditions, principally class relations.

> The ideas of the ruling class are in every epoch the ruling ideas: i.e., the class which is the ruling material force is at the same time its ruling intellectual force. (1845–6: 172)

Those that lack the physical means of material production also lack the mental means of ideological production. Ideology has two functions for Marx and Engels. It inverts and conceals the real relationship between symbolic representations and social conditions but, at the same time, it is also an idealized expression of those social conditions.

Just as people cannot be judged solely by what they think about themselves, so the transformation of material conditions ought not to be judged by what its leading institutions have to say about the process. Marx and Engels begin from where people are – 'their practical position in life, their job and the division of labour' – to explain ideological illusions and mystifications.

IDEOLOGY AND REALITY

Marx did not aim to expose religion as a faulty set of misconceptions. Rather, religious ideology depends on social conditions that create a need for the kind of illusions that it fosters. Religious ideology is an imaginary consolation for the social suffering of dominated classes. It is not primarily an irrational ideology but 'the sigh of the oppressed creature', 'the heart in a heartless world', 'the opium of the people':

> Religion is the *fantastic realization* of the human being inasmuch as the human being possesses no true reality. The struggle against religion is, therefore, a struggle against that world whose spiritual aroma is religion. Religious suffering is at the same time an expression of real suffering and a protest against real suffering. (Marx and Engels, 1845–6: 54)

Ideology expresses real torments not just illusions, real needs not just rational errors, protest as well as domination. Marx does not reduce ideology to a question of individual psychology or false motives. Against a one-sided emphasis on consciousness and ideas, Marx began from historically-produced social conditions. An ideological critique of religion led only to the 'theoretical bubble-blowing' of general categories about 'man' and 'humanity' rather than concrete analysis of social conditions. The result was a struggle about phrases rather than a critical examination of the connections between German philosophy and German reality. 'Instead we get a narrative based not on research but on arbitrary constructions and literary gossip' (1845–6: 167).

Rational criticism of religious belief remains trapped within 'the products of consciousness' in the belief that as soon as more rational concepts are established mistaken religious ideas and consciousness will be abandoned. 'The demand to change consciousness amounts to a demand to interpret reality in another way, i.e., to recognize it by means of another interpretation' (1845–6: 149). Material reality cannot be resolved by theoretical deductions about ideology.

THE DOMINANT IDEOLOGY

Ideology reduces history to a universal struggle over principles and ideals. The aristocracy appear to rule through ideal concepts like honour, duty and loyalty. Bourgeois rule expresses the superiority of other ideal concepts like equality, freedom and democracy. A newly ascendant class is forced in its struggle with the declining ruling class to represent its interests as being representative of much wider swathes of society.

key concepts in
classical social theory

Every new class, therefore, achieves its hegemony only on a broader basis than that of the ruling class previously, whereas the opposition of the non-ruling class against the new ruling class later develops all the more sharply and profoundly. (Marx and Engels, 1845–6: 174)

As it extends its social power, the ruling class generally produces ideas covering the whole range of ideological production: art, mass media, religion, law, politics and so on. These remain dominant only insofar as the ruling class also remains dominant.

The dominant ideology is not a seamless unity. It possesses a certain amount of autonomy from the economically dominant class. One part of the ruling class is more concerned with the business of economic rule, while another part specializes in ideological rule. This division of ideological rule from economic rule can result in 'a certain opposition and hostility between the two parts' (1845–6: 173).

Marx (1973: 245) later noted that the ideology of freedom and equality is an idealized image of a society premised on market exchange. Everything seems to be free and equal: exchange value for the employer (profit); the means of subsistence for the worker (wages). The reciprocity of exchange gives market relations the appearance of individual freedom and equality but actually conceals the real compulsions underlying the class society (1973: 248). In fact, should the worker wish to turn their means of subsistence into wealth they can only do so, Marx argues, by cutting back on consumption, working longer hours, or working more intensively – the opposite of freedom.

IDEOLOGY AND CLASS CONFLICT

If ideology is always partial, in both senses of the word (as biased and incomplete), it inevitably becomes a field of struggle. Only through ideological images can people attempt to make sense of class conflict 'and fight it out'. Marx gave a stirring account in the *Eighteenth Brumaire of Louis Napoleon* (1852) of how ideology makes sense of the bourgeois revolution in England in the 1640s by draping itself in the language of the Old Testament. Just when people are involved in transforming everything 'they timidly conjure up the spirits of the past to help them; they borrow their names, slogans, and costumes' and present the new stage in world history in time-honoured disguises and borrowed language: 'The tradition of the dead generations weighs like a nightmare on the minds of the living' (1852: 147).

As capitalism matures, harking back to earlier ideals becomes unnecessary. The dominated class, Marx argued, can only succeed in ridding itself of 'all the muck of the ages' through the practical activity of revolutionary change. Any future revolution would not 'take its poetry from the past but only from the future'. Capitalism severely tests the ability of ideology to keep up with reality:

> all that is holy is profaned, and man is at last compelled to face with sober senses his real conditions of life, and his relations with his kind. (Marx and Engels, 1848: 38–9)

Ideological misrepresentations about class, gender, race, nationality, religion and so on are displaced as the conditions that gave rise to them are transformed by capitalist rationality itself.

FALSE CONSCIOUSNESS

In Marx's mature work the concept of ideology is largely absent. Engels relapsed into a view of ideology as 'false consciousness' that they had both criticized 50 years earlier.

> Ideology is a process accomplished by the so-called thinker consciously, it is true, but with a false consciousness. The real motive forces impelling him remain unknown to him; otherwise it simply would not be an ideological process. Hence he imagines false or apparent motives. Because it is a process of thought he derives its form as well as its content from pure thought, either his own or that of his predecessors. (1893: 766)

False consciousness has three aspects to it: deficient knowledge, deceptive knowledge and idealism. First, knowledge is deficient because individuals lack knowledge about the primary causes governing their lives. Second, knowledge is deceptive because illusory ideas are accepted at face value. Third, knowledge is idealist because the world seems to be moved primarily by the force of beliefs and ideas.

Engels' concept of false consciousness is often taken to define Marxism's approach to ideology. In fact, Marx (1854) only used the term on a single occasion (in a very obscure pamphlet) to defend himself against the charge of false consciousness. Engels rarely used the term. While some have attempted to see false consciousness as a useful, productive concept (Pines, 1993), it runs counter to most of what Marx and Engels had to say about ideology as the expression of real needs and a contradictory field of struggle.

CRITICAL DEVELOPMENTS

Non-Marxists like Durkheim sometimes used the term 'ideology' where an object of study is mistaken for pre-given concepts (Durkheim, 1895:

60). For orthodox Marxists like Georg Lukacs (1923), Marxism itself is an ideology. Lukacs exerted a great influence over the inter-war generation of critical thinkers like Karl Mannheim. In *Ideology and Utopia* (1929), Mannheim separates ideology into, first, 'particular ideologies', specific deceptions and distortions, and, second, 'total ideologies', more wide-ranging worldviews structured around the collective life of entire classes.

Most famously, Gramsci (1971) developed the idea of ideological leadership, or 'hegemony'. Ideology succeeds because it makes some partial sense of the world and provides rules for action. Ideology is always contradictory, pulling between illusory ideals and a recalcitrant reality. He further distinguished between 'arbitrary ideologies' that do not correspond directly to objective class interests and 'organic ideologies' that emerge out of the interests of contending classes. For Gramsci this meant transforming the arbitrary ideology of common sense into a critical, organic ideology of 'good sense'.

A profusion of studies about ideology appeared in the 1970s and 1980s. These were typically either a defence of Marxism or a critique. This is despite the fact that Marx's concept of ideology had to be reconstructed from scattered passages and that his view of ideology often differed from its later usage. Much of this moved away from an argument about the (false) class content of ideology to an examination of how ideology functioned as a social process (Therborn, 1999).

Many were enthused or greatly exercised by the analysis of ideology produced by the French Marxist, Louis Althusser (2008). His main conclusion was that ideology's practical function in society is more important than its (false) theoretical knowledge. Ideology, or the 'Ideological State Apparatus' as Althusser called institutions like school, church, mass media, advertising, trade unions, is always relatively autonomous from the centralized state itself. Ideology, for Althusser, cannot be a deliberate manipulation involving 'beautiful lies' by a cunning ruling class out to deceive the masses. Subjects are hailed or 'interpellated' by ideology (Althusser, 2008). Through interpellation ideology is accepted into 'one's heart of hearts' or else it fails to function.

All this theorizing about ideological domination was rudely interrupted by an empirical study by Nicholas Abercrombie, Stephen Hill and Bryan S. Turner (1980). Their research showed that ruling class values have a limited and contested purchase in working class lives. Instead, the routine structures of paid employment are often enough to subordinate dominated classes. Importantly, Abercrombie, Hill and Turner (1980) argue that capitalism is highly pragmatic and adaptable, and has no essential ideology of its own. Of all socio-economic systems, capitalism is compatible with any number of ideological systems from democracy to fascism.

In this vein, the social psychologist Michael Billig (1991) has shown in a substantial body of work that ideological dilemmas are negotiated in routine, everyday discourses and arguments between people. Billig's approach to the contested discourse of ideology has some parallels with Valentin Volosinov's (1973) theory of language from the 1920s. Ideology is always subject to dispute and argument. If ideology always involves argument, it cannot command the passive obedience of participants. For others like Terry Eagleton (2007) it is important to remember that many ideological claims are plain wrong, prejudicial and clearly in the overall interest of dominant groups, sometimes all three at once. Regardless of whose material power they reflect, claims, for instance, that 'Men are naturally superior to women' or 'Muslims are fanatical terrorists' or 'The Irish are thick' are simply false.

RELATED CONCEPTS

Alienation; Base and Superstructure; Class; Collective Representations; Historical Materialism; Value Freedom

FURTHER READING

Terry Eagleton's *Ideology: An Introduction* (2007) is engaging and written with characteristic wit and verve. A useful collection of key articles is *Mapping Ideology*, edited by Slavoj Žižek (1994).

Legitimate Domination

Throughout his writings Max Weber used the terms 'domination', 'legitimation' and 'authority' to understand how power works. Perhaps more than any other classical social thinker, a concern with the operation of power in large-scale societies and organizations is central to Weber's thought. *Power* concerns the capacity of an individual to impose their will regardless of the views and feelings of less powerful individuals or groups, who may resist or oppose its use. Weber's famous definition states that power is

the probability that one actor within a social relationship will be in a position to carry out his own will despite resistance, regardless of the basis on
which this probability exists. (1978: 53)

Power in this amorphous sense is not the same thing for Weber as
domination or *discipline*. Domination concerns the probability that a
command will be obeyed. It turns into 'discipline' only when, through
habit and routine, obedience becomes unthinking and automatic.

LEGITIMACY

On the one hand, power, broadly understood, is imposed against the will
or interests of others. Domination, on the other hand, is more narrowly
conceived by Weber as involving a certain level of voluntary acceptance
or compliance with the right of the powerful to rule and to be obeyed.

> The merely external fact of the order being obeyed is not sufficient to
> signify domination in our sense; we cannot overlook the meaning of the
> fact that the command is accepted as a 'valid' norm. (1978: 946)

This is quite different from economic domination by market forces and
money. Few would take orders from a banker or a stockbroker in the
way that they might obey the monarch out of a sense of duty or comply
with the demands of a civil servant following a written procedure on,
say, making a benefits claim.

Weber calls this '*legitimate domination*'. An order is 'legitimate' or
'valid' when it is followed as 'binding' because of the prestige attributed
to the institution or individual issuing it (1978: 31). Weber's idea of
legitimate domination addresses the exercise of power in modern societies. Even the most brutal dictatorship always makes some effort to
legitimate its rule.

How a legitimate 'right to rule' over others is acquired varies historically. Some societies were dominated by a king or queen, others by war-
riors and soldiers, or religious leaders, or slave-owning citizens. Each form
of domination had its own distinctive mode of legitimacy, type of obedience, administrative organization, and mixture of direct and indirect rule.

In order to clarify the essential differences between the basic forms of
legitimate domination Weber drew up three pure *ideal types*:

- legal-rational domination
- traditional domination
- charismatic domination

LEGAL DOMINATION

Weber begins with the most recent and therefore most familiar example: *legal domination*. This kind of legitimacy is highly rational. It is expressed in legal rules, codes and procedures. A 'legal-rational' system of domination relies on 'a belief in the legality of enacted rules and the right of those elevated to authority under such rules to issue commands' (1978: 215). Its most perfect expression is the modern, large-scale bureaucracy.

A series of inter-connected principles provides legal authority with its legitimacy. First, obedience to the rules or legal norms is demanded of everyone coming under its jurisdiction. Second, conduct is governed by the consistent application of abstract rules. Third, even those in positions of authority, such as elected politicians or state officials, are themselves subject to the abstract rules. Fourth, 'members' of a legally constituted institution agree to obey 'the law'. Finally, obedience is owed only to the impersonal position of authority rather than to any particular individual who occupies the post. Commands that fall outside of legal rules are illegitimate and arbitrary, and can be legitimately resisted or disobeyed even if they are issued by a superior.

TRADITIONAL DOMINATION

Second, *traditional domination* is based on 'the sanctity of age-old rules and powers' (Weber, 1978: 226). In its most simple form, obedience is generated through personal loyalty to a patriarch, an elder or a master passed on through a common background, such as family, clan or nation. Traditional leaders acquire prestige in the eyes of the ruled through inherited rights or titles. They are tradition personified.

Intense personal devotion contrasts diametrically with the impersonal legal domination of the modern bureaucracy:

> The person exercising authority is not a 'superior', but a personal master, his administrative staff does not consist of officials but of personal retainers, and the ruled are not 'members' of an association but are either his traditional 'comrades' or his 'subjects'. (1978: 226)

Traditional customs and myths impose limits on the leader's discretion. If traditional constraints are breached he may be personally overthrown while the system of traditional privileges is preserved.

Weber develops three sub-types of traditional authority. First, through a *patriarchal* system, a patriarch or master of the household exercises an absolute hold on power through customs and obligations that are held to be sacred. No explicit rules are needed, allowing considerable scope for the master or chief. Nor is there any need for a personal retinue or permanent staff.

Second, a more widespread form of *patrimonial* domination combines the personal obligations and customary basis of patriarchal authority with a more stable administrative and military structure, organized according to the pecking order of the master's personal favourites. Coming under the absolute authority of the master's will this administrative order is quite different from the modern bureaucracy.

Third, in *feudal* domination a sworn oath functions as a rudimentary contract freely entered into by both the feudal lord and his vassals. Despite the idea of a free contract, a reciprocal sense of rights and obligations, and a stable administrative structure, feudal domination retained a direct personal relationship between lord and vassal, not the impersonal one in modern bureaucracies.

CHARISMATIC DOMINATION

With *charismatic domination* individuals seem to possess some exceptional quality through which they attract devoted followers and disciples:

> he is considered extraordinary and treated as endowed with supernatural, superhuman, or at least specifically exceptional powers or qualities. These are such as are not accessible to the ordinary person, but are regarded as of divine origin or as exemplary, and on the basis of them the individual concerned is treated as a 'leader'. (Weber, 1978: 241)

In earlier societies, such magical qualities were attributed to prophets, legal or medical counsels, hunt leaders or war heroes. 'Pure' charisma appears indifferent to everyday material or economic considerations. At least in the eyes of the devoted, the charismatic leader ought to be above that sort of thing.

In some ways, charismatic authority can claim to be the only pure type of legitimacy, uncontaminated by worldly interests and wholly dependent on the grace of their followers (Parkin, 2002: 84). How such individuals are viewed by their 'followers', 'disciples', 'devotees' or, as we might say today, their 'fans' is completely decisive for the exercise of charismatic authority. A charismatic leader must always be prepared to perform some 'brilliant display' in order to demonstrate their extraordinary gifts to the devoted followers. Failure to do so can result in a psychological crisis among followers leading to a full-scale loss of authority.

ROUTINE CHARISMA

Pure charismatic domination is incompatible with either legal domination or traditional domination. However, because charismatic authority is unstable and transitory it will inevitably acquire the trappings of either traditional authority or rational authority, or some combination of all three. This is what Weber (1946: 246) calls 'the routinisation of charisma'.

As a 'community' becomes more firmly established around the charismatic leader, a series of material interests in a more secure social position begins to emerge, especially among the most dedicated disciples of the inner group like advisors, administrators or party workers. Underlying tensions between an ascetic existence and material stability are revealed during leadership struggles to succeed a dead or declining charismatic leader. They are also evident when charismatic authority begins to come into contact with state bureaucracy or patrimonial forms of administration. This is bound to be a conflict-ridden affair. However, accusations of selling out the charismatic ideals and calls for a return to an uncorrupted past, Weber believed, will tend to keep any further bureaucratization in check.

CRITICAL DEVELOPMENTS

Weber's ideal-types of legitimate domination have proved useful for shedding light on different aspects of authority. Moreover, the focus on legitimation means that Weber understands the underlying sources of authority in custom, reason and devotion rather than simply re-describing ruling institutions like parliaments, armies, parties, and corporations as in 'realist' studies of power.

Charismatic authority has been applied to dictators like Adolf Hitler as well as celebrities, pop stars and film stars. Indeed, there is considerable debate concerning Weber's prophetic hopes for a 'Fuhrer' as a charismatic leader to rescue Germany from parliamentary mediocrity (Radkau, 2009: 401). Traditional authority has been consciously recreated through the invention of national traditions and the heritage industry in order to bolster the prestige of privileged strata like the aristocracy or the monarchy (Hobsbawm and Ranger, 1983).

Numerous critics have called the ideal-types into question. First, as an analytical device for classifying his three types of domination, Weber seems to be largely indifferent to the political ends they serve, whether democratic or tyrannical. Second, his focus is mainly on how elites consolidate their rule rather than how compliance among the lower orders is achieved in reality (Parkin, 2002). Third, Weber's ideal types of legitimate domination fail to account adequately for the fact that some kind of coercion, force or violence always underlies the question of power.

Fourth, neither does he account adequately for the crisis of legitimate domination, for instance during periods of revolutionary upheaval or popular discontent. Weber has been accused of throwing in charisma as 'a wild card' because he lacked a satisfactory theory of political change (Allen, 2004: 111). Wide-scale political protest and changes in consciousness cannot simply be reduced to the accidental appearance of a charismatic leader.

RELATED CONCEPTS

Bureaucracy; Class, Status and Party; Ideal-Types; Ideology; Rationality and Rationalization

FURTHER READING

The relevant sections on legitimate domination can be found in Chapter III of Weber's *Economy and Society* (1978). See Weber's summary account 'The three pure types of legitimate rule' in Sam Whimster, *The Essential Weber* (2004). Weber's biographer Joachim Radkau (2009) fills in the personal and political background to Weber's concern with legitimate domination. Chapter 3 of Frank Parkin's *Max Weber* (2002) contains a useful critical discussion of domination and legitimation, while Chapter 7 of Kieran Allen's *Max Weber* (2004) offers a Marxist critique of the concept.

Mechanical and Organic Solidarity

How are diverse individuals held together by society? Durkheim's answer is that individuals are bound together by two types of social solidarity – mechanical and organic. Perhaps surprisingly, Durkheim gave the name 'mechanical' to pre-industrial societies and 'organic' to industrial societies, reversing the usual order of meaning applied to these terms by Ferdinand Tönnies among others. *Mechanical* social bonds are, for Durkheim, based on similarity. *Organic* social bonds are based on difference. In the former case, collective life predominates while in the latter case individuality prevails. The nature of social interdependency changes as the division of labour develops. It may seem paradoxical that as the division of labour breaks up long-established social bonds into isolated atoms of specialized occupations and functions, the more it creates the general conditions for social cohesion and integration.

MECHANICAL SOLIDARITY

In mechanical solidarity individuals are strongly attracted to each other through what Durkheim calls 'resemblance'. An integral solidarity based on a similarity and a common identity reaches its highest stage through the *conscience collective* which exercises a strong centripetal pull on individual members. Personal identity and collective identity become fused: 'From this results a solidarity *sui generis*, which, born of resemblances, directly links the individual to society' (Durkheim, 1933: 106). This is found in highly cohesive, relatively small-scale societies based on kinship relations and cooperation.

Typically reaching for naturalistic analogies, Durkheim compares mechanical solidarity to the molecules of inorganic bodies that have no independent existence of their own.

> We call it [mechanical solidarity] only by analogy to the cohesion which unites the elements of an inanimate body, as opposed to that which makes a unity out of the elements of a living body. What justifies the term is that the link which thus unites the individual to society is wholly analogous to that which attaches a thing to a person. The individual conscience considered in this light, is a simple dependent upon the collective type and follows all of its movements, as the possessed object follows that of its owner. (1933: 130)

In extreme cases of mechanical solidarity the individual personality is completely submerged by an undifferentiated homogeneous social mass. Any infringement of mechanical solidarity is met with brutally repressive sanctions. This type of solidarity is expressed in a large number of repressive laws against any violation of the collective will.

Mechanical solidarity is 'positive', direct, unconditional and unmediated. It produces inner unity through collective feelings of inclusion and belonging. Durkheim (1933: 179) gives the example of the Iroquois tribes of North America as an almost 'pure' example of a people who live without specialized functions or privileged hierarchies or private property in a sort of early communism. The individual is wholly absorbed by the clan.

key concepts in classical social theory

The same basic clan structure is repeated across 'a segmental society', defined by strong similarities:

> For segmental organization to be possible, the segments must resemble one another; without that they would not be united. And they must differ; without this, they would lose themselves in each other and be effaced. (1933: 177)

In some cases they form a simple linear series of contiguous groups like families or villages. In others cases, several clans form a definite and distinctly new union, like a tribe or a confederation. Mechanical solidarity is most sharply defined when the *conscience collective* is expressed through the medium of a defined focal point of family or kin, 'a community of blood'. Durkheim tried to avoid idealizing early societies and noted the existence of despotic forms of mechanical solidarity under the unilateral centralized power invested in a chief or master.

ORGANIC SOLIDARITY

In societies where the main form of solidarity is 'organic' individuals are engaged in specialized functions in an advanced division of labour. Here individuals cohere precisely because of their difference or dissimilarity from each other. Durkheim names this solidarity 'organic' from another analogy drawn from nature.

> Each organ, in effect, has it special physiognomy, its autonomy. And, moreover, the unity of the organism is as great as the individuation of the parts is more marked. (1933: 131)

On one side, the more labour is socially divided, the more dependent individuals become on society. On the other side, the more labour is socially divided, the more uniquely personal and specialized it becomes. Social heterogeneity expresses the development of peculiar, unique personalities. Compared to the almost total control exercised over individuals by mechanical solidarity, the organic variant allows for greater individual autonomy, spontaneity and enterprise. Social obligations are not quite so repressive and limiting. Individuals are linked by particular functions, primarily occupation, rather than by kinship structures. Functional integration of occupational specialization displaces and opposes alternative traditional sources of integration such as heredity.

Integration based on specialized function strengthens personal conscience at the expense of the *conscience collective*. Occupational structure assumes a more central place for coordinating social cohesion. Occupational morality is not subject to the same harsh punishments as breaches of public morality. Restitutive law becomes more widespread than repressive law. Occupational functions depend upon cooperation and compromise rather than coercion and repression.

> Consequently, even where society relies most completely upon the division of labour, it does not become a jumble of juxtaposed atoms, between which it can establish only external, transient contacts. Rather the members are united by ties which extend deeper and far beyond the short moments during which the exchange is made. Each of the functions that they exercise is, in a fixed way, dependent upon others, and with them forms a solidary system. (Durkheim, 1933: 227)

Spontaneous cooperation in the advanced division of labour is intrinsically moral in nature. A new 'moral or dynamic density' emerges from the growing size of population, urban living and improved communications.

TYPES OF SOLIDARITY

	Mechanical solidarity	Organic solidarity
Basis of solidarity	Resemblances	Differences
Nature of society	Pre-industrial	Industrial
Substratum	Segmental	Organized
Population	Low volume	High volume
Moral and physical density	Low	High
Interdependence	Low	High
Social bonds	Weak	Strong
Law	Repressive	Restitutive

Source: Adapted from Lukes, 1992: 158
Lukes, S. (1992) *Emile Durkheim: His Life and Work: A Historical and Critical Study*. London: Penguin.

TRANSITION FROM MECHANICAL TO ORGANIC SOLIDARITY

Mechanical solidarity is prior historically to organic solidarity. Although it might seem otherwise, mechanical solidarity, for Durkheim, produces a weaker social bond than organic solidarity. Since individuals or sub-groups have absorbed society within themselves they are potentially more mobile and able to carry society within their person as they move elsewhere. Moreover, because outsiders do not threaten specialization within the group it is also easier for mechanical collectives to adopt or assimilate strangers.

There begins a shift from the closed system of the self-sufficient clan towards a more geographically dispersed population. In the village the clan is gradually reduced to people who happen to occupy the same territory. Social organization decisively upscales the geographical level of collective groups into territorial districts, cities and counties, and political administration based on wards or assemblies.

> When a person is born into a clan, he can in no way ever change his parentage. The same does not hold true of changing from a city or a province. (Durkheim, 1933: 186)

Segmental organization lost ground, literally, as occupational groups like merchants and artisans became more mobile. Organic solidarity only becomes an independent reality when individuals are compelled to specialize because of an acute competition for resources. Cities begin to specialize their functions – university cities, manufacturing cities, government cities, mercantile cities and so on – within an inter-regional division of labour. This all-round cooperation and social dependency on the organic whole weakens the *conscience collective*.

Social life becomes more general and relationships become more numerous. Due to the weakening of the *conscience collective*, subversive tendencies occur more frequently but are also much less catastrophic for the social order (Durkheim, 1933: 380). The centralized state reminds individuals of their common bonds in the nation. It meets with less resistance from local organs, which it begins to assimilate and dominate. As the state becomes more centralized and society more individualized, it intervenes more frequently and directly to regulate the instabilities created by individual liberty.

POSITIVE AND NEGATIVE SOLIDARITY

Mechanical and organic solidarity are examples of 'positive solidarity' based on a mutual cooperation between people. 'Negative solidarity', on the other hand, unites things to people rather than people to people. Things are always part of society. Durkheim talks about a 'solidarity of things'. In law, the 'real right' of indivisible ownership over things takes precedence over the 'personal right' of moral claims. The law of property in its different forms – employment, commercial, industrial, financial, artistic, inheritance and so on – is the 'solidarity proper to things'. 'Real rights' such as these can be exercised in complete isolation from other people. It specifies a demarcation line for private property. Moreover, negative solidarity depends on positive solidarity; in order to recognize that others have rights, individuals must limit their own.

Herbert Spencer (1971) similarly attempted to characterize shifts in collective solidarity from 'forced cooperation' for the defined ends of a hierarchal command structure of 'militant' or 'military' society to the spontaneous, automatic solidarity of contractual exchange by individual interests in 'industrial society'. Spencer argues that if contractual solidarity is spontaneous, then there is no need for a coercive apparatus like the state or similar institutions to produce or maintain it. Against Spencer's spontaneous social order Durkheim argues that state intervention is needed to regulate the relations between diverse specialized functions.

While Durkheim accepts that contract plays an increasingly prominent part in modern society, Spencer neglects the various ways that contract solidarity always presupposes non-contractual relations in a set of underlying 'normal conditions' of social functions (Perrin, 1995). Contrary to liberal individualism, the individual personality is not 'congenital with humanity' (Durkheim, 1933: 195). Durkheim evinces a sense that society under an advanced division of labour is increasingly subject to positive regulation and controls of organic solidarity, sweeping away Spencer's unreal picture of spontaneous solidarity through free individuals exchanging contracts.

CRITICAL DEVELOPMENTS

Durkheim's two types of solidarity echo that of Ferdinand Tönnies' concepts of *Gemeinschaft* and *Gesellschaft*. But Durkheim's concept of organic solidarity had much less to say about capitalism and class than Tönnies'. In his short review of Durkheim, Tönnies criticized Durkheim for confusing ideal concepts with material conditions (Cahnman, 1973). Durkheim constructed his 'pure types' as analytical devices where both types of solidarity would be found in any concrete society. 'They are two aspects of one and the same reality, but none the less they must be distinguished (Durkheim, 1933: 129).

Durkheim's story about organic solidarity growing out of mechanical solidarity depends on an intellectual 'fable' (Hirst, 1975: 132). Far from being immanent to mechanical solidarity the division of labour depends on external factors such as an increased population volume, dynamic density and competition for resources. These were imported from the

key concepts in classical social theory

outside by Durkheim to account for organic solidarity. Another concern is that Durkheim selects criteria from his binary opposition as the situation demands: similarities or differences; society or individual; a single and strong *conscience collective* or multiple and weak *conscience collectives*; complementary values or antagonistic self-interest. Durkheim is also inconsistent about whether it is functions or individuals, a part or the whole, he is dealing with.

While some aspects of mechanical solidarity are returned to in Durkheim's later work, the multiple difficulties with organic solidarity as a pure type of integration – its origins, its relation to the substratum and to collective beliefs, its normative resources, its 'normal' consensual functioning, its inverse relationship to mechanical solidarity – make the concept vague and largely immune to empirical testing.

RELATED CONCEPTS

Anomie; Conscience Collective; Division of Labour in Society (Durkheim); Normal and Pathological; Social Morphology; Suicide

FURTHER READING

Durkheim discusses his conceptual pair in *The Division of Labour in Society*, available in different versions. Lukes (1992: 147–163) puts them into a historical and intellectual context, while Susan Stedman Jones (2001: Ch. 5) focuses on the nature of solidarity in modernity.

-------------------------------- Metropolis --------------------------------

One of the most famous essays in the history of sociology is Georg Simmel's (1971) 'The metropolis and mental life'. Based on a lecture for a municipal exhibition held in Dresden in 1903, Simmel analyses the nature of and possibilities for individuality in a large, modern city. This essay on the metropolis is closely related to his wider studies of modernity, money, social space, aesthetics and fashion. A focus on the metropolis brings together the major themes of Simmel's sociology: abstraction, calculation, individuality, differentiation, sociation and culture. It also touches on other classical concepts such as alienation, anomie, the division of labour, pathology, reification and commodity fetishism.

His theme is literally the metropolis *in* mental life (Frisby, 2001: 143). How urban reality becomes internalized is related to Simmel's more general concern with the relationship between subjective culture and objective culture in modernity. In the modern city the material products of objective culture are concentrated in space. What effect might this fact have on the inner life and emotional capacities of urban types?

QUALITY INTO QUANTITY

It is no accident that the metropolis is 'the seat of the money economy'. Money and the city are bound together by an impersonal, intellectual rationality. Both are indifferent to subjective culture and the qualitative differences between things. Both money and the rational intellect will reduce everything to quantity and deal with people objectively as anonymous, interchangeable numbers and amounts. The city becomes a mathematical formula. People's needs and desires are met through the city's capacity to expand the market for commodities based on the rational calculation, weighing and measuring of costs and benefits, indifferent to the personal attributes of the producer or the consumer.

In a money economy all qualitative distinction is reduced to the most efficient question: 'how much?' Everything floats along without distinction in the urban stream. Over-stimulation by the concentration of commodities in a single place turns into its opposite: indifference towards the objective culture and the devaluation of personality. Emotions and intellect become dissociated. The rounded personality gives way to the one-sided, specialized function. As Simmel (1971: 327) says of London, it may never have been 'the heart' of England but it has often been its intellect 'and always its money bag'.

Metropolitan life acquires a precision about it, reflected in the greater use of clocks, watches, timetables and contracts. Exact punctuality becomes a dominant principle. Without standard time complete chaos would reign:

> If all the watches in Berlin suddenly went wrong in different ways even only by as much as an hour, its entire economic and commercial life would be derailed for some time. (1971: 328)

Encounters are brief. Even when sitting on a crowded bus together people make only fleeting eye contact. Blank facial expressions are read for clues about the inner self (Simmel, 1997: 112). Conversations are codified to 'get to the point' quickly. Language is abbreviated, with today's text messaging perhaps its most developed form.

THE BLASÉ ATTITUDE

Paradoxically, exact calculation and precision in the city give rise to 'a *chaos* of *impressions*, shocks and *interactions*' (Frisby, 2001: 250). Above all, the objective structure of the city has serious implications for the mind and the body. The punctuality, precision and calculation demanded by urban rationality inhibit irrational emotionality and sensuality. Large cities bombard the senses, moment to moment, with rapidly changing external stimuli – crowds, buildings, queues, traffic, shop windows, lights, advertisements, cafes and bars, noise, smells, street vendors and so on.

A bewildering range of objects demands the attention of distracted spectators. Under this barrage of stimuli it appears impossible to assert any sense of individuality. Indeed, individuals face nervous collapse, psychic exhaustion or mental breakdown from 'the rapid telescoping of changing images, pronounced differences within what is grasped at a single glance, and the unexpectedness of violent stimuli' (Simmel, 1971: 325).

Yet, urban types seem able to adapt and even thrive under these excessive conditions. This is because, for Simmel, rationality and the intellect take over. In contrast to small towns, where life is much slower and predictable, and feelings and emotions predominate, in large cities people develop a self-conscious, reflexive awareness as a 'protective organ' against unexpected disruptions, discontinuities and fluctuations. They become de-sensitized, moved less by emotional responses than by detached calculation.

This indifference towards the distinction between things Simmel calls 'the blasé attitude'. Since people are unable to re-adjust to each and every stimulation, they become blasé at the point when their nerves start to fray. Metropolitan types adopt a reserved attitude as a form of self-protection, somewhere between constant responsiveness and total indifference to external stimuli. Such reserve may seem cold, rude and detached to outsiders. It borders on aversion and antipathy in 'a mutual strangeness and repulsion which, in a close contact which has arisen in any way whatever, can break out into hatred and conflict' (1971: 329).

But the blasé attitude also has a positive side for Simmel. It incomparably enlarges the scope for personal freedom. People are released from the oppressive, interfering cohesion of small social circles of family, village or religion, with their 'trivialities and prejudices'. In the city, multiple, reciprocal interactions weaken rigid group boundaries and allow greater individual freedom of movement and expression. Physical proximity and a lack of space in a dense city crowd make personal distinctions between individuals palpable. The fact that individuals may experience loneliness in a big city only means that freedom does not guarantee a pleasant existence.

QUANTITY INTO QUALITY

Not only does the money economy transform quality into quantity. The city also produces the opposite process: quantity becomes quality. As Adam Smith and Adam Ferguson had earlier recognized and Simmel confirms, endless monotony in production gives rise to an endless variety in consumption. Mutual indifference is far from total. City types move from a blasé attitude to a restless quest for excitement and distraction. Where the quantitative increase in things creates difficulties for personal differentiation, individuals seize more radically on qualitative distinctions.

Social games, the play form of sociability, are perfected in the metropolis (Frisby, 2001: 156). Urban groups set or adopt the latest trends and fashions, become eccentrically fastidious or quirky, in order to get noticed and 'be different' from the crowd. Qualitative uniqueness rather than traditional roles become the measure of human value. On the one hand, the individual floats without much effort on a sea of objective material culture, things, institutions, technology, buildings and the state. On the other hand, objective culture exacts a high price for individuality in highly exaggerated tastes, effects, styles, distractions and fashions.

As economic, personal and intellectual relations in the city develop and grow in numerical size an endless number of threads are spun. Urban life becomes more cosmopolitan, autonomous and many-sided, developing well beyond its physical bounds. This 'functional magnitude' is, for Simmel (1971: 335), the 'most significant aspect of the metropolis'. An extension of the division of labour allows incomparable personal differences to find expression in a specifically urban form of life. As producers continually specialize they create ever new, differentiated and refined needs in their consumers, which the metropolis continually satisfies.

The city becomes a battle zone between quantity and quality, objective and subjective culture, collective and individual, fragmentation and cohesion, difference and identity. As a 'typical' metropolitan intellectual himself, Simmel (1971: 339) prefers to keep a distance from value judgements about the positive or negative aspects of city life: 'it is our task not to complain or to condone but only to understand'.

METROPOLITAN INVISIBILITY

Simmel (1997: 47) neglected the gendered nature of the metropolis, which, as the seat of objective culture, he sees as thoroughly male. While objective culture reflects the typical propensities of men to be detached, calculating and indifferent, women are seen by Simmel as culturally more rounded, indivisible and subjectively attached to people and things. There are exceptions to this – working-class women and prostitutes – but they are compelled to adapt to a male-centred objective culture.

He also had little to say specifically about class divisions in the city. Spatially, his focus is on the urban centre of the metropolis rather than working-class neighbourhoods. Economically, his focus is on what the division of labour means for the circulation and consumption of goods rather than their origin in the production process. Culturally and politically, different classes may have a different relationship to the 'levelling' tendency of objective culture in the city.

It might also have been possible for Simmel to consider the relative amelioration of religious, national or ethnic differences in the city. His famous essay on 'the stranger', someone 'who arrives today and stays tomorrow', gives some indication of what this might involve (1971: 143–149). The presence of the stranger in urban space introduces a tension between near and far, and inside and outside: the 'one who is close by is remote' while the 'one who is remote is near'. Because the stranger is physically close but culturally distant, a more objective relationship is possible to all local interests and feuds. At the same time, their alien origin means that strangers become stereotyped more readily and blamed for all manner of things.

CRITICAL DEVELOPMENTS

While Simmel identifies a positive as well as a negative side to the city, the emphasis is overwhelmingly placed on the loss of feeling and numbness through urban chaos and shock. In some ways this hollowed-out urban life corresponds to what Durkheim might see as the *pathological* form of the anomic city (Frisby, 2001: 250). In other ways, it is reminiscent of Marx's concepts of alienation and commodity fetishism. Individuals are dominated by their own creations in the city, which possess an autonomous power to intensively assault the senses. In response, the blasé attitude feigns indifference and goes looking endlessly for distraction and excitement.

Simmel's distinctive contribution to the sociology of urbanism was eclipsed by more historical, empirical and positivist accounts of the modern city. Max Weber (1978: 1212–1374) was certainly familiar with Simmel's approach to the city. In Weber's ideal-type of the city he wandered far and wide over every kind of historical content while Simmel restricted to himself to the problem of fragmented individuality within metropolitan modernity.

Simmel's influence over urban sociology was felt more directly in America with the Chicago School of Sociology in the 1920s and 1930s. Louis Wirth's celebrated essay 'Urbanism as a way of life' (1938) drew on Simmel, as well as Durkheim, to formulate the intensity of city life in terms of size, density and heterogeneity. However, few followed Simmel's lead in a substantive direction.

An exception here is Walter Benjamin's various studies of urban modernity. In his studies of nineteenth-century Paris, Benjamin saw the urban proletarian as a 'shock absorber' and discovered a blasé social type – 'the flâneur' – strolling through busy Paris streets. Unfortunately, Simmel's concept of the metropolis is more usually seen as a fascinating diversion rather than a major road that urban sociology might travel.

RELATED CONCEPTS

Capital; Fashion; *Gemeinschaft* and *Gesellschaft*; Modernity; Money; Rationality and Rationalization

FURTHER READING

Simmel's essay 'The metropolis and mental life' is included in a number of collections including, *The Sociology of Georg Simmel* (Wolff, 1950), *On Individuality and Social Forms* (Levine, 1971), and *Simmel on Culture* (Simmel, 1997). A fascinating account is given in Chapter 3 of David Frisby's *Cityscapes of Modernity* (2001). A sense of Simmel's place in the wider field of urban sociology can be found in Chapter 11 of Bryan S. Turner's *Classical Sociology* (1999).

Mode of Production

Marx inherited from the Scottish Enlightenment a 'stages theory' of human development. In this model society passes through a historical series of stages of 'modes of subsistence' – hunting, pastoralism, agriculture and commerce (Meek, 1967: 39). Marx changes the Scottish emphasis on modes of subsistence to one of 'modes of production'. The major historical modes of production are: tribal or communal, ancient or classical, feudal, capitalist.

Every mode of production is a combination of the 'forces of production' and the 'social relations of production'. Within any society people enter into definite social relations that are always independent of their will. These relations correspond to a certain stage of technological and organizational development of the forces of production. In each mode of production the labour process is indelibly stamped by how the prevailing social relations appropriate surplus labour.

FORCES OF PRODUCTION

Marx is often accused of holding a 'technological determinist' view of society. This implies that technical change causes social change, through ascribing autonomy to technical change as if machines, not people, make history (Axelos, 1976). As Marx put it:

> In acquiring new productive forces men change their mode of production; and in changing their mode of production, in changing the way of earning their living, they change all their social relations. The hand-mill gives you society with the feudal lord; the steam-mill, society with the industrial capitalist. (1847: 102)

Marx frequently asserts that the productive forces predominate over the social relations of production. It appears that the productive forces take on a life of their own, independent of or even against social relations: 'the revolt of modern productive forces against modern conditions of production, against the property relations that are the conditions for the existence of the bourgeoisie and its rule' (Marx and Engels, 1998: 41).

However, the term 'productive forces' does not fully express the sense of human agency in Marx's original German term, *Produktivkrafte*, which roughly translates as 'productive powers' (Wood, 2004: 66). Forces of production constitute both the production process and the wider infrastructure of knowledge (or *techne*), communications, transport, energy and so on (Axelos, 1976). Productive forces are not narrowly conflated by Marx with machines or technology but include labour-power, knowledge, organization, skills, training; in short, technique and knowledge as well as technology.

SOCIAL RELATIONS OF PRODUCTION

Every society creates distinctive institutions in order to perpetuate its own material reproduction. Society, community and the individual are the subjects of production as well as their ultimate objects.

> The purpose of the community, of the individual – as well as the condition of production – [is] the reproduction of these specific conditions of production and of the individuals, both singly and in their social groupings and relations – as living carriers of these conditions. (Marx, 1973: 541)

Marx conceives the social relations of production as a definite form of class domination and exploitation, the 'hidden' and 'innermost secret' of civil society and the state. The distinctive method for extracting additional work from the direct producers varies from one mode of production to another.

> It is always the direct relationship of the owners of the conditions of production to the direct producers – a relation always naturally corresponding to a definite stage in the development of the methods of labour and thereby its social productivity – which reveals the innermost secret, the hidden basis of the entire social structure, and with it the political form of the relation of sovereignty and dependence, in short, the corresponding form of the state. (Marx, 1959: 791)

One class forces another class to produce an extra amount beyond what is needed to reproduce themselves 'in order to produce the means of subsistence for the owner of the means of production' (Marx, 1976: 345)

'PRIMITIVE COMMUNISM'

'Primitive communism' based on mobile hunter-gatherer groups is the earliest mode of production. Nomadic groups were organized communally around the family. Neither classes nor private property nor women's oppression existed (Engels, 1884). In 'primitive communism', individuals stand as natural members of the community or clan and its land. Since there was no accumulated private property to pass on inter-generationally, relations between the sexes were egalitarian. Insufficient means existed for a ruling class to emerge to take control of surplus wealth.

TRIBAL MODE OF PRODUCTION

Societies first divided into classes when urbanization took hold around 5,000 years ago in places like Mesopotamia (Iraq). Settled societies increased the stock of wealth in the form of crops and cattle, which was gradually appropriated and transformed into private property by a privileged, priestly section of society. Urban settlement also stimulated innovation in and rational exploitation of new means of production like metallurgy, the wheel, the cart, the pack-ass and sailing ships (Childe, 1964).

The tribal mode of production had colossal implications for gender relations. Engels (1884: 736) located the *world-historic defeat of the female sex* and the rise of the patriarchal family in tribal struggles over the male inheritance line for passing on stores of wealth.

CLASSICAL MODE OF PRODUCTION

Out of tribal conquest the institution of slavery asserted itself in Greece and Rome as the basis for the ancient or classical mode of production around 2,500 years ago. Although not a majority class in ancient society, slave-labour characterized this mode of production because it produced the surplus products on which the rest of society – freeman, plebeian, citizen or noble – ultimately depended. In Rome slaves had to be constantly replenished by wars of conquest and the resources secured to support an expanding military apparatus. Here begins the political domination of the city over the country.

FEUDAL MODE OF PRODUCTION

Feudalism is Marx's third mode of production. Feudalism reversed the dominance of the city in ancient Greece and Rome. With the collapse of the Roman Empire, large amounts of the productive forces were destroyed. Feudal units of production lay scattered across wide territories. Slavery gave way to the small-scale peasant labouring away at subsistence-level agriculture. In the towns, the guilds monopolized small-scale craft production. Neither the guilds nor the lords had much cause or means to raise the level of productivity through technical innovation. Instead, the peasants were forced to surrender a significant proportion of what they produced to support 'the organized robber nobility' and the church.

TRANSITION TO CAPITALISM

Two inter-related divisions of labour prepared the ground for capitalism within feudal society. One was the separation of material and mental labour while the other was a separation of town and country. Only the emerging urban middle-class burghers – or bourgeoisie – with their networks of commercial and industrial capital were able to challenge the limits of the feudal ruling class. Manufacturing and commerce escaped the restrictions of this feudal society through the increased mobility of capital. By extending commerce and trade to the level of a world market on the basis of large-scale industry the bourgeoisie was able to more permanently harness all the innovations and science embodied in the productive forces. Free competition within nations was secured politically by the 'bourgeois revolutions' of 1640 and 1688 in England and 1789 in France.

CAPITALIST MODE OF PRODUCTION

As a mode of production capitalism is unique. All other modes of production made use-value its aim; capitalism makes exchange-value and profit the whole point of production. It is the most technologically advanced society in human history but also, paradoxically, the most destructive society ever. Periodic crises eliminate large amounts of the productive forces, including unemployed labour and machinery.

> The capitalist mode of production and accumulation, and therefore capitalist private property as well, have for their fundamental condition the annihilation of that private property which rests on the labour of the individual worker himself; in other words, the expropriation of the worker. (Marx, 1976: 940)

This Marx identifies as the historical tendency of capitalist accumulation. On the one hand, the globalization and centralization of capital and, on the other hand, the organization and socialization of workers as a class enslaved by capitalist production but also in revolt against it.

Marx recognizes the gains for humanity made by the capitalist mode of production; the *Communist Manifesto* (Marx and Engels, 1998) is a veritable hymn to the achievements of the bourgeoisie. They socialized production and established 'universal interdependence' in a world market, making a new global culture possible. Spatial separation and distances have been overcome by capitalism's efficient use of time, what Marx called 'the annihilation of space by time':

> Capital must on one side tear down every spatial barrier to intercourse, i.e., to exchange, and conquer the whole earth for its market, it strives on the other side to annihilate this space with time, i.e., to reduce to a minimum the time spent in motion from one place to another. (1973: 539)

Marx also argued that capitalism had brought society to the threshold of a more advanced culture, socialism. The only alternative to socialism Marx thought was a descent into barbarism, with 'the mutual ruin of the contending classes'.

FETTERS AND 'THE BAD SIDE'

Every mode of production, Marx (1847: 113) argues, develops through the 'bad side' of antagonistic class relations: 'It is the bad side that produces the movement which made history, by providing a struggle'. This has been the case for every previous mode of production. Classes first rise to dominance over society as revolutionary classes. But once installed in unchallenged power, they stifle the potential of the productive forces in order to protect their rule.

Marx and Engels (1845–6: 194–5) echo their scientific hero Charles Darwin in viewing the forces of production in evolutionary terms: 'in the place of an earlier form of intercourse, which has become a fetter, a new one is put, corresponding to the more developed productive forces and, hence, which in its turn becomes a fetter and is replaced by another'. In the *Communist Manifesto*, Marx and Engels surveyed the wreckage of the feudal mode of production, destroyed by conditions created through maturing contradictions between the forces and relations of production.

> The means of production and of exchange, on whose foundation the bourgeoisie built itself up, were generated in feudal society. At a certain stage in the development of these means of production and of exchange, the conditions under which feudal society produced and exchanged, the feudal organization of agriculture and manufacturing industry, in one word, the feudal relations of property became no longer compatible with the already developed productive forces; they became so many fetters. They had to be burst asunder; they were burst asunder. (1998: 41)

As capitalism develops, a new 'bad side' emerges in the shape of class struggle and capitalist crises. Periodic crises under capitalism occur not because of scarcity but because of its opposite: excessive abundance in the over-production of commodities. The productive forces have become too powerful for the social relations of bourgeois society. Each crisis is resolved through the destruction of a significant part of the productive forces, preparing the way for even more extensive crises.

It is not autonomous technology that revolts against capitalist social relations. A certain level of technological development is the necessary but insufficient precondition for the transformation of social relations. Marx asserts that the working class must actively overcome 'the fetters' of capitalist private property:

The monopoly of capital becomes a fetter upon the mode of production which has flourished alongside it and under it. The centralization of the means of production and the socialization of labour reach a point at which they become incompatible with their capitalist integument. This integument is burst asunder. The knell of capitalist private property sounds. The expropriators are expropriated. (1976: 929)

Only the 'socialization of labour', not technology per se, Marx argues, can overcome the limits imposed by capitalist social relations as a necessary step towards the free development of humanity.

CRITICAL DEVELOPMENTS

Each mode of production and the transition between them has produced countless scholarly studies and disputes. Debates have raged over whether the transition to capitalism occurred either through the driving force of market exchange, class struggles between serfs and lords or mainly out of the emerging production forces. Non-Marxists prefer to use other terms like 'industrial society' or 'modern society' rather than capitalism as a mode of production.

Modes of production must be analysed in their own right rather than assumed to be inevitable mechanical 'stages' of development. A mechanical 'stages' view of modes of production became widespread among later Marxists who accepted that progress inevitably flows from advanced technologies. A positivist belief in the progressive role of technology was largely abandoned after the catastrophes of industrialized warfare, the 'murder factories' of Nazi concentration camps, and nuclear weapons. This distortion of the liberating potential of the productive forces by hostile social relations was memorably described by the unorthodox Marxist, Walter Benjamin (1940), as a 'storm blowing from paradise'.

RELATED CONCEPTS

Base and Superstructure; Capital; Civil Society; Class; Historical Materialism; Primitive Accumulation

FURTHER READING

Modes of production are scattered throughout Marx's writings but see especially the *Communist Manifesto* (Marx and Engels, 1998). For a sweeping and highly accessible Marxist account of world history see Chris Harman's *A People's History of the World* (2008).

'Modernity' does not refer so much to a distinct time period as to new forms of experience, new ways of life, new forms of production and consumption, new political movements, and new modernist cultures. The term 'modernity' was first minted by the poet and critic Charles Baudelaire in the 1850s. Baudelaire dramatized modernity as 'the fantastic reality' of what is temporary and transitory in everyday life – 'the ephemeral, the fugitive, the contingent'. For Baudelaire's contemporary, Karl Marx, modernity was identical to the wild rhythms of capitalism where 'all that is solid melts into air' (Berman, 1983).

Modernity overthrew all previous beliefs, relationships and systems of authority. Society no longer stood still but was in constant upheaval. Life speeded up. Huge distances were overcome by new forms of transport and communications systems. Machinery replaced people. Technology eased the conditions of life. Gigantic cities sprung up, teeming with the most diverse commodities for sale. While many changes were exhilarating, they were bought at a high cost. For Marx, the price of modernity was exploitation, anarchy and alienation. For Weber, it was the rise of the 'iron cage' of rationalization. For Durkheim, it was widespread anomie during the transition to organic solidarity. For Tönnies, modernity meant the artificial society of *Gesellschaft* dominating the natural community of *Gemeinschaft*. While most classical theorists were ambivalent about modernity, they nevertheless recognized that there was no way back to the stable harmony of a pre-modern world.

SIMMEL'S MODERNITY

Few classical social theorists were more attuned to the ambiguities of modernity than Georg Simmel. Simmel has been called 'the first sociologist of modernity' (Frisby, 1985: 39). Simmel does not describe the entire historical development of modernity but tries to isolate individual fragments of modern life to reveal the totality of society. In studies of money, fashion and the metropolis, the primary sites of modernity, Simmel freezes the surface appearance of things in order to reveal their innumerable connections to the fleeting experiences of modern life.

Modernity is lived as a fragmented series of 'snapshots'. A restless search for excitement and diversion breaks up the mundane routines of an indifferent everyday life. Leisure time is set aside as a special period to be filled up by seemingly unique activities. Adventure, sports, tourism, gambling, sexual affairs and travel allow modern types to temporarily rupture the mundane flow of time. For Simmel this punctuation of everyday life represents the suspension of historical time, of living without a past or a future, 'obliterated in the rapture of the moment' (Simmel, 1997: 224).

OBJECTIVE AND SUBJECTIVE CULTURE

Modernity is characterized by Simmel as the domination of 'objective culture' over 'subjective culture'. Objective culture is embodied in independent things, objects like products, buildings, technology or works of art. By subjective culture Simmel refers to the active assimilation of material culture by individuals through their will, intelligence and emotions. For Simmel, what is valuable in culture is the development of the individual human personality. Subjective life must be the 'overriding final goal' of any truly living, dynamic culture (Simmel, 1997: 58).

Modernity, however, widens the gap between people and things. People become alienated and dominated by the things of 'objective culture'. As society becomes more technological 'people are capable only to a lesser degree of deriving from the improvement of objects an improvement of their subjective lives' (1997: 45). Objective material improvements take place at the expense of subjective human values: 'The intrinsic worth of material things has advanced much more rapidly than the intrinsic worth of men' (Simmel, 1902: 5).

More and more cultural objects are acquired which have less and less value for us. Life is burdened with 'a thousand superfluous things' that cannot be assimilated by an individual personality. Quantity destroys quality. The rigid split between objective and subjective culture is 'the real tragedy of culture'. Instead of synthesizing personal values and material culture they are kept apart. Objective culture does our thinking and feeling for us. Like Marx's idea of commodity fetishism, objects created by and for human beings through the division of labour become alienated from their origin and purpose.

'Real culture', subjective development, must be realized in an objective definite form. Modernity is tragic because the dominance of independent objects denies the subjective side of culture. A conflict ensues between the products of culture and the processes of culture.

> There thus emerges the typical problematical condition of modern humanity: the feeling of being surrounded by an immense number of cultural elements, which are not meaningless, but not profoundly meaningful to the

individual either; elements which have a certain crushing quality as a mass, because an individual cannot inwardly assimilate every individual thing, but cannot simply reject it either, since it belongs potentially, as it were, to the sphere of his or her cultural development. (Simmel, 1997: 73)

The finished product is incapable of being assimilated by the subject as part of the process of human self-development. Individual experience is reduced to the commands of objective culture. Dominating external objective culture, money transforms inner life, helping to form our desires and needs, not least by making rational calculation seem like second nature to us (Simmel, 1900).

TECHNIQUE AND APPEARANCE

Modern life revolves around improving things through 'technique', forgetting that technique is only a means to an end, not an end in itself. In modernity, technical efficiency becomes its own final goal. The dominance of objective technique over subjective experience does not just affect everyday things. In science, the striving for improved technique led to the general dominance of positivism and materialism. This extols only those material things available to the senses and rejects any deeper reflection about ultimate cultural, ethical or spiritual values. Technique in research methods becomes everything in the social sciences. Simmel considered social research techniques 'essentially worthless' and 'unimportant' where they do not deepen human values.

Finance and commerce, machinery, large businesses, state bureaucracy, science and the technical side of art all underwent unprecedented formal improvements with no corresponding growth in personal or cultural qualities. As the object is perfected through technique so the imperfections of the subject are revealed. In the age of the cell phone and the Internet Simmel's comments still have a contemporary feel:

as though telegraphs and telephones were in themselves things of extraordinary value, despite the fact that what men say to each other by means of them is not at all wiser, nobler, or in any way more excellent than what they formerly entrusted to less rapid means of communication. (1902: 6)

modernity

The external world of things invades our internal world of thoughts, feelings and sensations. It becomes more difficult to comprehend the socially produced knowledge embodied in objective culture 'in which a comprehensive intellectuality is accumulated, but of which the individual mind can only make minimal use' (Simmel, 1900: 449). Even modern education is less concerned with stimulating subjective development than it is with transmitting objective knowledge as something distant from individuals.

The 'practical materialism' of modernity is reflected in the decorative facades of houses, fashion, photography and travel. Attention to the appearance of things was stimulated by the power of the rising middle classes. Always looking for 'new sensations', sections of the middle class even dabbled with revolutionary socialism.

FEARS OF 'LEVELLING'

Modernity allocates social positions increasingly on the basis of ability and energy, indifferent to the inherited privileges of wealth or background. Compared to the higher classes, which 'seem in many cases to be so decadent, so exhausted and neurasthenic [depressed], as to be unable to bear the future upon their shoulders', the 'less refined' lower classes seem more energetic and dynamic (Simmel, 1902:12). Because they stand far down the cultural scale the working class will drag down the better educated to a cultural level far beneath them. One of the 'tragedies' of modernity, Simmel (1902: 16) claims, is 'that which elevates the lowest groups lowers the highest'.

Modernity promotes a cult of 'individualism'. Simmel connects individualism to the philosopher Friedrich Nietzsche (1844–1900). Nietzsche opposed 'social levelling' which makes all individuals equal and defended the natural superiority of elites. If everyone is made to conform to the average values of 'the herd', then nothing great or worthwhile will be achieved by outstanding individuals. With its motto of living for today, modernity is deeply nihilistic, caught up in a permanent present. Nietzsche called this the 'eternal recurrence of the ever-same', without meaning or direction.

Nietzsche's philosophy was used to justify an arrogant, selfish individualism – 'the right of the strong and unusual character to be a law unto itself' – against other moral values like social justice and solidarity. But Nietzsche objected equally to the vanity of superficial and mediocre bourgeois individualism as having nothing in common with the cruel, violent individuality of innately superior aristocratic elites. Neitzsche's sentiment was memorably put by Harry Lime, the character played by Orson Welles in the classic film *The Third Man* (1949):

> Like the fella says, in Italy for 30 years under the Borgias they had warfare, terror, murder, and bloodshed, but they produced Michelangelo, Leonardo da Vinci, and the Renaissance. In Switzerland they had brotherly love – they had 500 years of democracy and peace, and what did that produce? The cuckoo clock.

Instead of cultural achievements of this magnitude, for Nietzsche modernity produces only servile elites, forced to pander to stupidity and ignorance in the lowest common denominator of the masses. In order to avoid the truth about mediocre individualism, people take refuge in illusions, subterfuges, politeness, fashion, ephemera and the empty opinions of the passing moment. Simmel sees Nietzsche as an aristocratic opponent of modernity, representing purely spiritual values against the demands for social justice for the working class.

CULTURAL FREEDOM

However, Simmel did not succumb to Nietzsche's pessimism about modernity. He concluded that modernity contained within itself a corrective to an over-mechanical, anti-spiritual world. By the end of the nineteenth century, Simmel argued, positivism began to lose its appeal for science and philosophy. Some types of knowledge are formed beyond what is given by material facts, metaphysically, by imagination, ideas and beliefs. Historical materialism transformed history from the study of princes and heroes to the study of the objective conditions of class conflict, but also had the effect of restoring the ethical or subjective side of capitalism.

Simmel allows technique a special role in modernist music, art and poetry, to the extent that it serves to enhance subjective values, higher feelings and critical thought. But even here an interest in art is in danger of becoming a fad. Cultured people try to overcome the fragmentation experienced in modern life with the more profound unity of meaning found in a work of art. Then, as now, a search for cultural meaning in a modernity that lacks unified values can result in quasi-religious revivals and mystical mumbo jumbo like spiritualism (Simmel, 1997).

The flux of modernity also transformed the situation of women in society. Simmel gives more attention to the position of women in modernity than other European male sociologists. The position of women varied with class. Industrial production drove working-class women out of the home and into the factory and office. It also supplied all the objects for domestic consumption that kept middle-class women in the home. Middle-class women formed the modern women's movement to demand greater freedom and rights outside the home, while working-class women were exposed to exploitation and oppression – 'a monstrous social injustice' – in the workplace: 'the woman of the proletariat has not, as the middle class woman, too little, but on the contrary too much social freedom – however badly it may stand with her individual freedom' (Simmel, 1902: 17).

modernity

CRITICAL DEVELOPMENTS

Simmel forensically reveals what is significant about the myriad inter-connections hidden in the transient, fugitive and fragmentary surfaces of modernity. Because of this, many of Simmel's contemporaries argued that he lacked any coherent view of society (Frisby, 2002). Weber was annoyed by what he saw as Simmel's attempt to turn sociology into a search for 'the meaning of life'. Many others agreed, demanding that sociology produce more systematic explanations about modernity rather than engage in making speculative connections in the style of Simmel.

His influence extended to Georg Lukacs, Siegfried Kracauer and Walter Benjamin, who produced some of the most dazzling analyses of moder-nity in the twentieth century (Frisby, 1985). Kracauer (1995: 251–2) is particularly perceptive about the 'irregular' legacy of his teacher's insist-ence on the interconnectedness of all things in modernity. Kracauer com-pared Simmel's perspective to that of a frog: 'a world view from below instead of above' (quoted by Frisby, 1992a: 132). Other students like Georg Lukacs and Karl Mannheim compared him to an 'Impressionist'. They objected to his failure to understand modernity as a totality and the magisterial distance that he took from real social conditions.

Simmel's approach to modernity has some affinity with recent social theory. The regularities and systems of 'grand' social theory have been widely criticized in favour of more specifically cultural approaches. Theories about modernity are considered passé, superseded by a recent 'postmodernism' of cultural detachment, irony and fragmentation, with some seeing Simmel as a precursor (Weinstein and Weinstein, 1993). Recent social theory sees a very different world from that of classical social theory, one that neither conforms to a single overriding dynamic nor to rational prediction and scientific control. While such typical char-acterizations of classical social theorizing about modernity could be disputed in a number of ways, accusations of reducing modernity to a single factor or positivist controls most certainly do not apply to Simmel's pioneering approach to modernity.

RELATED CONCEPTS

Alienation; Anomie; Commodity Fetishism; Fashion; Metropolis; Money; Rationality and Rationalization

FURTHER READING

Extremely useful is the collection *Simmel on Culture* (Simmel, 1997) edited by David Frisby and Mike Featherstone. At a more introductory level David Frisby's short book

Georg Simmel (2002) forms an excellent starting point. More ambitious is Frisby's stunning comparison of Simmel, Kracauer and Benjamin's theories of modernity in *Fragments of Modernity* (1985).

Money

Money plays an unrivalled role in the structuring of social life. What seems strange is that money as a physical object – as coin, banknote or credit card – has no intrinsic value or usefulness. Coins, notes and plastic cards cannot be eaten or worn. Money's value must come from something else. In classical social theory, two major contributions to the sociology of money were made by Karl Marx and Georg Simmel. In some ways, their respective concepts of money complement each other, though in other ways they diverge.

MARX

In the 1844 manuscripts Marx gave a memorable statement of the power of money. Money is 'the pimp' mediating between human needs and their satisfaction in an object. Money both binds people to and separates them from society; it is 'the bond of all bonds' as well as 'the world upside down'. Money transfers whatever exists in 'the objective world' to the owner of money. It turns personal limits into their opposite through the 'universal inversion of individualities'. 'Money is the highest good and so its possessor is good' (Marx, 1844: 109). If the owner of money is ugly they can buy beauty; if the owner is dishonest and stupid, money can buy honesty and intelligence.

In *Capital* (1976), Marx examines money as a necessary social convention and the ultimate commodity fetish. Only society makes money, a particular commodity, into the measure of all other commodities. Money arises out of the social need for the mutual comparison of different products of labour against a fixed measure. This function of money Marx calls the 'universal or social equivalent'. Only through money can the products of labour become commodities. All labour is social labour embodied in discrete commodities that can only be obtained by means of money.

135

Gold traditionally performed the universal function as the 'social equivalent' in two ways. First, because of the uniform qualities of the metal, gold could act as the material embodiment for equalizing different kinds of social labour. And, second, because it can be divided and re-assembled in different amounts, it flexibly expresses different quantities of labour stored up in different commodities.

As a commodity, money embodies both exchange value and use value. As use value, money functions as both a store of value and a means of payment that allows all other commodities to circulate. As exchange value, money itself becomes the object of exchange, independent of all other commodities. Money is 'pure exchange value' (1976: 180). Money is put into circulation to generate even more money.

Money is the starting point and end point of capital accumulation. It appears as if 'money begets money', obscuring the source of money in social labour. In this process, money starts with the capitalist, 'or rather his pocket', where it constantly returns. This constant chase after money is common to both the capitalist and the miser; 'but where the miser is a merely a capitalist gone mad, the capitalist is a rational miser' (1976: 254). While the miser hoards his money the capitalist throws it back into circulation over and over again.

Workers earn money wages which entitle them to a certain amount of the social product in the shape of other commodities. The value of real money wages depends on the price of goods, which fluctuate across society. Prices are merely the money-name for an imaginary or ideal expression of social labour objectified in a commodity. The number on the price label of a coat expresses a quantity of money, an ideal symbol for the social labour embodied in the coat. Marx says 'ideal' because the price number cannot simultaneously be both a real coat and real money.

SIMMEL

Simmel's (1900: 56) stated aim in his masterpiece *The Philosophy of Money* was 'to construct a new storey beneath historical materialism'. He wanted to locate the economic base of society within the 'ideal depths' of individuals, history and culture. Simmel begins from the surface details of economic life in order to arrive at what he sees as the most essential movements and values of individuals, culture and history.

Characteristically, Simmel (like Marx) does not begin with a chronological, descriptive history of money from its origins to the present. Instead, he analyses money as a logical concept.

Money is simply a means, a material or an example for the presentation of relations that exist between the most superficial, 'realistic', and fortuitous phenomena and the most idealized powers of existence, the most profound currents of individual life and history. (1900: 55)

In the first 'analytical' part of the book, Simmel reveals the underlying connections of money. These general relationships can only be explored through abstract concepts. In the second 'synthetic' part, he explores the logical structuring of life and culture in an ideal money economy.

THE VALUE OF MONEY

Money depends on how value comes to be invested in it. Simmel develops a theory of value that is simultaneously subjective and objective. Value cannot be solely *subjective* because it always stands in relation to an object. And it cannot be solely *objective* because it always involves an active process of valuation. Value is not a quality inhering in things but a judgement made upon them by a subject. What people consider valuable can vary considerably depending on subjective feelings, dispositions, wants, desires and so on. A starving person will place more value on a piece of bread than a rare jewel.

Value stems from our distance and separation from the desired object. Value is attached to external objects that can be realistically acquired through effort, sacrifice, frustration, costs and labour. Easy virtue has low value. If things are put too easily within our reach they have little value for us; if they are too far away, if the price is exorbitant, then their absolute distance also lowers their value for us. 'Objects are not difficult to acquire because they are valuable, but we call those objects valuable that resist our desire to possess them' (1900: 67).

EXCHANGE

Echoing Marx, money for Simmel represents 'the congealed form' of concrete exchange among people. It creates a unified, self-enclosed world, pulling into its orbit innumerable disparate things and people, all held together by the functional contingency of exchange (Simmel, 1997: 255–8). Money for Simmel has a dual nature: substance and function. On the one hand, it is a concrete substance and, on the other hand, it is 'the complete dissolution of substance into motion and function, [which] derives from the fact that money is the reification of exchange among people, the embodiment of a pure function' (Simmel, 1900: 176).

Simmel compares the accumulation drive of capitalists to hamsters that pile up objects of every kind without any direct interest in them as things. Money stores up future 'possibilities' in both senses of the word, as latency, what can be done with money but hasn't yet, and, second, as uncertainty, money provides security against what is unknown about the future.

Money measures the exchange of one object for another. It represents a special kind of value: abstract value. It is the value of things of value: 'the value of all things without the things themselves' (1900: 121). Money brings every thing that possesses value into a relationship with every other concrete value (thing) and with itself as abstract value (money). It is 'the stable pole' that expresses the distance between subjective desire and objective value. Everything submits to the power of money. It has become a god which unifies every contradiction and difference, centring the entire universe around itself.

In economic exchange something is acquired and something is surrendered. The object is not only valuable for me but for others too, independent of my own desire. Everybody gets something and sacrifices something. In this way exchange combines a change in ownership to everyone's mutual advantage. Economic exchange is only the most concentrated case of general social interaction found in every human encounter, conversation, glance, game, social advance and social withdrawal. Simmel even considered production to be a form of exchange between people and nature, although what 'nature' desires and acquires in return for its sacrifice is difficult to see.

MEANS AND ENDS

Money is neutral and colourless with no intrinsic qualities of its own, only those given to it by social organization. Because of the difficulty in tracing its origins, money's anonymity makes bribery and secrecy more effective and tempting (Simmel, 1900: 385). With money in charge, personal obligations are replaced by impersonal functions. Money is a means through which individuals can acquire definite ends which they could never attain alone.

Because of its lack of specific content, money is able to spread itself in every direction for endlessly diverse uses. Unlike other commodities that are restricted to a definite form, money is infinitely flexible and available for unlimited purposes. This ubiquity gives it a value that transcends all other values. 'Money is the purest reification of means, a concrete instrument which is absolutely identical with its abstract concept; it is a pure instrument' (1900: 211).

Money is the most extreme case of a means becoming an absolute end in itself (Simmel, 1997: 233–42). Because it can be used at any time for almost any purpose, money allows its owner more freedom than any other commodity. The abstract character of money, lacking any intrinsic qualities, 'supports an objective delight in money, in the awareness of a value that extends far beyond all individual and personal enjoyment of its benefits' (1900: 241).

QUANTITY TRUMPS QUALITY

Money as a number and amount is the universal symbol of life's domination by quantity. Life is determined by the question 'how much?' Commodities for sale are forced to adopt fixed standards. If 'time is money' then a more exact measure of time becomes imperative. Precision is demanded to gauge the exact price we are prepared to pay in our daily transactions. Time becomes an abstraction to be counted by the precision of the clock and the watch. In politics, votes are counted and the balance of power is weighed.

Diverse objects are valued solely according to the amount of money that they cost. Because money shatters the totality of life into small individual parts, commodities can be recombined into any arbitrary arrangement, as in a shop window, in the home, in a share portfolio and so on. This abundance of disparate products provides the raw material for modern individualism (Simmel, 1900: 276). But instead of individual qualities becoming paramount, money reduces quality to quantity.

A corollary of the domination of quantity over quality is that life becomes subject to continuous calculation (Simmel, 1997: 243–53). In measuring the cost of everything the world is transformed into a huge arithmetical problem without a solution. A calculating rational intellect predominates over impulsive emotions. Costs and benefits, pleasure and pain, have to be weighed and a calculus of utility established. Calculation always promotes self-interest rather than wider human values.

MONEY AND SOCIETY

Money helps to reify 'society' by giving it independence, solidity and coherence. 'The function of exchange, as a direct interaction between individuals, becomes crystallized in the form of money as an independent structure' (Simmel, 1900: 175). As exchange becomes general and public rather than specific and private, money asserts itself as a claim upon society. Society is called upon to honour the value of money by generating relations of trust to make monetary exchange possible in the first place.

money

At the back of money transactions always stand concrete individuals engaged in social interaction. We are dependent on the function that money buys not the individual person, whether salesperson, money-lender or hairdresser (1900: 296). Money makes us more dependent on society as a whole to satisfy our needs and to specialize in a particular function. But it also allows us to be remarkably independent of and indifferent towards specific people, whose function could be performed just as well by any number of wholly different people. Functions mediated by money represent only a fragment of the whole personality. 'The content of a representation does not coincide with the representation of contents' (1900: 65). Money reduces people to social types: the wealthy, the stranger, the worker, the prostitute, the miser, the spendthrift, the thrifty, the poor, the cynic and the blasé urbanite.

But money is also inherently ambiguous. On the one hand, it is indifferent to specific commodities, say this brand of beans over another. On the other hand, money allows greater discrimination between specific objects. The object acquires a greater significance for the subject. Subjective feelings are subdued by money's greater regard for objective culture. We become more detached and respectful towards objects when their distance from us might be overcome by exchanging scarce money.

CRITICAL DEVELOPMENTS

Contemporaries hailed *The Philosophy of Money* (Simmel, 1900) as a pioneering work. Georg Lukacs (1991) praised its subtle, many-sided analysis. It made possible other developments in German sociology. Tönnies recognized its importance for sociology and Weber drew from it liberally (if critically) in making rationalization central to his own understanding of modernity. Simmel compared his own diffuse intellectual legacy to money. As he famously wrote in his diary:

> My legacy will be like cash, distributed to many heirs, each transforming his part into use according to his nature – a use which will no longer reveal its indebtedness to this nature. (quoted by Levine, 1971: xiii)

Some saw the influence of Marx in Simmel's concept of money. But although he emphasizes money's central role for objective culture, Simmel tends to adopt a subjective theory of value determined by individual desires. So while there is some overlap, Simmel has little to say about Marx's distinction between exchange value and use value or the objective nature of the labour theory of value based on socially necessary labour time (Frisby, 1992b: 80–97). He also prefers to use the concept of 'money economy' rather than 'capitalism'. And while Simmel shows how money shapes the experience of modernity he says little concretely about how it shapes relations between the social classes.

The increased role of credit and the financial crisis of recent years give Simmel's theory of money a continuing relevance. While there has been an explosion of interest in the sociology of consumption Simmel's sociology of money has not yet been widely assimilated. Money, finance and credit continue to restructure and mediate lifestyle, shopping, consumer culture, indeed every kind of social relation, in ways not unlike those explored a century ago by Simmel.

RELATED CONCEPTS

Alienation; Capital; Class; Commodity Fetishism; Fashion; Metropolis; Modernity; Protestant Ethic and the 'Spirit of Capitalism'; Rationality and Rationalization

FURTHER READING

The Philosophy of Money (Simmel, 1900) is a demanding read. Better to start with shorter outlines such as Bryan S. Turner's summary in his textbook *Classical Sociology* (1999) and David Frisby's concise discussion in *Georg Simmel* (2002). A longer but accessible essay is Gianfranco Poggi's, *Money and the Modern Mind* (1993). A brilliant discussion of the meaning of money is James Buchan's *Frozen Desire* (1998).

Normal and Pathological

Durkheim attempted to establish sociology as a scientific discipline by constructing mutually-exclusive dualisms (Lukes, 1992: 16–30). These are pairs of conflicting concepts like 'individual' and 'society' fixed at opposite ends of the scale. Durkheim's conceptual dualism 'normal' and 'pathological' makes knowledge about society analogous to knowledge about medicine. Normal social phenomena are 'healthy' (therefore good), while pathological social phenomena are 'sick' or 'diseased' (therefore bad). Sickness refers not to every misfortune that befalls an individual but to anything 'avoidable which is not intrinsic to the normal constitution of the living creature' (Durkheim, 1895: 88). Durkheim reasons that what is general or average across society must count as 'normal' (or 'physiological') while what is exceptional or deviant must count as 'pathological'.

SOCIAL HYGIENE

Durkheim (1895: 91) constructs hypothetical 'normal' types from 'the most frequently occurring characteristics of the species in their most frequent forms'. Social practices and institutions are good or bad relative to the average appropriate to a certain stage of development. In this evolutionary model, the 'normal' is that which successfully adapts to the prevailing conditions of collective life. 'Normality' is grounded in the nature of things, above all environmental conditions (1895: 96). A given social fact may be assumed to be necessary (normal) or accidental (pathological) to the social structure depending on the stage of development.

Conversely, pathology does *not* inhere in the nature of things. Pathology is an unnecessary deviation from environmental conditions. Any deviation from the average type is considered by Durkheim (1895: 91) to be morbid, an exceptional deviation from the more general or 'healthy' social facts. Durkheim (1895: 93) claims that the average social type is never pathological since society typically resists and repels the causes of its own destruction. Deviant pathological cases will have great difficulty surviving in the midst of healthy norms.

Social hygiene, for Durkheim, is not an absolute thing that inheres in institutions. This principle of healthy adaptation applies only when society is well integrated and stable. A social fact is 'normal' if it represents a general response to a particular set of conditions. But if conditions change then the same social fact becomes morbid. For instance, if the social structure that gave rise to market economies still exists then market competition is healthy and normal. If its social supports have disappeared then the market is morbid and abnormal.

When society is in transition and a new stability has yet to be established the normal-pathological dualism cannot function. Norms that fitted well with earlier social conditions no longer correspond to the new or changing situation:

> It therefore has only the appearance of normality, and the generality it displays is deceptive; persisting only through the force of blind habit, it is no longer the sign that the phenomenon observed is closely linked to the general conditions of collective existence. (1895: 95)

PATHOLOGICAL DIVISIONS OF LABOUR

Under 'normal' conditions, the division of labour results in a new moral density generated by labour's mutual interaction, purpose and value. Organic solidarity will become the 'normal' state of society, even if it was passing through a pathological transitional phase in Durkheim's lifetime. Transformation was so rapid that new, often antagonistic interests lacked time to adapt to each other and restore a new equilibrium. Durkheim identifies three 'abnormal forms of the division of labour': anomie, forced and disorganization.

First, anomie becomes evident in a pathological absence of regulation, rules and coordination, resulting in economic crises and class conflict. Second, Durkheim distinguishes 'normal' inequalities based on the average value of individual abilities from the 'abnormal' inequalities of a 'forced division of labour'. An inequality of inherited wealth 'falsifies the moral conditions of exchange':

> If one class of society is obliged, in order to live, to take any price for its services, while another can abstain from such action thanks to resources at its disposal which, however, are not necessarily due to any social superiority, the second has an unjust advantage over the first. (Durkheim, 1933: 384)

Rather than seeing this as the normal condition of capitalist society Durkheim views it as artificial and 'forced', a pathological deviation from natural justice. Finally, commercial and industrial enterprises lack the continuous functional organization of a 'normal' division of labour. Work is thereby less valuable, more wasteful and prone to industrial unrest. Durkheim is remarkably vague about 'the exceptional circumstances' that cause this pathological situation.

NORMAL CRIME AND SUICIDE

Crime is commonly seen as pathological. For Durkheim, however, crime is a 'normal' social fact. All societies produce criminality, albeit understood in widely diverse ways. Crime only becomes 'morbid' when it reaches unusually high or excessive levels. Crime is 'normal' for society since it is bound up with the moral conditions of collective life.

> Thus crime is necessary. It is linked to the basic conditions of social life, but on this very account is useful, for the conditions to which it is bound are themselves indispensable to the normal evolution of morality and law. (Durkheim, 1895: 101)

normal and pathological

143

Surprisingly, crime helps to integrate a normal society. In conditions where violent crime declines, society becomes more sensitized, exacting and reactive about the slightest infractions. As with the recent redefinition of 'anti-social behaviour', as violent crime falls relatively minor acts are considered 'criminal'. Crime can also be socially useful when it points towards a change in morality. What was earlier defined as 'pathological' may later become 'normal', as when yesterday's heretics become today's heroes.

In Durkheim's famous study, suicide shows a 'normal' 'healthy' pattern. The whole – society – is more than the sum of its parts – individuals. So long as society remains stable and the density of association is maintained suicides are less likely. So long as society is prone to crisis and association thins out suicides become more likely. Normally, the three currents of egoism, altruism and anomie offset each other, producing 'a state of equilibrium' in any single individual. But if any one becomes dominant pathological suicidogenetic tendencies are released.

HYGIENIC REFORMISM

Durkheim wanted to use scientific knowledge to maintain science in its 'normal' state and purge it of what he considered to be unnecessary maladies. If 'objective criterion' can be unearthed by medical science, then pathological social facts might be rectified by medicalizing society:

> The duty of the statesman is no longer to propel society violently towards an ideal which appears attractive to him. His role is rather that of the doctor: he prevents the outbreak of sickness by maintaining good hygiene, or when it does break out, seeks to cure it. (Durkheim, 1895: 104)

Unlike the neutral diagnosis of medicine, the health of society is bound to involve value judgements of some kind. Against the kind of value-neutrality advocated by Weber, Durkheim argues that it is necessary to make judgements about social facts if science is to have any positive effect on the health of society. For Durkheim (1895: 86) a choice always has to be made between different paths towards a given goal. From a certain point of view ends can become means and means ends. Durkheim clearly thought that the most desirable end was a healthy, stable, 'normal' society.

CRITICAL DEVELOPMENTS

Many critics objected to Durkheim's use of medical terms to characterize society. Durkheim was well aware of the limits to the analogy and highlighted the more unpredictable nature of moral norms in human societies. By his own admission the analogy does not operate when society is undergoing rapid change. The normal state is assumed to be relatively static, subject only to incremental movements in collective life. As Hirst argues:

> Normality and pathology are defined in a purely nominal and circular fashion; what is the norm is the given social practices and codes which are the average in a particular social species. (1973: 27)

Neither are such vague generalizations particularly useful for explaining societies where economic restructuring, rising suicides, depression, alienation and anomie are relatively widespread and stable phenomena. Are such societies healthy in a structural or a purely nominal sense?

Durkheim dodges the issue by appealing to some future perfect of a 'normal' society that has not yet existed. A deeper problem lies in the ideal correspondence between social facts and social structure. Durkheim seems to conservatively equate what is normal with whatever exists at an average level. Steven Lukes summed up the extent to which Durkheim departed from his own scientific principles:

> As a result, he tended to idealize societies he thought of as integrated, ignoring the tensions and conflicts within them, while seeing the realities of his own society only as pathological deviations from its future, normal, ideally integrated state. (1992: 30)

In fact, Durkheim saw his own society as tending towards 'a veritable sociological monstrosity' of endemic sickness. As society becomes more complex and disorganized, the centralized nation-state attempts to impose order from above and outside society:

> A society composed of an infinite number of unorganized individuals, that a hypertrophied State is forced to oppress and contain, constitutes a veritable sociological monstrosity. For collective activity is always too complex to be able to be expressed through the single and unique organ of the State. (Durkheim, 1933: 28)

A further problem is that the normal-pathological distinction undermines the concept of social facts. Social facts are premised on the 'normal' force of external constraints acting on individuals. But generality and the average type may in fact be pathological (Gane, 1992: 67–8).

The normal-pathological dualism may be a useful preliminary methodological device for thinking about means and ends in social theory and research. However, as an explanatory concept it is too vague, deeply misleading and arbitrary to appeal to many sociologists today.

RELATED CONCEPTS

Anomie; Conscience Collective; Division of Labour in Society (Durkheim); Ideal-Types; Social Facts; Social Morphology; Suicide

FURTHER READING

Durkheim discusses pathological social facts in Chapter 3 of *The Rules of Sociological Method* (1895). Useful summaries and context can be found in Lukes (1992) and Jones (1986). A detailed consideration of pathology as a metaphor is offered by Paul Q. Hirst's 'Morphology and pathology' (1973).

.... Positivism ....

Positivism is a shortened term for the 'positive philosophy' strongly associated with the nineteenth-century French thinker Auguste Comte (1798–1857). Positive philosophy has had a deep impact on the development of sociology and influenced generations of thinkers. Indeed, Comte invented the term 'sociology' (on 27 April 1839) to replace what he had previously called 'social physics', as a major, though not the only, element of positive philosophy (Pickering, 1993: 615). While positivism is widely used as a term of abuse today, some of its assumptions about a science of society are still common currency.

UNIFY THEORY, UNIFY SOCIETY

Positive philosophy was described by Comte (1998: 75) as the attempt 'to regard all phenomena as subject to invariable natural laws' through exact discovery and a reduction to 'the smallest number possible'. He assumed that sociology would sit atop and synthesize a unified hierarchy of knowledge. Comte's model was the precise mathematical formulae of the natural sciences, especially physics, as a universal ideal for measuring the success of the new science of sociology. Individual phenomena could be explained only if these were integrated into the most general laws of social development.

Positivism was set up in opposition to what Comte saw as 'negative philosophy'. Comte (1998: 9) wanted to resist what he thought were the destructive forces of social disintegration, above all 'moral and political anarchy'. Since he believed that ideas govern the world, 'social anarchy' reflected a lack of scientific understanding about the laws of society and philosophy's over-critical and speculative principles about humanity, freedom and equality.

Endless philosophical speculations about the ultimate point of human life and the nature of society would be displaced from now on by positivist sociology. This represented an ambitious attempt to limit sociology to the study of 'positive facts'. Positivism should not prejudge the kind of knowledge about the world that science might produce (Kolakowski, 1972). It should confine itself to setting down rules and criteria for judging the validity of concepts. Comte showed little interest in the empirical study of society, preferring to set out general laws of development.

SOCIAL STATICS AND SOCIAL DYNAMICS

Comte wanted to scientifically heal the 'social anarchy' following the French Revolution and subordinate individuals to a unified conception of 'society'. He advocated a positive balance between the two principles of conservative order and radical progress. Society is broken into two distinct spheres in his 'positivist' theory of society, on the one hand, 'social statics' (order) and, on the other, 'social dynamics' (progress):

1 Social statics: a concept of social order, stability, and integration.
2 Social dynamics: a concept of social change, fragmentation and progress.

Social statics studies society at rest in a fixed space. Social dynamics studies the laws of motion as things change over time. This follows a similar division in biology between fixed anatomy and changes in physiology. Statics, or 'social anatomy', and dynamics, or 'social physiology', may be divided for purposes of scientific analysis but in practice they are always inseparable.

Social statics are those 'laws of harmony of human society', involving the core institutions of the family, the state and, ultimately, humanity (or at least the 'white race' as Comte, 1998: 263, put it). Statics refer to the essential capacities of all types of societies – forms of social organization, intellectual culture, material production and moral norms. Statics are therefore more basic than dynamics. Social dynamics refers to the necessary progress of society from more simple to more complex forms of social organization through the successive stages of conquest, trade and production. There can be no laws of social development without movement.

COMTE'S THREE STAGES

Society is viewed as an abstract totality that passes through three modes of knowledge (not Adam Ferguson's 'mode of subordination' nor Karl Marx's 'modes of production'). 'The Law of Three Stages' includes, first, theological or fictitious knowledge, second, metaphysical or abstract knowledge and, third, scientific or positive knowledge (Comte, 1998: 71).

Knowledge begins by trying to explain things on the basis of supernatural phenomena (theology). This is then challenged by the negative critique of philosophy (metaphysics). Finally, the entire process culminates in positive science. Intellectual stages correspond to three stages of social organization from a warrior-military society (theological), a professional-commercial society (metaphysical), to a human-industrial society (science). This 'Law' is seen as an inevitable series of evolutionary stages that every (Western) society is fated to pass through as it progresses from the childhood of the family unit to the adolescence of the state before reaching maturity by covering the whole of humanity.

COMTE'S THREE STAGES OF THEORETICAL KNOWLEDGE

Form of knowledge	Social basis	Organization	Social type
1. Theological	The family	Military	Warrior
2. Metaphysical	The state	Commercial	Lawyer
3. Positive science	Society/ Races/ Humanity	Industrial	Scientist

Source: Comte, 1998

SOCIAL PHYSICS

Before Comte invented the term 'sociology' he advocated what he termed 'social physics'. Social physics works from the social world, not abstract theoretical postulates. Society is assumed to operate according to certain natural laws, which the social scientist discovers through unbiased or 'value-free' study.

Comte was at pains to stress that society's injustices are as inevitable as a law of nature. While they can be ameliorated through gradual planned reforms ultimately injustices must be endured as natural. Once positive sociology proves scientifically that poverty and exploitation are 'incurable evils' Comte expected peace to reign between the social classes.

The positive spirit tends to consolidate order by the rational development of a wise resignation to incurable political evils … A true resignation – that is, a permanent disposition to endure, steadily, and without hope of compensation, all inevitable evils – can proceed only from a deep sense of the connection of all kinds of natural phenomena with invariable laws. (Comte, 1998: 213)

Elites trained in positivism would reconcile society to its 'natural' divisions and inequalities. Positivism even set up its own church under Comte.

CRITICAL DEVELOPMENTS

Despite writing elaborate volumes, Comte spent little time actually clarifying what 'positivism' itself might mean. Beyond some general comments about observation, experiment, comparison and history, little indication was given of what positive philosophy meant for substantive sociological studies. It is not the case, however, as is widely believed, that Comte felt that the facts could speak for themselves. Comte's theory of science attempted to show that facts always depend on their selection and interpretation by some theory or other at a certain point in its historical development (Heilbron, 1995).

Subsequent critiques of positivism would fill an entire library. Positivism has come to mean two essentially different things (1995: 198). First, it refers to the various ways that the social sciences imitate the methods of the natural sciences. Second, positivism also refers to restricting social science to the empirical testing of statements or hypotheses. Comte was a positivist in the second sense and warned against forcing social science into a natural sciences mould. His ambition was to *synthesize* knowledge, social and natural, in a scientific hierarchy rather than *reduce* all knowledge to a single model.

Few sociologists have registered their debt to Comte. However, many have sharpened their own version of positivism against Comte's (Abrams, 1968). Herbert Spencer, the second positive sociologist, shifted away from Comte's focus on adapting individuals to the whole of the social organism to one which stressed the 'natural' competition between individuals (Turner, 2001). Comte also enjoyed the public support of leading figures like John Stuart Mill, who advocated a systematic empirical study of society. Acceptance of the positivist creed was widespread by the early twentieth century among British sociologists like Patrick Geddes and L.T. Hobhouse.

Perhaps the most illustrious figure in sociology to critically assimilate Comte's legacy was Emile Durkheim. Durkheim had some sympathy with positivism's appeal to the natural sciences as providing a model for the social sciences and its progressive role in social reform. Unlike Comte's closed system, however, Durkheim demonstrated what this meant for empirical sociological investigation. Alasdair MacIntyre (1986) argues that Durkheim's positivism is evident in his study of suicide, which did not start from what individuals thought they were doing but instead tried to establish general measurable laws. In response, Robert Strikwerda (1997) argues that Durkheim can be considered a positivist only in the broadest sense of using rigorous scientific methods.

Later positivists like Ernst Mach (1838–1916), Henri Poincaré (1854–1912), and Pierre Duhem (1861–1916) were more concerned with clarifying the universal rules and criteria for a scientific method than with constructing large-scale theories about society. In the 1920s a group of thinkers known as the Vienna Circle, including Rudolf Carnap (1891–1970) and Otto Neurath (1882–1945), developed what became known as 'logical positivism'. Logical positivists wanted to clarify the scientific method by eliminating anything that was not consistent with logic, observation or concepts. They hoped for a universal language of science restricted to logic or facts. This emphasis on verification was rejected by Karl Popper (1902–1994). Popper argued that science must allow itself the possibility of being disproved or falsified rather than positively verified through a neutral scientific language.

From the 1920s critical theorists, above all Max Horkheimer, Theodor Adorno and Herbert Marcuse, found positivism intellectually and politically objectionable. Building on Marx and Weber, they saw in positivism an intellectual version of brutal inhumanity that would result in Fascism in the 1930s. As a neutral science of factual progress positivism is unable to formulate any critique of oppressive social structures and simply justifies the existing state of things (Adorno, 1976). Sociology should not merely collect and organize facts into 'laws', it should also contribute critical images of a different world. If natural laws govern the social world then society is neither rational nor historical (Marcuse, 1941: 344).

As late twentieth century sociology turned towards more qualitative, interpretative and phenomenological approaches, which stressed the role of meaning in agents' own account of social action, positivism's large-scale ideas about invariant social laws fell out fashion (Halfpenny, 2001). Feminist ideas about the specific experience and standpoint of women in society reject positivism as an archetypal male-centred form of knowledge – universalizing, controlling, reductive, impersonal – in contrast to feminist knowledge that emphasizes particularity, empathic, embodied and expressive sociological participants.

Bureaucracy; Ideal-Types; Rationality and Rationalization; Social Facts; Value Freedom; *Verstehen*

FURTHER READING

Larry Ray provides a concise summary of positivism in *Theorizing Classical Sociology* (1999). Comte's main writings on positivism are available in a single edited volume, *Auguste Comte and Positivism* (1998). Mary Pickering's intellectual biography *Auguste Comte* (1993) places the origins of positivism in a historical context. Johan Heilbron's *The Rise of Social Theory* (1995) is an important re-evaluation of Comte's contribution to a historical theory of science.

Primitive Accumulation

Part eight of Marx's *Capital* Volume 1 (1976) is concerned with the 'so-called primitive accumulation of capital'. His aim here is to establish the historical preconditions for the emergence of the capitalist mode of production from local beginnings in a few places in Europe to the creation of a world market. Capitalism seems to lack any historical beginnings and presupposes its own existence:

> the accumulation of capital presupposes surplus-value; surplus-value presupposes capitalist production; capitalist production presupposes the availability of considerable masses of capital and labour-power in the hands of commodity producers. (Marx, 1976: 873)

But how were 'masses of capital and labour-power' created? One class was dispossessed of its traditional means of production and forced to labour for wages while another class took into its possession all the means of production. Primitive accumulation is 'so-called' because it functions as a 'just so' story of classical liberal theory to legitimize class inequalities. One class of people invested their wealth wisely, enabling it to grow, while another class simply squandered it on immediate pleasures. While the bourgeoisie are awarded all the virtues of a diligent, sober and frugal elite, the dispossessed class have all the vices of a lazy, dissolute mob, squandering their income through 'riotous living'.

primitive accumulation

151

CAPITALISM'S VIOLENT ORIGINS

Against the 'insipid childishness' of imagining two congenitally differ-ent sorts of people existing in an idyllic state of nature in an original 'social contract', Marx uncovers the tormented history of the origins of capitalism. Capital, Marx (1976: 926) declares, comes into the world 'dripping from head to toe, from every pore, with blood and dirt'. With the historical rise of capitalism 'it is a notorious fact that conquest, enslavement, robbery, murder, in short, force, play the greatest part' (1976: 874).

In the form of money-rich farmers, the capitalist class can locate its origins in the agricultural revolution. What had been produced for the direct consumption of the peasant family was now produced as com-modities for the market. This did not spring from the spontaneous, peaceful operation of free market forces. Rather, it depended on the coercive force of the state to fight commercial wars against other states and wars of colonial conquest. 'Force', Marx (1976: 916) argued, 'is the midwife of every old society which is pregnant with a new one. It is itself an economic power'.

Primitive accumulation was not confined to the core regions of early capitalism like England. Pillage and brutality on a global scale attended the dawn of capitalism:

> the discovery of gold and silver in America, the extirpation, enslavement and entombment in mines of the indigenous population of that continent, the beginnings of the conquest and plunder of India, and the conversion of Africa into a preserve for the commercial hunting of blackskins. (1976: 915)

END OF THE COMMONS

Marx's historical chapters in *Capital* (1976) make grim reading. He takes England as the classic example of forcible expropriation. By the late fifteenth century, the feudal lords were evicting the peasantry from the shared land known as 'the commons'. Private ownership of the earth was imposed through the 'enclosure of the commons' and consecrated by legal edict. In this transitional period, feudal rights of the peasants to productive land were challenged and overthrown, exposing them to the terrors of becoming landless and propertyless. The result was mass des-titution, poverty, begging, robbery and insecure seasonal employment.

Primitive accumulation's main task was to forcibly separate labour from the means of production. This was possible only through widespread use of force and fraud. With the destruction of feudal relations, serfs and indentured labourers were set free to sell their labour power through a brutal process of expropriation – 'forcibly torn from their means of subsistence, and hurled into the labour-market as free, unprotected and rightless proletarians' (1976: 876).

When Marx talks about the 'sprit' of Protestantism he draws the opposite conclusions from Weber's ascetic, civilizing function. Common lands were seized on a colossal scale in the aftermath of the Glorious Revolution in the late seventeenth century. During the Reformation, the Catholic monasteries that previously sheltered the poor were dissolved, forcing their inmates into the propertyless proletariat. Landowners reduced the burden imposed by the Elizabethan Poor Law by locking up and working the poor intensively as a lesson against claiming Poor Relief. By the mid-eighteenth century the last independent agricultural labourer, the yeomanry, had disappeared along with the final trace of common land.

HIGHLAND CLEARANCES

In such ways, Marx (1976: 895) notes sarcastically, the 'idyllic methods of primitive accumulation ... conquered the field for capitalist agriculture, incorporated the soil into capital, and created for the urban industries the necessary supplies of free and rightless proletarians'. To meet the growing demand for labour, especially in remote factories driven by water mills, small children were procured and made subject to 'the most exquisite refinement of cruelty' (1976: 923). Constant waves of dispossession swelled the ranks of the proletariat, forced down wages, and intensified the competition for paid work.

Early nineteenth-century land clearances in the highlands of Scotland – 'the promised land of romantic novels' – crystallized, for Marx (1976: 890), a process that lasted centuries in England. Here the process was more systematic, on a larger scale and rested on the peculiar land ownership system of clan chiefs. Marx alights on the example of the Duchess of Sutherland who, in line with the current economic theory of the time, sought to 'improve' the land by transforming it into an efficient and profitable enterprise. Marx recounts the devastation in the county of Sutherland, with thousands of families evicted, villages destroyed and an old woman burnt to death in her home (but see Richards, 2000). Human suffering in the Highlands was essential to make way for more profitable businesses like sheep farming, reforestation and deer preserves.

STATE AND CAPITAL

Marx gives the state a prominent part in the development of capitalism, in contrast to Weber who, curiously, relegated it in his account of the rising 'spirit of capitalism'. Emerging capitalism resorted to the state to enforce its rule through 'extra-economic' legal methods for attacking early trades unions and lowering wages. Through the national debt and taxation regime, the state also plays a decisive part in the making of the financial system. State-backed, the slave trade allowed cities like Liverpool to gorge themselves in unprecedented prosperity: 'the veiled slavery of the wage-labourers in Europe needed the unqualified slavery of the New World as its pedestal' (Marx, 1976: 925).

However, the colonies in America presented a major problem for capitalism. Too few free labourers were available for hire and far too many European settlers were getting by as independent domestic producers. They had not been separated forcibly from their own small-scale means of production and 'public land' was abundant. As soon as immigrant wage-labour established itself in the American colonies they deserted the capital-relation to become small independent producers in their own right. The real independence of small producers in the colonies exposed the idea of a 'free contract between buyer and seller' in the home country as a 'beautiful illusion'. But by the time Marx had written *Capital* in 1867 America had ceased to be 'the promised land' for emigrating workers. Stimulated by the Civil War and land speculation capital grew in scale, squeezing out small producers. Bringing primitive accumulation in America to a close, the future face of large-scale capital accumulation could be recognized.

CRITICAL DEVELOPMENTS

Marx's account of the origins of capitalism has been the subject of fierce debate. It centred on whether the nature of 'the transition from feudalism to capitalism' arose primarily out of production or exchange. Some like Maurice Dobb (1946) followed Marx's account closely and stressed the shifts in sixteenth-century rural England towards capitalist production as wealthier peasants began to employ wage labour on a growing scale, turning themselves into capitalist farmers. Paul Sweezy (1950) responded that capitalism develops from an urban merchant class concerned with market-based trade and exchange. However, Dobb also pointed out that the interests of this merchant class seemed fully compatible with feudal society.

Robert Brenner (1977) later emphasized the role played by colonial merchants. They organized production as well as exchange in the colonies. Brenner argued that the crisis of late mediaeval society was resolved in England by the political events of the 'bourgeois revolution'. Brenner views the political coherence of the English ruling class as the decisive factor in clearing away, albeit unevenly, the obstacles of feudal society to capitalist forms of rule.

More was involved than an internal struggle among the ruling class. Popular agency played a critical part in the English Revolution of the 1640s. Discontent of 'the middling sort' surged forwards and backwards against the Royalist ruling class (Manning, 1991). It is unclear if bourgeois political leaders were self-consciously attempting to bring about a capitalist society (Mooers, 1991). Primitive accumulation was driven more by immediate self-interest, which had the 'unintentional consequence' of unleashing capitalism as a globally dominant system.

In the twentieth century, Rosa Luxemburg (1913) developed the idea that capital could only expand by dominating and exploiting precapitalist societies, leading to imperialism and warfare. More recently, this has been adopted by the Marxist geographer David Harvey (2005) in what he calls 'primitive accumulation by dispossession' to account for 'neoliberalism' in the shift since the 1970s from public forms of state services to private forms of market services, profit, private property, finance and credit.

Primitive accumulation remains a real process in the world today. In many parts of the developing world primitive accumulation continues to see the destruction of peasant societies, massive human displacement and unemployment in the concentrations of human misery in the slums of the South (Davis, 2006). Masses of dispossessed labour lack capitalist employment opportunities. One exception to this is China, the world's most dynamic economy (Arrighi, 2007). There millions have been driven off the land into the cities to find employment. China's strategy of primitive accumulation was stimulated directly by the active intervention of the state.

RELATED CONCEPTS

Capital; *Gemeinschaft* and *Gesellschaft*; Historical Materialism; Mechanical and Organic Solidarity; Protestant Ethic and the 'Spirit of Capitalism'

FURTHER READING

Start with Part 8 of Stephen Shapiro's *How to Read Capital* (2008) supplemented by the corresponding Part 8 of *Capital* (Marx, 1976). Rodney Hilton's *The Transition From Feudalism to Capitalism* (1978) contains the debate among Marxist historians. See also David Harvey's *A Brief History of Neoliberalism* (2005) on the neoliberal form of primitive accumulation and Giovanni Arrighi's *Adam Smith in Beijing* (2007) for an account of the process in China.

Protestant Ethic and
the 'Spirit of Capitalism'

Max Weber's 1904–05 study *The Protestant Ethic and the Spirit of Capitalism* is an audacious work of historical reconstruction. Weber (1930) explores how a certain type of religious commitment, Calvinism, gave rise to a certain type of rational value structure, an industrious work ethic, which unintentionally nurtured the development of capitalism as an economic system.

Weber's central problem was to explain why capitalism first arose in the West and not in other parts of the world. Core features of capitalism, 'the impulse to acquisition, pursuit of gain, of money, of the greatest possible amount of money', had been around for a long time and in many places. 'Unlimited greed' cannot be the defining feature. In fact the opposite may be the case: 'Capitalism *may* even be identical with the restraint, or at least a rational tempering, of this irrational impulse' (1930: 17).

Something else lay behind the 'peculiar rationalism of Western culture'. 'Capitalism', according to Weber, existed in other societies like China, India, Babylon, in the classical world and in the Middle Ages. But in each case the road to economic rationalism was barred. By what? 'Magical and religious forces' obstructed the development of rational capitalism according to Weber. They lacked a guiding idea, an 'ethos' or a 'spirit' favourable to rational capitalism. Crucially, only in the West did 'the rational capitalist organization of (formally) free labour' appear (1930: 21). Free labour is decisive for Weber: 'Exact calculation – the basis of everything else – is only possible on a basis of free labour' (1930: 22).

WHAT IS THE 'SPIRIT' OF CAPITALISM?

Essentially, the 'spirit of modern capitalism' expresses an attitude dedicated to the methodical, rational pursuit of profit (Weber, 1930: 64). Capital is subject to the rational calculation of profit-and-loss bookkeeping. Business and work became separated from the household and organized on a rational basis. The entire social structure of capitalism rests on 'the rational organization of free labour under regular discipline' (1930: 23).

Weber illustrates his 'somewhat pretentious phrase', the 'spirit of capitalism', with a series of homilies from Benjamin Franklin: 'Time is money'. 'Idleness' is only money 'spent, or rather thrown away'. 'Credit is money'. 'Money begets money'. This is not simply a lesson in business sense, Weber notes. It is an entire 'ethos', summing up the stern morality and miserly personality of the capitalist. Every virtue – honesty, frugality, industry, punctuality – is worthwhile only so long as it helps to grow piles of money.

Weber identified the main bearers of the capitalist spirit as 'the rising strata of the lower industrial middle classes' (1930: 65). Other wealthy commercial and aristocratic strata might have managed banks, putting-out businesses and other large enterprises for profit. Yet these were run in the 'traditional spirit' of trade monopolies and legal privileges. Business was often conducted in a leisurely style in the convivial atmosphere of pubs and taverns. Weber contrasts the commercial opulence of Florence in the fourteenth and fifteenth centuries which barely tolerated 'the spirit' of capitalism with the relative backwater of underdeveloped Pennsylvania in the eighteenth century where the capitalist ethos dominated personal conduct (1930: 75).

In contrast to Marx's account of the violent origins of free wage labour, Weber invents an entirely fictitious story about how this happened:

> some young man from one of the putting-out families went out into the country, carefully chose weavers for his employ, greatly increased the rigour of his supervision of their work, and thus turned them from peasants into laborers. (1930: 67)

In Weber's story about the origins of capitalism *spirit* is the animating force. Hostility from traditional producers could only be endured by the unusually strong self-control, self-belief and high ethical conduct of an individual thoroughly imbued with this spirit.

> men who had grown up in the hard school of life, calculating and daring at the same time, above all temperate and reliable, shrewd and completely devoted to their business, with strictly bourgeois opinions and principles. (1930: 69)

Weber's ideal type bourgeois is neither the commercial type nor the decadent social climber. Weber's bourgeois is a humble and modest ascetic for whom wealth is not a means to something else but an end in itself, for whom rational money-making has become 'a calling'.

Weber rules out the possibility that capitalist rationality might be related to the wider revolution in scientific, artistic, philosophical and legal rationalism. Some countries like England had a high degree of capitalist rationality but a low level of legal rationality, while Southern Europe came under the rational principles of Roman Law but was nevertheless underdeveloped economically. Weber once more contrasts 'the spirit' of capitalism with the Marxist emphasis on the material conditions of capitalism: 'To speak here of a reflection of material conditions in the ideal superstructure would be patent nonsense' (1930: 75).

Ideas are not simply a reflection of economic interests. Rather, ideas are themselves moving forces. Weber also understood the role played by economics (just as Marx grasped the role played by ideas) and claimed that he did not wish 'to substitute for a one-sided materialistic an equally one-sided spiritualistic causal interpretation of culture and history' (1930: 183).

WHAT IS THE PROTESTANT ETHIC?

In the West the 'spirit of capitalism' showed a special affinity with 'the rational ethics of ascetic Protestantism'. Calvinism and the Puritan sects did not express 'the spirit of capitalism' in a direct way. If they had any effect on the capitalist spirit, as Weber believed, then it was unintended and completely unforeseen. It even contradicted some of their core beliefs. Weber therefore 'imputed' the capitalist spirit to Calvinism by working out the 'correlations between forms of religious belief and practical ethics' (1930: 91).

Weber begins from a sociological fact then current in Germany:

> the fact that business leaders and owners of capital, as well as the higher grades of skilled labour, and even more the higher technically and commercially trained personnel of modern enterprises, are overwhelmingly Protestant. (1930: 35)

This is traced back to the Reformation in the sixteenth century when many wealthy districts came out on the side of Protestantism. An entirely new way of life was established by the new religion. Protestantism involved 'a regulation of the whole of conduct which, penetrating to all departments of private and public life, was infinitely burdensome and earnestly enforced' (1930: 36).

This leads Weber to 'those psychological sanctions which, originating in religious belief and the practice of religion, gave a direction to practical conduct and held the individual to it' (1930: 97). The tyrannical strictures of Calvinism were embraced, not repudiated, as something 'heroic' by the rising bourgeois class. Scottish and Dutch Calvinists and English and American Puritans repudiated 'the joy of living' and adopted a harsh and unyielding abstemious lifestyle.

> The spirit of hard work, of progress, or whatever else it may be called, the awakening of which one is inclined to ascribe Protestantism, must not be understood, as there is a tendency to do, as joy of living nor in any sense connected with the Enlightenment. (1930: 45)

Calvinism developed a forceful form of 'psychological sanction' in the militant doctrine of 'predestination'. Its essential idea is that human beings are at the mercy of God's will. Human action is incapable of changing the individual's chances of eternal salvation. Individuals were on their own, alone with God, not knowing if they were saved or damned for eternity. God would save only the elect few. Any lack of self-belief or certainty was a public demonstration of a lack of God's grace. Worldly activity dispenses all such doubts and solidifies certainty.

Just as Weber had taken Benjamin Franklin as representative of the spirit of capitalism so he takes the English Puritan Richard Baxter as a representative type for the Protestant ethic. Baxter warned about the dangers of relaxing the Puritan prohibition on sensuous pleasure and the arts. Time-wasting, indolence, sociability, idle talk, luxury consumption and over-sleeping were deadly sins. Baxter exhorted good Puritans to maintain hard physical or mental labour: 'Work hard in your calling' (1930: 159). Calvinists were prone to arrogant self-righteousness, expressed in the individualist credo: 'God helps those that help themselves' (1930: 115).

RELIGIOUS 'CALLING' AND HARD WORK

Purposeful labour serves the greater glory of God. The 'end' for Protestant asceticism was intelligent hard work under rational self-control. This also meant breaking labour from traditional attitudes, which emphasized comfort and indolence. Work must be transformed into an end in itself and become 'a calling'. In Puritanism hard work could be used to justify all manner of oppression. Oliver Cromwell, for instance, subjugated Ireland in 1650 by 'calling God to witness, on the fact that English capital has taught the Irish to work' (1930: 213). Puritan contempt for landless labourers and the destitute also informed the cruelty of English Poor Laws.

A 'calling' is 'a task set by God' (1930: 79). Weber finds its Protestant origins in Martin Luther's 'this-worldly' stance as against the 'other-worldliness' of Catholic monasteries. But Luther's calling could not serve 'the spirit of capitalism'. Luther rejected both the capitalist motives of selfish acquisition and peasant rebellions in favour of divinely-ordained 'stations' in the status quo.

Calvinism more directly made the capitalist spirit into a calling. Weber considers other varieties of Protestantism – Pietism, Methodism and the Baptist sects. It is only the 'iron consistency' of Calvinism that represents the purest, most extreme form of 'the calling'. Insofar as work becomes more productive and specialized it serves God. Above all, profit-making is reserved as the greatest calling: 'For if God, whose hand the Puritan sees in all the occurrences of life, shows one of His elect a chance of profit, he must do it with a purpose' (1930: 162). With this comes the responsibility to avoid waste and to increase money through unstinting efforts. Puritanism opposed the organic social organization of 'merrie old England' in favour of free, rational market competition.

TOWARDS THE 'IRON CAGE'

Calvinism had contradictory effects. On one hand, it restricted personal consumption by making enjoyment of possessions a sin. On the other hand, 'it had the psychological effect of freeing the acquisition of goods from the inhibitions of traditionalistic ethics' (Weber, 1930: 171). Profit which could not be wasted in luxury consumption had to be reinvested back into production. But religious dogma gave way to utilitarian dogma of the greatest pleasure for the minimum pain. Rather than the harsh measures of seventeenth-century asceticism, a comfortable bourgeois lifestyle could be enjoyed through voracious and ostentatious consumption.

Weber (1930: 181–3) finishes his essay with compelling imagery of what this transition means today. First, 'the Puritan wanted to work in a calling; we are forced to do so'. We are compelled to work under technological and bureaucratic 'instrumental' rationality. Second, instrumental rationality has become an 'iron cage' offering few means of escape. Third, instrumental rationality has set in train the blind destruction of nature 'until the last ton of fossilized coal is burnt' (1930: 181). Fourth, 'victorious capitalism' no longer needs any overall ethos or restraint:

> The rosy blush of its laughing heir, the Enlightenment, seems also to be fading, and the idea of duty in one's calling prowls about in our lives like the ghost of dead religious beliefs. (1930: 182)

Fifth, Weber wonders if 'new prophets' will arise or if the future will be one of unstoppable 'mechanical petrification':

For of the last stage of this cultural development, it might well be truly said: "Specialists without spirit, sensualists without heart; this nullity imagines that it has attained a level of civilization never before achieved". (1930: 182)

After this lyrical lapse, Weber remembers himself as an objective social scientist and proposes the need for a wide-ranging study of ascetic rationalism and its implications for practical social ethics.

CRITICAL DEVELOPMENTS

Over the past century a huge literature has debated the strengths and weaknesses of Weber's thesis. A sympathetic critic like Frank Parkin (2002) suggests that Weber at various points poses alternately a strong or a weak relationship between Protestantism and capitalist rationality. The strong thesis suggests that the pure religious beliefs of Calvinism directly created capitalist rationality. The weak thesis suggests that there was far less of a direct causal relationship than a vague correlation or affinity between them. On balance, Weber adopts the weak thesis of a general correspondence between his two ideal-types. This leads to a further complication: how valid is Weber's ideal-type and how might it be evaluated against other explanations of capitalism's origins in the West?

Weber isolates instrumental rationality as the common denominator shared by both ideal-types. Seventeenth-century Puritanism is taken as the representative specimen for three centuries of religious belief across two continents. Weber's comparative method tries to hold 'constant' the institutional structures of the West and East to show that both posses similar material preconditions necessary for capitalist take-off. Their sole difference, Weber argues, is religious belief. But, as Parkin (2002: 66) argues, 'it is on this crucial point that Weber is at his most maddeningly inconsistent'. Across his writings, Weber often showed how the institutional conditions differed markedly between the West and the East. Weber's ideal-types seem loaded from the start to arrive at precisely the Eurocentric explanation of the mental superiority of Western rationality over Eastern superstition and 'magic'.

On the other hand, there is little evidence to suggest that Calvinism as a mind-set was uniquely predisposed to capitalist rationality. Indeed, the opposite conclusion might be entertained given Calvinism's antipathy to anything resembling a capitalist spirit. A crucial test case for Weber's thesis was Scotland, where Calvinism under the leadership of John Knox took deep root by the end of the sixteenth century. Against even Weber's weak thesis, capitalism did *not* emerge in any systematic way in Presbyterian Scotland for another two centuries (Marshall, 1980).

In constructing his ideal types as largely peaceable and always rational Weber ignored Marx's account of how capitalism was brought into existence through the organized violence of primitive accumulation, colonialism, slavery, civil war and dispossession.

RELATED CONCEPTS

Capital; Primitive Accumulation; Rationality and Rationalization; Sacred and Profane; Social Action; *Verstehen*

FURTHER READING

Weber's (1930) book remains a powerful testimony to the sociological imagination. In Part 1 of *The Essential Weber* (2004) Sam Whimster provides an accessible introduction to Weber's thesis as well as a representative selection of Weber's writing on the sociology of religion. Chapter 2 of Frank Parkin's *Max Weber* (2002) sets out the key issues. Weber's own defence of his thesis against contemporary critics is presented in David Chalcraft and Austin Harrington's *The Protestant Ethic Debate* (2001).

Rationality and Rationalization

Rationality and rationalization are fundamental themes of Max Weber (Eldridge, 1971). The term 'rationalization' appears hundreds of times throughout the CD-ROM edition of Weber's collected works, even in the context of Weber's sociological study of music (Radkau, 2009: 369). In his ideal-types of social action Weber begins from what the rational course of action should be before examining concrete cases. In the Introduction to *The Protestant Ethic*, Weber (1930: 13–26) compiles a list of seemingly unrelated achievements to support his claims about a peculiarly Western rationalism. These include:

- rational proofs in Western geometry inherited from the ancient Greeks
- rational concepts in Western philosophy since Aristotle

- rational jurisprudence of Western legal systems based on Roman law
- rational chemistry underpins European medicine
- rational music in Western instrumentation, harmonies and notation
- rational aesthetic in Western art and architecture
- rationalized literature fostered by rational European print technology
- rational Western science is specialized, logical and systematic
- rational administration and rational written constitutions of state bureaucracies in Europe.

This veritable hymn to western rationalism leads Weber into his main theme of Protestantism and the capitalist ethos in Europe as the expression of rationality.

TYPES OF RATIONALITY

Rationality seems to be a deceptively simple concept but Weber is concerned to formally draw out its many nuances, subtleties and tensions. At least 16 types of rationality are present in Weber: 'deliberate, systematic, calculable, impersonal, instrumental, exact, quantitative, rule-governed, predictable, methodical, purposeful, sober, scrupulous, efficacious, intelligible and consistent' (Brubaker, 1984: 2). More usually this is reduced to just four basic types: formal rationality, practical rationality, substantive rationality, and theoretical rationality.

First, 'theoretical rationality' through the clarification of abstract logical concepts in science and mathematics: '[Rationalism] means one thing if we think of the kind of rationalization the systematic thinker performs on the image of the world: an increasing theoretical mastery of reality by means of increasingly precise and abstract concepts' (Weber, 1946: 293). Second, 'practical rationalism' or 'instrumental rationality' calculates the most efficient means to achieve a desired end through 'the methodical attainment of a definitely given and practical end by means of an increasingly precise calculation of adequate means' (1946: 293). Third, 'formal rationality' is used by Weber to refer to the unambiguous numerical expression of economic needs through quantitative calculation and accounting. Fourth, 'substantive rationality', 'on the other hand, is full of ambiguities' since it refer to the 'ultimate ends', whether these be 'ethical, political, utilitarian, hedonistic, feudal, egalitarian or whatever'.

Weber also calls this latter type 'value rationality' since it selects certain criteria to judge the outcomes of action, whether these be socialist values of social justice or militarist values of war-making. Formal and substantive rationality may coincide, although the formal rationality of the free market is indifferent to any end other than profit (Weber, 1978: 108).

RATIONALIZATION

Although they are inter-related, the concept of rationality is separate from the concept of rationalization. By 'rationalization' Weber attempts to capture the underlying process that drives modernity in the distinctively instrumental direction of an all-embracing rule-bound order. By 'rationality' Weber refers to an ideal or optimum representation of social action, although Weber sometimes conflates 'rationality' with 'instrumental rationality'. Rationality represents freedom while rationalization represents its absence. Rational action represented for Weber the highest 'feeling of freedom' (1949:124). Rationalization, on the other hand, removes control from individuals and raises it to the level of a machine-like system.

Rationalization standardizes beliefs and places greater areas of social life under instrumental principles, with the loss of belief in ultimate ends such as God or nation. It substitutes 'the unthinking acceptance of ancient custom' for a 'deliberate adaptation' to reality in terms of instrumental 'self-interest', encouraging moral scepticism or relativism. It sweeps everything along in its path, even music, as Weber shows in his fascinating discussion of the piano as a rationalized machine for striking major chords attuned to bourgeois drawing rooms (Eldridge, 1971; Runciman, 1978). Indeed, it was his detailed study of music, rather than, say, his work on the stock exchange, that led Weber to appreciate, unexpectedly, the power of rationalization (Radkau, 2009: 370).

Administratively, this process finds expression in the increasing bureaucratization of society. Economically, capitalist rationalization is furthered by accounting techniques like rational double book-keeping (Weber, 1978: 92). However, the conflict between formal and substantive rationality produces an overall structure of *irrationality* as rational profit-making and ultimate values of justice and equality impede each other.

PROGRESS AND DISENCHANTMENT

Only rational knowledge about the world can deliver individuals out of a stupefied state of nature and into meaningful existence. For Weber the problem here is that a consciously guided rationality was being submerged by impersonal social structures. Rationalization is too often celebrated as 'progress' or 'modernization' when it results in a loss of meaning or an overall goal for life. Weber notes that the rise of secular rationalism makes the modern working class largely indifferent to religious or superstitious beliefs:

For the modern proletariat the sense of dependence on one's own achievements is supplemented by a consciousness of dependence on purely social factors, economic conjunctions and power relations guaranteed by law. (1978: 485)

This general rationalization of modern life leads to what Weber called, following the philosopher Schiller, 'the disenchantment of the world' in the loss of magical beliefs and the increasing loss of traditional customs and ways of life. As Weber put it in his famous lecture 'Science as a vocation':

> there are no mysterious incalculable forces that come into play, but rather one can, in principle, master all things by calculation. This means that the world is disenchanted. One need no longer have recourse to magical means in order to master or implore the spirits, as did the savage, for whom such mysterious power existed. Technical means and calculations perform the service. (1946: 139)

Weber claims that people serving a rationalized money economy know considerably less about the forces that govern their daily lives compared to earlier societies that knew how their food was produced and which tools to use for every task in life. He also allowed a certain relativity into the concept of rationalization in that what might appear as rational from one viewpoint, say science, might seem irrational from another, say mysticism.

CRITICAL DEVELOPMENTS

Weber's rationalization thesis has had a huge and contentious impact on social theory. It was given a Marxist twist in Georg Lukac's (1923) theory of the objective domination of the working class by a rationalized capitalist world. It also led to the idea of a 'one dimensional society', totally administered through instrumental reason in the Critical Theory of Horkheimer, Adorno and Marcuse. In America, Weber's rationalization thesis informed the systems theory of Talcott Parsons that dominated an entire generation of post-war sociology.

Weberian rationalization theory was reconstituted as a formal system by Jurgen Habermas in Volume 1 of *The Theory of Communicative Action* (1984). For Habermas, rationalization still offers the best explanation for the multiple problems of a capitalist modernity. However, Weber left too many gaps and inconsistencies, limited rationalization to instrumental reason, or 'purposive-rationality', and neglected what Habermas calls 'moral-practical' and 'aesthetic-expressive' rationality.

Once these alternative sources of rationality are accounted for, especially what he calls 'communicative reason', it can be seen that rationalization is always an incomplete, internally differentiated process. Capitalism 'rationalizes not too much but rather too little', as the critical theorist Siegfried Kracauer (1995: 81) once put it.

According to Habermas, Weber conflated the instrumental capitalist 'system' with the looser 'lifeworld' rationality of everyday life. Habermas, like many commentators, tends to conflate formal and instrumental rationality when they are quite distinct in Weber's schema. Donald Levine (2005: 116–17) challenges the 'simplistic' idea that Weber assumed that rationalization leads to the world becoming flattened and more homogeneous. Since rational action occurs in different spheres – religious, military, artistic, educational, scientific, economic and so on – and in distinctive ways – conceptual, practical, formal, instrumental, substantive – Weber's talk about an 'iron cage' is misleading since he, more than most, recognized the multiple sources and effects of rationalization.

RELATED CONCEPTS

Bureaucracy; Ideal-Types; Legitimate Domination; Modernity; Social Action; *Verstehen*

FURTHER READING

A useful starting point is Weber's introduction to *The Protestant Ethic* (1930). See also Part III of the recent collection *The Essential Weber*, edited by Sam Whimster (2004). John Eldridge (1971) provides a brief overview of rationalization in Weber and an excerpt from Weber's sociology of the piano.

Sacred and Profane

According to Durkheim (2001) all religious belief systems, from the most basic to the most complex, fundamentally divide the world into two mutually exclusive spheres: the sacred and the profane. The sacred represents the ideal that society sets for itself in contrast to the profane world of private egos and mundane interests. Any object might be considered sacred – a tree, a rock, a house, an animal, human hair, ashes and so on – as might any words, phrases or gestures carried out by a specially consecrated person. The sacred can be 'superimposed' on a wide range of objects (2001: 175). Since nothing is inherently 'sacred' this quality must be acquired from somewhere else.

In religion everything can be assigned to a class of sacred things radically divided from a class of profane things. Religious belief structures the world into the pure and impure, holy and sacrilegious, divine and diabolical, consecration and contamination. Durkheim takes this as the starting point for understanding how all human groups are based on a radical duality that assigns dignity, privilege or distinction to one thing, not given by palpable experience, over other things that are based in more practical and mundane activities of everyday life. When things are considered sacred they are arranged into a unified system.

> Every homogeneous group of sacred things, or indeed every sacred thing of any importance, constitutes a centre of organization around which a group of beliefs and rites, a particular cult, gravitates. And no religion, however unified, fails to recognise the plurality of sacred things. Even Christianity, at least in its Catholic form, includes, in addition, to the divine being – the Virgin, angels, saints, souls of the dead, and so on. (Durkheim, 2001: 40)

This same mental structure later gives rise to scientific knowledge set apart from ordinary common sense. Because this basic duality has survived for millennia it cannot be illusory but must fulfil a profound human need. That need is society. What makes a thing sacred is the collective feeling that attaches to it. Collective life 'awakens' religious thought in order for society to remake itself. Sacred objects will disappear over time, but society will return again and again to create sacred replacements to reaffirm its collective unity.

WHAT IS SACRED?

Durkheim defines religion in the following way:

> a religion is a unified system of beliefs and practices relative to sacred things, that is to say, things set apart and surrounded by prohibitions – beliefs and practices that unite its adherents in a single moral community called a church. (2001: 46)

Sacred here refers to a 'single moral community' founded on 'things set apart' and absolutely forbidden by prohibitive beliefs and practices.

When we unpack Durkheim's definition of the sacred it possesses five core properties: sacred essence, sacred prohibition, sacred contagion, sacred rituals and sacred institution.

Sacred essence

For Durkheim the sacred and the profane are distinguished by their 'heterogeneity'. By this he means that they are completely separate from each other and cannot be combined together without destroying what they are. 'There is no other example in the history of human thought of two categories of things so profoundly differentiated or so radically opposed to each other' (Durkheim, 2001: 38). While good and evil, or health and sickness, are thought to be polar opposites in fact they derive from the same source or 'genus', morality or life respectively. Unlike these examples, the sacred and the profane do not share a common point of origin. They are completely different in kind and not just different by degree. They cannot be brought together and still keep intact their essential nature. Such a radical dissociation can lead to hostility between the two worlds, as when pious people withdraw from the corrupted profane world into monasteries and religious retreats.

Sacred prohibition

Strict prohibitions protect the sacred from contamination by the profane. 'Sacred things are those things protected and isolated by prohibitions; profane things are those things to which such prohibitions apply and which must keep their distance from what is sacred' (Durkheim, 2001: 40). This sense of distance gives sacred objects an aura about them. The principle of prohibition ensures that the sacred and the profane stand in an inverse relationship to each other; the more intensely one is felt the more it will drive out the other.

Because they prevent mixing and contact, prohibitions or 'taboos' make negative demands rather than taking a more positive form of reverence (2001: 221). Durkheim calls this a 'negative cult'. He also identifies a more 'positive cult' that pulls believers towards the sacred, and which also pulls gods – the personification of society – back towards the worshippers.

Sacred contagion

The plurality of sacred things belongs to a whole that gives it an overarching meaning. Sacred things possess a remarkable mobility and contagiousness that spreads their holy quality through mutual contact

(Durkheim, 2001: 237). Since the sacred is not bound to any specific material form it is easily transmitted, as when souls, which have no tangible form, are said to migrate. This promiscuous nature of the sacred helps explain the strict nature of the prohibitions. Things that are worshipped are not just feared by believers but also acquire a singular 'majesty' in their eyes (2001: 56). Without this unity isolated fragments lose the power to express something sacred, although they may survive as profane folk rituals.

Sacred rituals

Against the profane world, the sacred combines both the pure and impure, good and evil, sanctified and contaminated, saint and sinner. This ambiguity means that the passage from the profane world to the sacred one needs to be carefully regulated by complex rituals and ceremonies. Rites of passage symbolize the death of the profane and a rebirth into the sacred. Ritualistic control is essential because the sacred is deeply ambiguous. For instance, some religions prohibit the eating of pork, but it is unclear if this is because it is forbidden as something impure or as something holy (Durkheim, 2001: 305).

Sacred institution

Religion seems to share much of this with magic, which it resembles superficially. But religion differs from magic insofar as it celebrates the collective group in a 'church' that institutionalizes a common moral order and conception of the sacred world (Durkheim, 2001: 43). Magic, on the other hand, has no church that binds its followers to each other. By 'church' Durkheim does not just mean an institution with a formal bureaucratic clergy but any organization that arranges sacred things collectively. Since it issues in a church, religion is fundamentally collective, whereas magic is always personal.

PROFANE WORLD, SACRED SOCIETY

It is not only entities called gods or spirits that might be considered sacred. Society is constantly in the process of inventing 'new sacred things' and setting these apart from profane things. It establishes its own dogmas, symbols and holidays. Nation, Freedom, Humanity, Reason, Progress and Democracy are consecrated as sacred, which it would be a sacrilege to flout.

> Society's capacity to set itself up as a god or to create gods was nowhere more visible than in the first years of the [French] Revolution. In the general

sacred and profane

enthusiasm of that period, things were transformed by public opinion into sacred things: homeland, liberty and reason. (Durkheim, 2001: 161)

High social positions are routinely invested with a quasi-sacred majesty that demands respect and deference. People in dominant social positions, at a remote distance from instrumental labour, are approached like gods, the social gulf is respected, precautions are taken, and a different language is adopted from that used normally when ordinary mortals converse with each other.

The sacred is always social in absolute opposition to the 'pre-social' world of the profane. The profane resides in the mundane or physical aspects of daily life, above all labour. Work is profane because it satisfies mere utilitarian and physical needs: 'work is the pre-eminent form of profane activity: its only apparent aim is to meet the secular necessities of life; it connects us exclusively with ordinary things' (2001: 228). Of course, labour is 'social' in a certain sense. But the self-interest and instrumentalism inherent to profane labour, Durkheim supposes, make it radically distinct from the exclusively social nature of the sacred. In this sense, profane work is anti-social or pre-social, while holidays (or holy-days), as a cessation of work, are sacred and truly social.

Durkheim further divides life into profane and sacred time periods. At certain times the aboriginal population is scattered in small independent family groups that spend their time providing for their basic needs. At other times, the population is concentrated into larger clan groups that hold collective ceremonies. 'Society can revive its sense of itself only by assembling. But it cannot remain perpetually in session' (2001: 259). When the population is dispersed life is 'rather monotonous, lazy and dull', but when it is concentrated emotional life becomes more intense, sacred and collectively effervescent.

CRITICAL DEVELOPMENTS

Emile Durkheim's concept of the sacred is seen by some as one of the boldest contributions to sociology. As the conservative-minded sociologist Robert Nisbet (1993: 243) put it, 'Of all the concepts and perspectives in Durkheim the sacred is the most striking and, given the age in which he lived, the most radical'. Despite a range of criticisms, Durkheim's contemporaries also found the sacred-profane device useful. It influenced a generation of anthropologists and 'structural-functionalists' who were intent on producing something like a natural history of the collective representation of the sacred.

Although it comes in waves, the influence of the sacred-profane concept is still being felt. It is both a sociology of religion and a religious theory of society (Cladis, 2001). Outside of the sociology of religion, perhaps the most influential recent use of the sacred-profane binary has been the social theory of Jurgen Habermas. In an elaborate thought-experiment, Habermas (1987) is concerned to demonstrate that under modernity the utilitarian drives of the profane will eclipse and dominate the moral consensus of the sacred, what Habermas terms the colonization of the 'lifeworld' by 'the system'. As well as building on his achievements, Durkheim is criticized by Habermas for neglecting the inter-subjective medium of speech acts in favour of the impersonal medium of symbolic rituals. Another important difference is that modern legitimacy requires self-conscious collective deliberation and dialogue rather than reverence and awe in the face of the sacred symbol.

Durkheim's sacred-profane binary was also criticized on numerous other empirical and conceptual grounds. First, Durkheim failed to see the ways in which the sacred and the profane might be interdependent rather than mutually exclusive. For instance, a spear may be used in a sacrifice but later also be used for the profane activity of hunting for food (Evans-Pritchard, 1965). Second, reasons other than the self-worship of society may exist for keeping sacred objects at a distance. For some critics it was Durkheim that made society sacred, not aboriginal religion. Third, as a concept, the profane is a residual category made up of whatever is left over from the sacred such as the 'commonness' of the anti-sacred or non-sacred. Fourth, the profane is too disparate to classify a coherent group of things or feelings.

Fifth, the sacred and profane dichotomy is not the most basic structure, as Durkheim asserts, but is derivative of the dichotomy between the social and the individual (Lukes, 1992: 26). The sacred is another way of counterposing society as a collective to the profane as the personal sphere of the individual ego, and therefore falling outside the field of sociology proper. Sixth, the sacred-profane couplet is circular: the sacred is always identical to the social, while the profane never is, or only residually.

Seventh, Durkheim applies his own value judgements with the idea that profane labour is pre-social while the term 'sacred' is reserved for everything that Durkheim wants to elevate as social. It might seem obvious that the sacred has superior powers over the profane and that ordinary people caught up in the routines of everyday life are inferior to and dependent on the sacred. But this ignores the fact that religion also depends on ordinary life. Any dependency between the sacred and the profane is mutual not purely hierarchical. Even gods need followers.

Eighth, Durkheim fails to establish why society's collective representation of itself should necessarily be 'sacred' in nature. Finally, if science is merely secularized religion then perhaps sociological concepts function as a sacred cloak against the profane concepts of common sense.

RELATED CONCEPTS

Collective Effervescence; Collective Representations; Conscience Collective; Normal and Pathological; Social Facts; Totemism

FURTHER READING

The key text is Durkheim's *The Elementary Forms of Religious Life*, available in a number of editions. As a way into this begin with Robert Nisbet's chapter on 'the sacred' as one of the core 'unit ideas' of sociology in his lively textbook *The Sociological Tradition* (1993). A further useful context and summary of the concept is provided in *Durkheim's Sociology of Religion*, by W.S.F. Pickering (1984).

Social Action

Max Weber (1978: 4) states that 'sociology is a science concerning itself with the interpretative understanding of human social action'. Social action derives from the meanings and interpretations individuals, on average, would ideally give to their interactions. Social action was understood by Weber as a meaningful 'probability' that could be imputed rationally to individuals in concrete settings. Weber's emphasis on *individual* action distinguishes him from the emphasis on *social* facts or the reciprocal interaction of other classical social theorists (Levine, 2005). Weber claims that an abstract clarification of the concept of social action is the only appropriate scientific approach.

> The apparently gratuitous tediousness involved in the elaborate definition of the above concepts is an example of the fact that we often neglect to think out clearly what seems to be obvious, because it is intuitively familiar. (1978: 44)

This is closely related to Weber's ideal-types of rationality, where action is treated as fully conscious and explicit, even if in reality fully conscious action proves to be the exception rather than the rule.

IDEAL-TYPES OF SOCIAL ACTION

Weber identifies four ideal types for social action: instrumental-rational, value-rational, affectual and traditional. First, *instrumental-rational* refers to the relationship of means and end: 'action is instrumentally rational (*zweckrational*) when the end, the means, and the secondary results are all rationally taken into account and weighed' (Weber, 1978: 26). Such conceptions of instrumental rationality were familiar to Weber from the Austrian 'marginalist' school of economics (Levine, 2005). In challenging Marxism 'the marginalists' focused on an ideal individual subjectively calculating between means (price) and ends (consumption) (Swedberg, 1998: 25–30; Therborn, 1976: 290–95).

Second, *value-rational* behaviour, or substantive rationality, refers to a self-conscious belief in the intrinsic value of some ethical, artistic, intellectual or religious purpose. Regardless of the costs to an individual, value convictions are a guide to action for their own sake.

Third, *affectual* action refers to the stimulus to action provided by emotional or psychological feelings: 'Action is affectual if it satisfies a need for revenge, sensual gratification, devotion, contemplative bliss, or for the working off of emotional tensions' (Weber, 1978: 25). Affectual action lacks the self-consciousness of value rationality, although both transcend ulterior or instrumental motives.

Fourth, *traditional* action refers to habitual, customary, almost automatic reflexes in the practical action of everyday life. As such, it represents a borderline case. It can shade into unthinking imitation (non-social action) or it can merge into value rationality as it becomes more self-conscious and meaningful (pure social action).

IDEAL-TYPES OF ORIENTATION

Weber attributes no substantive content or normative meaning to social action, which may range from violent conflict to peaceful cooperation. Meanings are likely to stabilize where they are subject to explicit codification, as in a business contract, than where they are formed on the basis of affectual action, such as erotic attraction or personal loyalty. Mutual agreement or consent stabilizes social action through a predictable framework of trust and reciprocity.

Typical modes of social action throw up definite patterns and regularities. Weber identifies three ideal 'types of orientation': usage, custom and self-interest. First, 'usage' is social action based on routines, conventions and fashion. Second, if usage endures over time it becomes 'custom':

> Today it is customary every morning to eat a breakfast which, within limits, conforms to a certain pattern. But there is no obligation to do so, except possibly for hotel guests, and it has not always been customary. (Weber, 1978: 29)

social action

173

Third, Weber calls social action 'self-interest' where it selects the best means to realize a given end. Since self-interest does not follow the norms of usage or the duties of custom it tends to promote uniform outcomes since individuals will react to similar situations in similar ways (1978: 30). Orientations conflict or support each other. For instance, self-interest in making money might rely on usage or custom.

NON-SOCIAL ACTION

Weber (1978: 23) discounts 'merely reactive imitation' in order to emphasize the rational basis for his conception of meaningful social action: 'It is not proposed to call action "social" when it is merely the effect on the individual of the existence of a crowd as such and the action is not oriented to that fact at the level of meaning'. Individuals may be *causally* induced to act but this is not meaningful in Weber's sense of subjective action.

If two cyclists collide their relationship stands outside of social action until they begin to argue or fight over whose fault it was. Then it becomes meaningful. Individuals who separately put up an umbrella if it starts raining or read the morning papers are not engaged in social action because their meaning is not oriented to others. On the other hand, passive acquiescence may be social action if it is determined by the actual or expected behaviour of other individuals or groups. Things are also implicated in social action, as when commodities are oriented to others as producers or consumers.

COMMUNAL ACTION

In an echo of Tönnies *Gemeinschaft* and *Gesellschaft*, Weber distinguished 'communal action' from 'social action':

> Communal action refers to that action which is oriented to the feeling of actors that they belong together. Societal action, on the other hand, is oriented to a rationally motivated adjustment of interests. (Weber, 1946: 183)

'Social action' is premised on 'associative relationships' rather than 'communal relationships' (Weber, 1978: 40). These stand at opposite ends of the rationality axis. Associative relationships rest on judgements about either the value-rationality of ultimate ends or the instrumental rationality of expedient means, as in a free market exchange or voluntary associations. Communal relationships, on the other hand, are based on a subjective feeling of collective solidarity, which can be either affectual or traditional, with Weber taking the family as its prototypical 'natural unit'. Trade unions might bridge between communal and social action where they grow affectively out of a common 'class situation' but are also oriented rationally to worker self-interest.

CRITICAL DEVELOPMENTS

Weber's concept of social action relies on a rather impoverished 'Robinson Crusoe' model of the isolated rational actor (Gerth and Mills, 1946: 56). It also rests on underlying 'pre-scientific' assumptions about 'the disguised naturalism of community' (Radkau, 2009: Ch. 15). Weber adopted a transhistorical sense of social action based on a supposedly fixed human nature. His point of departure for the study of social action had been 'primitive communities' rather than an abstract discussion of the concept as it appeared later in *Economy and Society* (1978). As a formal concept, social action hardly figured in Weber's own substantive work (Levine, 2005).

Positively, Weber's naturalism allowed him to resist adulatory claims about the intrinsic superiority of his own society and to allow other human societies to stand the comparison with his own. Compared to Tönnies' nostalgic view of affective communities, Weber took a more detached, ironic and 'stone-cold sober view' of the often harsh, violent, not to say 'brutal social Darwinist' nature of pre-modern communities (Radkau, 2009: 415). Negatively, he subjected these to law-like analyses of social action and treated meaning and rationality as pre-given rather than historically specific.

While Weber was well aware of the dangers of elaborating formal concepts such as social action, Talcott Parsons (a translator of Weber) had no such inhibitions about building abstract models. His book's title, *The Structure of Social Action* (1949), took up Weber's theme directly. Ironically, Parsons transformed social action into an objective social structure that robbed actors of meaningful action other than functional compliance. Parsons is not widely read today. From Parsons' failure to develop Weber's insights into social action in substantive directions, some sociologists have argued that it is high time to give up any 'general theory' of social action altogether (Holmwood, 1996).

RELATED CONCEPTS

Gemeinschaft and *Gesellschaft*; Ideal-Types; Rationality and Rationalization; Social Facts; Social Forms and Sociation; *Verstehen*

Chapter 1 of Weber's *Economy and Society* (1978) deals directly with social action. This is reproduced in Sam Whimster's excellent collection *The Essential Weber* (2004). See Donald Levine's (2005) essay 'The continuing challenge of Max Weber's theory of rational action' for a qualified defence of rational social action.

Social Facts

For Durkheim 'social facts' are compelling moral forces that integrate individuals into collective life. A social fact is an objective reality, norm, representation, belief or practice found in the *average* life of a social group. 'Facts' refer specifically to *social* 'factors' or 'forces'. Durkheim gives social facts four core attributes: they are *independent* of, *general* across, *external* to and exercise a *constraint* on individuals.

> A social fact is every way of acting, fixed or not, capable of exercising on the individual an external constraint;

or:

> which is general over the whole of a given society, whilst having an existence of its own, independent of individual manifestations. (1895: 59)

INDIVIDUAL AND SOCIETY

Social facts lie along a scale ranging from fundamental structures that organize vast populations, communications systems and housing patterns to specific institutions like religion, education, occupation and politics, through to the great 'social currents' of social movements and popular moods. Examples of social facts include marriage, suicide, education, public meetings, birth rates and so on.

Durkheim constructs his concept on the basis of a fundamental opposition between the individual and society, which is, 'in a sense, the keystone of Durkheim's entire system' (Lukes, 1992: 22). Unlike Weber's social action, social facts are *not* the sum aggregate of individual actions. Social facts are found in individuals because they are part of the whole, rather than being found in the whole because they exist first in the individual parts. The whole is something different and something more than the sum of its parts. Social facts have their own autonomy, are trans-individual, and stand over and above individuals.

Society itself cannot be considered a social fact since social conditions are the precondition for the 'objective validity' of social facts. Society is conceived as something separate from individuals, constituting what Durkheim calls a 'reality *sui generis* [in itself]', which imposes its authority on individuals in the distinctive form of social facts. Individuals for Durkheim are much closer to a 'homo duplex'. By this he means that individuals are always two-sided, both inwardly self-interested but also outward facing toward society.

FACT AND FUNCTION

Durkheim's (1895: 45) minimum definition specifies that a social fact concerns whatever endures after social interaction has taken place: 'for a social fact to exist, several individuals at the very least must have interacted together and the resulting combination must have given rise to some new production.' This creates a 'superadded' thing-like quality in the social fact. To explain social facts at the psychological level is patently false for Durkheim. Durkheim (1895: 39) draws an analogy with the individual elements that compose physical substances: the softness of copper, tin and lead combine to form the hardness of bronze, while the gases hydrogen and oxygen produce the liquidity of water.

Although Durkheim is often portrayed as a 'functionalist' he does not limit social facts only to those functions that are useful to society. Social facts rely on deeper social conditions. Durkheim insists that the 'efficient cause' which produces social facts must be separated from the function it fulfils. At the level of scientific analysis, if not in reality, it is logical to uncover the causes of social facts before determining their effects or the precise nature of the relationship between them. 'As in biology, the organ is independent of the function – in other words, while remaining the same, it can serve different ends' (1895: 91).

Social facts are external

When we act, say as sister or brother, worker or boss, we inhabit roles that are defined externally, which exist outside, beyond and prior to us, pre-given by law or convention. From birth, we are compelled to accept and adopt local and national customs and values. Social facts are therefore external to the individual in a double sense. First, each individual is born into a ready-made society that profoundly shapes their development. Second, individuals interact with numerous external customs and rules such as paying bills with legal tender, speaking a comprehensible language and so on.

Social facts are independent

Independent social facts cannot be modified by a sheer force of will-power. Durkheim sees the independent power of social facts as 'essentially conservative'. This challenges fundamental ideas in Marxist theories of social revolution: 'How much more dangerous is the doctrine which sees social facts as the mere product of mental combinations which a simple dialectical artifice can, in an instant, utterly overthrow' (Durkheim, 1895: 32).

Social facts are constraining

As well as having an independent existence external to individuals, social facts also constrain them to act in certain prescribed ways. Every kind of resistance to social facts meets with the full power of external sanctions.

> If I do not conform to ordinary conventions, if in my mode of dress I pay no heed to what is customary in my country and in my social class, the laughter I provoke, the social distance at which I am kept, produce, although in an attenuated form, the same results as any real penalty. In other cases, although it may be indirect, the constraint is no less effective. I am not forced to speak French with my compatriots, nor to use the legal currency, but it is impossible for me to do otherwise. (Durkheim, 1895: 51)

Individuals amass social costs with every attempt to violate the integrity of social facts. This coercive authority is like a thing that has its own independent existence. It is not just formal rules but also, even more importantly, informal understandings, as in the 'social current' of a crowd.

Social facts are 'things'

Durkheim presented his claim that social facts are 'things' as 'the very basis of our method'. Like physical facts, social facts are things because we can only know them from the outside. From the most immediate observation through to much less palpable structures and processes, social facts acquire significance and authority in the eyes of the group. Hence they tend to become fixed and stabilized in 'institutions'.

Examples of such 'things' include legal rules, moral obligations, popular proverbs, social conventions, the family, the nation-state and so on. Socially approved 'ways of doing' are consolidated into stable 'ways of being'. Sociology, for Durkheim (1895: 45), is not so much a science of society than it is 'the science of institutions, their genesis and their functioning'.

Even material things like buildings or machinery are also social facts since they express collective representations at a certain point in their development. Less fixed are popular moods or social indignation, for example at a child murderer, where an aroused collective sentiment is imposed on countless individuals. Such episodes of popular mobilization recalibrate the coercive and external nature of the social facts and produce the definite forms, or 'fixed objects', of collective practices and representations.

CRITICAL DEVELOPMENTS

Durkheim's concept of social facts was meant to destabilize the taken-for-granted assumptions of his contemporaries. By specifying and constructing social facts as external, coercive things, Pierre Bourdieu and his colleagues (1991: 33) compared Durkheim's achievement in sociology to the scientific revolution which Galileo effected in physics. It certainly provoked a hostile response and continues to excite controversy.

Some charged Durkheim with idealism for emphasizing moral categories as social facts while others, in contrast, despaired variously at his metaphysics, positivism, empiricism or 'realism' (Lukes, 1992: 314). Durkheim himself preferred to emphasize the rationalism of his procedure. Many like Gabriel Tarde took exception to the comparison of social facts with things (see Lukes, 1992: 302–313, for the increasingly bad-tempered debate). As Durkheim noted, by declaring as fact the existence of social things he offended against an underlying individualism and psychological reductionism prevalent in modern societies. It might also be added, social facts offended against the dominance, until recently, of interactionist and structural-functionalist schools of sociology (see Remender, 1973). They saw the concept of social facts as obscuring concrete social interaction and turning human agency into a mystical object.

Undoubtedly, Durkheim deploys his criteria for social facts – externality, constraint, generality and independence – in ambiguous and inconsistent ways. His conception of social facts as external to individuals seems to reify the independence of society as a permanent, invariant aspect of human life rather than a historically-specific feature of modernity or capitalism (Frisby and Sayer, 1986: 95).

Durkheim's conceptual circularity depends on a fundamental mind-body dualism. Physical individuals are pictured as somehow pre-social biological creatures until their consciousness submits to the predominant social facts. Being restricted to using the local language or wearing appropriate fashions doesn't so much forcibly alter behaviour as influence it or even make it possible. In a later preface to *The Rules*, Durkheim (1895: 47, n.4) noted this tension between coercive obligations and a more positive attachment to social facts. Once general norms are internalized by individuals it becomes difficult to separate out individual consciences from independent social facts.

By emphasizing that fact-things unify social life, Durkheim also tends to obscure the divisions in society and presents conflict as existing between the individual and society rather than between unequal social groups like classes (Giddens, 1978). For instance, his example of punishment for crimes as reflecting the average social facts neglects the way that unequally powerful groups and the mass media can mobilize popular opinion.

Durkheim might have avoided much of the criticism had he not stated his concept of social facts in such a rigid way. Instead of claiming that individuals can only be explained by social facts, he might simply have argued that there was more to social facts than the sum of individuals or that individuals cannot be entirely separated from social influences. Social facts make individual actions possible in the first place and give them a defined purpose. In his defence, Durkheim clearly thought it 'absurd' to think that social facts had a completely separate existence apart from the individuals associated within it. Society may dominate and command us but we also need, desire and internalize society.

RELATED CONCEPTS

Collective Representations; Conscience Collective; Division of Labour in Society (Durkheim); Normal and Pathological; Positivism; Social Morphology; Suicide

FURTHER READING

The Rules of Sociological Method (1895) opens with the concept of social facts. Steven Lukes' incomparable biography *Emile Durkheim* (1992) sets down social facts in a critical theoretical context. Frisby and Sayer (1986), Jones (1986) Giddens (1978) and Thompson (2002) offer succinct readable summaries of the concept. A substantial discussion and informed defence of the concept is provided by Gane (1988).

Social Forms and Sociation

Georg Simmel asked what is it about 'society' that might be distinctively *social* rather than, say, psychological or historical? Simmel's answer was to abstract consistent patterns of social interaction that he called 'social forms' (Herberle, 1948). Social forms are seen by Georg Simmel as analogous to spatial forms in geometry. Ideal shapes like perfect circles, squares, octagons and so on are pure abstract creations of geometry that do not exist anywhere in nature. Similarly, social forms – subordination, competition, conflict, sociability, inclusion and exclusion, exchange, rendezvous, secrecy, sociability – are ideal abstractions from actual social interactions. Such forms give social relations their specific texture and gravity across widely varying historical contents.

Social theory, for Simmel, needed to dig below the major organs of society – family, religion, class, division of labour, state, military, prison and so on. These are merely the large-scale crystallizations of something far deeper: sociation. Sociation ranges in intensity and scale, from momentary events like a glance to the structures of the nation-state. At one extreme, it takes the pure form of being with and for one another in *sociability* and, at the other extreme, it underpins various degrees of being against one another in *conflict*.

SOCIATION

A thousand social threads are spun and broken every minute of every day. Simmel coins the idea of 'sociation' (*Vergesellschaftung*) to address these infinitesimal forms of interaction. Sociation refers to those stable and patterned forms of reciprocal interaction between individuals who are 'with-one-another, for-one-another, in-one-another, against-one-another, and through-one-another, in state and commune, in church and economic association, in family and in clubs' (Simmel, 1971: 127).

At every moment people look at each other, are jealous, write text messages, advertise on social networking sites, take lunch with each other, attend sports, gossip, dress up and adorn themselves (or dress down and appear casual):

all the thousands of relations from person to person, momentary or enduring, conscious or unconscious, fleeting or momentous, from which the
above examples are taken quite at random, continually bind us together.
(1997: 110)

Sociation is malleable, tenacious and reciprocal. Individuals form themselves and society through 'innumerable, specific relations and in the feeling and knowledge of determining others and of being determined by
them' (1971: 7).

Sociation emerges at 'the intersection of various social circles' and is
subject to their distinctive weave and woof (Simmel, 1976). Society and
individuality are merely different aspects of the same social reality:

> We perform the synthesis 'social being'. We are capable of constructing the
> notion of society from the very idea of beings, each of whom may feel him-
> self as the *terminus a quo* [starting point] and the *terminus ad quem* [end point]
> of his developments and destinies and qualities. And we do construct this
> concept of society, which is built up from that of the potentially autonomous
> individual, as the *terminus a quo* and *terminus ad quem* of the individual's very
> life and fate. (Simmel, 1971: 18)

Simmel develops a geometrical notion of social circles. In modernity
individuals belong to a wide range of social circles: family (parental,
spouses and self), occupation (superiors, subordinates, colleagues), club,
party, trade union, professional body, neighbourhood, voluntary group,
through to the widest circles of social class or national identity (Simmel,
1976: 97). Points of contact between social circles shift as individuals
join or leave, ensuring that the elements of objective culture are continually re-combined in new ways.

SOCIATION AND SOCIETY

Sociation is not the same thing as 'society'. Society cannot be grasped in
its entirety all at once. Simmel located his concept of sociation within
the standard dispute of his time about 'society':

> One side mystically exaggerates its significance, contending that only
> through society is human life endowed with reality. The other regards it
> as a mere abstract concept by means of which the observer draws the
> realities, which are individual human beings, into a whole, as one calls
> trees and brooks, houses and meadows, a 'landscape'. (1997: 120)

Society is not a thing-like substance. For Simmel (1971: 27) there is
no such thing as society 'as such' or interaction 'as such'. Society is

fundamentally a relational concept; it exists only in and through forms of sociation. Instead of treating society as an independent substance, as with Durkheim's social facts, for Simmel 'everything interacts in some way with everything else'.

It is only through specific social forms that society also emerges. Sociation is neither the cause nor the consequence of society; it *is* society. Society as a complex whole is not the sum of individual people in the same way that a collection of individual trees becomes a forest. Society is a 'synthesis' or a unity of individuals in countless interactions, connections and forms of association. While sociation extracts and distils into a definite *form* what is specifically 'social' the abstract idea of 'society' is merely a 'frame' which contains the innumerable contents of social life.

SOCIAL FORMS

What does Simmel mean when he suggests that sociation is a form? Sociation is not to be confused with the psychological *content* of interaction – interests, purposes or motives – but rather with those 'pure *forms*' through which interaction acquires some definite shape. We abstract from the physical content of the world only those forms that are relevant and meaningful for our purposes. When a photograph is reproduced in a newspaper, we are less interested in the physical properties of the print or the paper itself than with what the image signifies, its meaning and context.

Geometry, which determines what is purely spatial about objects through abstract forms, provides a model for Simmel. Sociology must similarly abstract the forms of sociation from their content: 'Abstractions alone produce science out of the complexity and unity of society' (Simmel, 1971: 25). Unlike geometry, there is no foolproof, logical method of distilling social forms from their complex, diverse content. While geometry can resolve the most irregular spatial shapes into a few simple formal axioms, such is the complexity of society that social forms only apply to a limited range of cases.

Forms of sociation represent an intermediate 'cross-section' of society, somewhere between universal laws and particular empirical examples. On one hand, the *same* form of sociation – say competition, sociability or authority – can be observed over a wide range of disparate contents, like the feudal court, art school, the family or a multinational corporation. On the other hand, *different* forms of sociation may express the same material content. Economic interests can take various social forms of competition or cooperation; religious belief can be centralized in a church or decentralized as private worship; sexual relations or family groups can take a wide variety of forms; education can have an authoritarian form or a liberal form; and so on. As Simmel states:

> Any social phenomenon or process is composed of two elements which in reality are inseparable: on the one hand, an interest, a purpose, or a motive; on the other, a form or mode of interaction among individuals through which, or in the shape of which, that content attains social reality. (1971: 24)

Content – individual interest, purpose or motive – is only realized through social forms. Subjective content, whether economic, ideal, warlike, erotic, religious, altruistic, leads to some definite social form, a social 'circle', state, church, trade union, family, club and so on.

Forms of sociation may be abstractions but they are not random. They must be identified from empirical examples, arranged systematically, explained psychologically, understood in their historical development and made susceptible to empirical verification, falsification or revision. Recurring forms of sociation are analysed by Simmel as 'eternal sociological snapshots' ('snapshots *sub specie aeternitatis*') (Frisby, 1992a: 102–31).

As such, there is always a risk of ambiguity as to whether something is categorized as an eternal social form or a specific content. For instance, the poor – who are always with us under vastly different historical conditions – may be understood in a permanent social form, poverty, or as a specific material fact, poor individuals (Simmel, 1971: 178).

SOCIABILITY

Pleasure is found in the special form of sociation that comes from being with each other for its own sake: sociability. Whether in 'play form', say card-playing or sports, or in 'art form', say music or painting, a special feeling of being together with other people arises from free association and company, of overcoming isolation and loneliness, of creating an 'ideal sociological world'. Sociability temporarily releases us from the serious business of life. This distance from worldly cares does not descend into an empty 'flight from life'. Pure sociability keeps us in contact with reality by suspending its serious side, where things are a means for something else, in order to play with life's aesthetic side for its own sake.

Sociability is the 'pure essence' of sociation. In play the stresses and strains of life fall away. Run of the mill frictions and conflicts are lifted into a purely symbolic realm. Since it involves no narrow ulterior motive, sociability is expansive and generous and, above all, equal. It is a game in which everyone acts as if each individual is of equal importance. Simmel (1971: 132) formulates the rule of pure sociability: 'everyone should guarantee to the other that maximum of sociable values (joy, relief, vivacity) which is consonant with the maximum of values he receives'. This principle of mutual playfulness is inherently democratic.

Because it is enjoyed purely for its own sake the pure form of sociability, for Simmel, transcends both the self-interest of individuals and the external weight of social structures. Pure reciprocity banishes both objective social position and subjective ego. Deviation towards either destroys sociability. On the one hand, external importance – wealth, social position, possessions, fame, honours – cannot play any part in the sociable circle. In sociability people do not come as the bearers of functions and interests but as personalities in their own right, with specific attractive qualities, witty, affable, agreeable and so on. On the other hand, purely personal affectations, moods or instrumental networking are disagreeable to the sociable gathering. Personal vanity takes a back seat.

Among sociable individuals conventions of tact and self-effacement impose restraints on personal egoism and cut worldly pretensions down to size. A model for this social ethic is the spontaneous forming of groups at parties as conversations develop, rise and fall, break off, take an unexpected turn and so on. It has no meaning beyond itself in the free 'give and take' of equal interaction, telling tales, anecdotes, puns, irony, teasing and witty banter. Similarly, erotic flirting as a sociological form is enjoyed in its own right as an ambiguous shadow play of sexual attraction and denial.

CONFLICT

Conflict is never entirely absent from sociation. But it also contains something positive for sociation. Except for marginal cases of conflict that tend towards outright annihilation, sociation places definite limits on violence. As an elementary form of sociation, conflict helps to resolve, rather than destroy, tensions between attraction and repulsion (Simmel, 1955). First, without conflict sociation would lack any dynamic. Second, it helps to integrate the social group, as when a marriage is strengthened through a certain amount of discord or a hierarchy functions through mutual hostility at all levels. Third, resistance to oppression is positive if it limits power over us, encourages mutual restraint and leaves us with a feeling of agency. Fourth, in the metropolis, a mutual repulsion and antipathy creates social distances that make a physical proximity to innumerable people bearable.

Sociation is always a dynamic totality, mediating between the poles of attraction and repulsion. Only in the concrete relationship itself do these two tendencies have a specific impact. Within a family, for instance, individuals tend to be wholly absorbed by its close intimacy. Under such intense intimacy the slightest friction assumes a disproportionate significance that it would not possess between complete strangers. In class struggles, personal animosity gives way to objective conditions. Yet the impersonality of class struggle does not lessen its intensity and violence. Simmel (1955: 40–41) gives the example of the 1894 workers' boycott of Berlin's breweries, which escalated into open violence but lacked any real personal hatred between the contending sides.

Simmel (1955; 1971: 70–95) recognizes that some forms of conflict will destroy any basis for sociation. In cases where conflict is undertaken in the name of a higher impersonal cause, political, moral or religious, it is fought with merciless militancy. Idealistic individuals feel entitled 'to make anybody a victim of the idea for which they sacrifice themselves' (Simmel, 1955: 39; 1971: 87).

Yet, even where fight and victory is the sole purpose as in games of skill or games of chance, all parties recognize their formal rules and norms. Similarly, the purest form of conflict is legal conflict because nothing enters into it which does not serve objectively the conflict between prosecutor and defendant.

CRITICAL DEVELOPMENTS

Simmel's concept of social form has had a wide-reaching, though often unacknowledged, influence on social theory (Levine, 1997). The concept of social form anticipates Max Weber's concept of ideal-types. Sociation seems close to Marx's dual sense of the individual as 'the ensemble of social relations' and society as reciprocal activity. Just as Marx saw class divisions as the underlying cause of conflict, Simmel (1971: 94) argued that 'separation does not follow from conflict but, on the contrary, conflict follows from separation'. Marx also examined forms of social life – the commodity, class, capital. Unlike Simmel, these were filled with definite historical content. Simmel was more concerned with the varying intensity of conflict and sociation rather than delineating their primary causes (Turner, 1994).

Many of Simmel's contemporaries viewed sociation as a rather speculative and vague concept that lacked any coherent view of society as a whole (Frisby, 2002). Durkheim, the pre-eminent theorist of large-scale social facts, sharply criticized Simmel's separation of social form from material content. However, as Simmel (1971: 24) himself put it: 'A social form severed from all content can no more attain existence than a spatial form can exist whose form it is.' The idea of pure sociation as play found an echo in Erving Goffman's 'dramaturgical' approach to social life as analogous to a theatrical production, although Goffman operated with a much more limited conception of interaction than Simmel (Smith, 1994).

David Frisby (1992b) emphasizes the specifically 'aesthetic dimension' of social form in Simmel's work. Like sociation, art depends on a sense of form, unity, harmony, symmetry, equilibrium and proportion. 'Sociological aesthetics' understands sociation in terms of abstractions, fragments, frames, impressions, distances, play, tensions, textures and perspectives. Simmel's sociological aesthetics of social form and sociation may enjoy a new lease of life as cultural perspectives are integrated into the mainstream of sociology.

RELATED CONCEPTS

Historical Materialism; Ideal-Types; Modernity; Social Facts; Social Morphology; Social Space

FURTHER READING

Simmel's writings on sociation are available in the collections edited by Donald Levine, *Georg Simmel, On Individuality and Social Forms* (1971), and the earlier volume, *The Sociology of Georg Simmel* (1950), edited by Kurt H. Wolff. On the culture of interaction, including the essay on sociability, see Part IV of *Simmel on Culture* (1997).

Social Morphology

With the concept of social morphology Durkheim classified the 'substratum' of society according to how human populations are distributed and organized across space.

The social substratum will differ according to whether the population is of greater or lesser size and density, whether it is concentrated in towns or scattered over rural areas, according to the way in which towns and houses are constructed, whether the space occupied by a society is more or less extensive, according to the nature of the frontiers which enclose it and the avenues of communication which cross it. (1899: 241)

For Durkheim, the 'facts of social morphology' always play a 'preponderant role' in collective life. Likewise, they must also be a principal factor in sociological explanations. Social morphology allows sociology to throw a bridge between what Durkheim called 'the fragmentary sciences' of geography (the science of space) and demography (the science of population) to create a unified science of sociology.

MORPHOLOGY AND PHYSIOLOGY

To go beyond the large-scale philosophical systems of predecessors like Montesquieu, Comte and Spencer, Durkheim envisaged a need for detailed studies of 'social morphology' and 'social physiology' before a larger synthesis or 'general sociology' might be attempted (see table below). In biology, morphology refers to the study of the form and structure of organisms and is sometimes used interchangeably with anatomy. This is distinct from physiology, which studies the functions of the inter-dependent parts of organisms. Structure and function in living organisms are always interrelated. Their separation is for purely analytical or classification purposes. Similarly, social morphology studies the 'substratum' of society while social physiology studies social functions, institutions and collective representations: religion, morality, economic sociology, legal sociology, political sociology, cultural sociology and sociology of language.

PRINCIPAL DIVISIONS OF SOCIOLOGY IN DURKHEIM AND MAUSS

	Durkheim	Mauss
SOCIAL MORPHOLOGY	The study of geographically-situated social organizations The study of population volume and density	Material structures
SOCIAL	Sociology of religion	Practices

PHYSIOLOGY	Sociology of morality	Representations
	Sociology of Law	
	Economic sociology	
	Linguistic sociology	
	Aesthetic sociology	
GENERAL	Abstract theoretical	Language and the
SOCIOLOGY	synthesis of special	symbolic
	sciences	Science
		Collective ethology
		Applied sociology
		and politics

Source: Adapted from Durkheim, 1909; Mauss, 1927.

Mauss, M. (1927) 'Sociology: Its divisions and their relative weightings', in M. Mauss (2005) *The Nature of Sociology*. New York and Oxford: Durkheim Press/Berghahm Books, pp. 31–89.

CLASSIFICATION

A common misunderstanding holds that Durkheim thought that society, the object of sociology, was like an organism, the object of biology. In fact, Durkheim objected strongly to simple evolutionary approaches to society. His analogy between biology and sociology was restricted to the question of methodology. Both biology and sociology study their respective objects at the level of organized wholes rather than isolated parts. Social morphology is restricted to 'that part of sociology whose task it is to constitute and classify social types' (Durkheim, 1895: 111).

Social morphology solves a fundamental methodological problem for Durkheim. On one side, it avoids forcing reality to fit with abstract concepts about humanity in general, as his predecessor Comte recommended. On the other side, it avoids merely describing unique events, as in ethnography or history.

It would therefore seem that social reality can only be the object of an abstract and vague philosophy or of purely descriptive monographs. But one escapes from this alternative once it is recognised that between the confused multitude of historical societies and the unique, although ideal, concept of humanity, there are intermediate entities: there are the social species. (1895: 109)

social morphology

189

The concept of 'social species' brings together both empirical diversity and scientific unity. Social species are not to be confused with historical phases, or economic or technological conditions. These are too transitory and unstable to provide a basis for classification. Social species refers to the more or less permanent essences of national societies.

> From its origins France has passed through very different forms of civilization. It began by being agricultural, to pass then to an industry of trades and small businesses, then to manufacturing, and finally to large-scale industry. One cannot admit that the same individual collectivity can change its species three of four times. (1895: 118)

Social species exist for the same reason as biological ones: they are varied combinations of the same anatomical unity. Social species are not part of an evolutionary sequence towards a higher order but represent merely one possibility from an infinite variety.

This intermediary category of (national) social species allowed Durkheim to construct a classification of social types based on a more precise initial definition of 'decisive or crucial facts'. Social physiology, 'the general facts of social life', is dependent on social morphology, the classification of social types. If society is a combination of previously separate parts, the principles of classification should follow the ways in which more simple societies combine together to create a more complex unity (1895: 115). A simple society is defined as indivisible, that is, it cannot be divided into anything smaller than itself.

Durkheim gives the example of 'the horde' as the simplest unit or segment, 'the protoplasm of the social domain and consequently the natural basis for any classification.' It is conceived as a pure type, the basis for all later combinations and the 'root source' of all social species. Internally, there is no segmentation, no stratification, no differentiation, and no division of labour.

> Once this notion of the horde or single-segment society has been assumed – whether it is conceived of as an historical reality or as a scientific postulate – we possess the necessary support on which to construct the complete scale of social types. (1895: 113–14)

Durkheim's idea of 'the horde' is simply a convenient fiction, with no basis in the historical record, on which to build a classification system of social types.

'NORMAL' MORPHOLOGY

What Durkheim considers as 'normal' *social facts* always corresponds to a determinate social structure. Under mechanical solidarity the social structure is conceived as a series of homogeneous segments whose form is more or less identical to each other. Mechanical solidarity is indivisible and static. It only becomes organic solidarity as more individuals come into contact with each other, creating a moral density and social volume. Normally, as contact between similar trades increases the competition between them also grows. To offset this, groups will tend to specialize, stimulating the re-division of labour still further. The advance of the division of labour has its 'decisive causes' in the density and volume of social morphology.

First, moral or 'dynamic' density is explained by the concentration of larger populations in urban space. Cities are sometimes seen as a threat to values of order and cohesion. But if cities have long been part of the social species then they cannot be 'pathological' for Durkheim. Urban density closes the moral gaps between segments through increased communication and transportation. Second, 'social volume' refers to the sheer size of the population. However, not all populous societies develop the division of labour in proportion to social volume. If the growing intimacy of urban density fails to erase the 'moral gaps' separating individual segments, the substratum remains essentially mechanical in nature. Social volume may amplify moral density but on its own does not necessitate an advanced division of labour (1895: 136).

SOCIAL MORPHOLOGY OF SUICIDE

Durkheim's study of suicide put social morphology to a more stringent test than speculations about the origins and development of the division of labour. The experience compelled him to revise the methodological priority given to social morphology. Given the inadequacy of official statistics, hastily collected on the basis of individualist and psychological assumptions about the causes of suicide, Durkheim needed to be inventive in order to wring out the hidden social causes contained within the existing data. Rather than being able to inductively build up models or types of the social causes of suicide from the substratum, the 'morphological' method, Durkheim was forced to reverse this procedure and deduce the social causes of suicide from their effects, the 'aetiological method' of classification.

Using the aetiological method Durkheim constructs his famous three types of suicide: egoistic suicide, altruistic suicide and anomic suicide. However, a major problem with the aetiological method is that the cart of classification is put before the horse of empirical evidence. Any arbitrariness in the construction of classification may be obviated, Durkheim (1952: 147) contends, by working between the two methods: 'we shall descend from causes to effects and our aetiological classification will be completed by a morphological one which can verify the former and vice versa'. Once this 'aetiological' classification of suicide was verified empirically to Durkheim's satisfaction, a morphological analysis becomes necessary since 'a deduction uncontrolled by experiment is always questionable' (1952: 278).

Having created his aetiological classification of suicide and subjected it to empirical analysis, Durkheim considers its implications for social morphology. Suicides generally occur among disparate and separated individuals. That one person rather than another is prepared to kill him/herself is the concern of the clinician; that each society produces a uniform and not a random pattern of suicide is explained ultimately by the social substratum.

Using this approach, Durkheim drops a bombshell: the actual suicide performed – drowning, hanging, gunshot, poisoning, asphyxiation – has no logical relationship to the underlying social cause. Customs, convenience and cultural acceptability decisively influence the suicide method. In France hanging was the most popular method in the 1870s but in Italy around the same time drowning and firearms were much more popular. In cities people jump from high buildings while in countries with a developed railway system people take the opportunity to throw themselves in front of trains.

CRITICAL DEVELOPMENTS

Among Durkheim's contemporaries, social morphology was taken up most notably by Marcel Mauss and Maurice Halbwachs in their respective efforts to mediate between materialist and idealist approaches to collective life. Mauss divides the study of society into two:

> The first phenomenon, i.e., the group and the things, corresponds to *morphology*, the study of material structures; the second, phenomenon corresponds to *social physiology*, i.e., the study of these structures in movement, in other words, their functions and the functioning of these functions. (1927: 55)

Mauss warns that social morphology should be stripped of any association with life sciences. Mauss abandoned this preoccupation with Durkheim's schema for his anthropological analyses of 'closed societies' in recognition of the problems with Durkheim's fictitious idea of an original 'horde' as society's fundamental segmentary unit (Allen, 2000). Earlier, in their brilliant study *Seasonal Variations of the Eskimo: A Study of Social Morphology* (1979), Mauss, with Henri Beuchat, directly applied Durkheim's strictures to a 'single decisive case study'. This short study has been described as 'one of the most remarkable ever produced by the Durkheimians' (Nielson, 1999: 158). Mauss explains that the collective life of Eskimos varies between summer and winter not simply because the environment changes dramatically but because the seasons represent two different classification systems for organizing the substratum. In winter society is concentrated and relations are intensely communal; in summer it is dispersed and social bonds weaken. This dual morphology affects the form and intensity of all other social phenomena in Eskimo society, including types of housing, family groups, ceremonies, sexual relations, property rights and moral life. Here, Mauss practically refutes the often made claim that social morphology is rigidly counterposed to collective representations.

Of Dukheim's followers, Halbwachs' studies of social morphology, class, suicide and demography are considered 'among the richest, most versatile and up-to-date in the group' (Karady, 1981: 39). Inspired by Durkheim, Halbwachs took a social morphology approach to the study of population and road networks in nineteenth-century Paris and summarized his ideas in his final book *Morphologie sociale* (translated as *Population and Society*). Halbwachs (1960) was especially taken by Durkheim's critique of geography's environmental determinism and the need to focus on what is distinctively social in the spatial distribution of populations (Lenoir, 2001). For Halbwachs demography is always laden with social meaning (Stoetzel, 2006).

Social morphology is related to collective representations as the 'material base' is related to the 'ideological superstructure' by Marx. But, as with Marx's simile, social morphology is often seen as 'a rather quaint doctrine' by modern sociologists (Hirst, 1973: 22). It has been taken to task for being a speculative construction, its changing role in Durkheim's sociology, its denial of historical specificity, and its formalism. First, morphological arguments that build from the horde as a pure simple, segmented society through to the role of density and volume in the modern division of labour rest on fictional foundations and speculative reasoning (Lukes, 1992: 171).

Second, the concept of 'social morphology' was deployed by Durkheim in different ways and given different emphases at different times. Durkheim initially emphasized function as the dynamic element which shaped structures. Morphology then moved from being a secondary function of something else to becoming a core explanatory variable to later being regarded by Durkheim as means to distinguish the boundaries of sociology as a discipline (Andrews, 1993). Although he did not renounce the morphological procedure set out in *The Rules of Sociological Method* (1895) Durkheim subsequently became preoccupied with collective representations and referred less explicitly to social morphology (Hawkins, 2004).

Third, where the metaphor of social species implies a stable, enduring nature that transcends historical shifts, Durkheim appears to have killed off historical development. Agricultural, artisanal, mercantile and industrial France are not defined by him as distinct historical societies but as carriers of the same permanent national essence of social species. Durkheim appears less concerned with empirical content than with formal structures. Morphological classification does not depend on establishing the facts but helps determine which facts to look for and how to make sense of them.

Durkheim's scientific method is not describing the surface appearance of reality. He is constructing a field of structural essences amenable to scientific study. As a biological analogy, morphology and social species have a more general import for understanding Durkheim's provisional construction of the object for scientific study. Durkheim is trying to establish the scientific credentials of sociology in a way quite different from Simmel's social forms:

> At first sight one might think that by *social forms* or *forms of association* Simmel means the morphological aspect of societies, namely, their geographical basis, their population mass and density, the composition of secondary groups and their distribution over the area occupied by a society. (1903: 191)

But, Durkheim argues, the examples of sociation that Simmel gives – division of labour, competition, individuals in groups, imitation and conflict – 'are in no way morphological phenomena'. They are over-generalized forms of sociation not their essential structural components.

While social morphology has not had much of a following in sociology, the idea of scientific knowledge as a 'construction' has made considerable headway in recent years, even if few today acknowledge a debt to the epistemological break initiated by Durkheim or find his biological language of morphology and species relevant (Bourdieu et al., 1991).

RELATED CONCEPTS

Base and Superstructure; Division of Labour in Society (Durkheim); *Gemeinschaft* and *Gesellschaft*; Mechanical and Organic Solidarity; Positivism; Social Facts; Social Forms and Sociation

FURTHER READING

Durkheim (1895) sets out his social morphology in Chapter 4 of *The Rules of Sociological Method*. Mauss and Beuchat's (1979) study *Seasonal Variations of the Eskimo: A Study of Social Morphology* is one of the greatest attempts to apply

Durkheim's principles. Bourdieu and colleagues (1991) in *The Craft of Sociology* defend what Durkheim attempted to achieve with the morphological method.

Social Space

In his essay 'The sociology of space' Simmel (1997: 137–70) plots what he calls a 'social geometry' to establish that space is the simultaneous precondition and product of social forms. Social forms presuppose relations of social space – inside and outside, breadth and narrowness, boundary points, large and small, intersecting circles, centre and margin, concentration and dispersal, fixity and mobility, sensory proximity and cultural distance. If sociation is 'the possibility of being together' then its spatial dimension needs to be accounted for. He sets out five dimensions of 'social space': unique space, boundaries, fixed or focal points, social distance, and mobility.

EXCLUSIVE SPACE

A first condition of sociation is that space is unique and exclusive. Only the nation-state and, to a lesser extent, the city enjoy exclusive authority over space. There can only be one state ruling over a particular space. While only one city at a time can occupy a certain location, it is permeated by a diverse range of influences and its influence, in turn, often extend far beyond the city boundary. At the other extreme of the spatial scale, the church potentially extends its influence over every space.

BOUNDED SPACE

A second condition for sociation is the demarcation of space by boundaries: 'The boundary is not a spatial fact with sociological consequences, but a sociological fact that forms itself spatially' (Simmel, 1997: 143). Like a picture frame, the boundary unifies what is inside against what is outside. Boundaries intensify sociation. A geometrical line between two neighbours has different implications than a natural boundary like a river or mountain. A sociological boundary pulses with latent tension since it might be contested and redrawn at any time.

But it also places a mutual limitation and self-restraint on neighbourly relations. The boundary has the sociological function of reinforcing the

centre of group life. Similarly, in ordinary interactions personal boundaries are constructed and negotiated. Sociological investment in a line in
space often becomes rigid when reciprocity becomes a routine fact of
life. If the boundary is more porous, individuals will feel that they have
more freedom of movement; where it is more constricted, the feeling of
compactness and overcrowding will compress individuality into an
homogeneous mass.

FIXED SPACE

Third, where a group or object is fixed in space it functions as a
'pivot-point' which keeps 'a system of elements in a specific distance,
interaction and interdependence' (Simmel, 1997: 147). The contrast
here is between the fixed spatial points of settled populations and the
changing spatial points of mobile or nomadic people. With the loan of
a mortgage, the creditor allows the debtor to occupy the property
precisely because it is physically fixed in space. On the other hand, a
shift from the pre-modern convention of giving names to houses to
the modern convention of numbering them sequentially indicates a
loss of belonging to a uniquely individual fixed point in space.

Among immigrant communities churches function as pivot-points to
organize scattered worshippers. Alternatively, churches may also be
centralized at a fixed point in space; for Catholics 'all roads lead to
Rome'. Rome represents the most extreme uniqueness as well as the
transcendence of all fixed spaces. Simmel gives the further example of
the rendezvous as a unique form of intense sociation. Because the illicit
encounter occurs as a breach of everyday life, the place arranged for the
rendezvous later becomes a fixed focal point for idealized memory.

DISTANCE AND PROXIMITY

A fourth condition of sociation is whether people are in close spatial
contact or separated by distance. Social distance in the form of impersonal, objective and functional relations is a central feature of modernity.
For Simmel physical distance or proximity does not have uniform
effects. People may feel closely bound to each other even if they are
spatially separated, as with members of a nation separated by considerable distances. In the metropolis, people are socially distant but spatially
close.

Sensory contact shapes sociation. At the interpersonal level, spatial
intimacy is often confused with emotional intimacy. Individuals show
excessive confidence in spatial intimacy and drop any sense of reserve.

When 'too much' is given up or demanded through spatial intimacy relations cool off. Such emotional closeness can never again be revived.

Beyond the immediacy of face-to-face contact, sociation relies on abstractions. An abstraction like national identity connects and unifies things that may be spatially remote. Spatial distance also reduces the intensity of the social encounter, whereas spatial proximity can heighten feelings of attraction and repulsion. But, again, *social* distance cannot be read off directly from *spatial* distance. Social distance is always relative to its content. Hence, instead of intense emotions, spatial proximity can lead to indifference and detachment, as in a big city. And rather than cool detachment, spatial distance can contribute to a fierce hostility towards foreign groups.

Close contact tends to destroy the abstract categories of spatial distance. If individuals see each other frequently but rarely have the chance to speak, as in a large workplace or on a regular bus journey, sociation is mediated by fleeting visual images. These can only build an imperfect picture of other people. If individuals speak to each other frequently the content and tone will give sociation a more definite, rich and individual texture than sight alone. Smell is usually a source of sensory repulsion, at least when it is attributed to socially distant groups, like the working class, foreigners, or ethnic minorities, by a dominant social group.

Minorities adopt different spatial strategies to resist hostile pressures from majority groups. If they are relatively few in number the greatest dispersal will allow evasion from attack; if they are relatively large then the greatest concentration of numbers facilitates resistance and protection. Jews adopted both survival strategies, on the one hand, dispersed by the global Diaspora and, on the other hand, densely concentrated into the 'solid, air-tight cohesion' of urban ghettoes. Simmel believed that spatial strategies could transform social weakness into a real strength:

> Thus, whereas the ghetto was a decided benefit and a strengthening factor for the Jews in that earlier stage of weaker forces that were generally dependent on defence, it seems extraordinarily disadvantageous now that the strengths and energies of Judaism have grown, and their dispersal throughout the population has increased their collective power most effectively. (1997: 158)

Written just 30 years before the Nazi genocide, Simmel's defensive social geometry of ethnic minorities has a tragic poignancy about it. Jewish ghettoes became staging posts on the way to mass annihilation in 'concentration camps'. With the exception of the heroic uprising of the Warsaw ghetto in 1944, resistance seemed utterly futile.

MOBILITY

Simmel's final dialectic of space and sociation concerns the consequences of movement from place to place. Different forms of sociation are appropriate to a wandering group compared to a sedentary group. Nomadism lacks the constant test of interaction that lets individuals know where the social boundaries lie. Since they transport their possessions with them along the journey their existence appears precarious.

In modernity, people in movement remain connected to and in contact with their fixed point of origin. Modern communications – letters, books, photography, mass media – keep the migrant or traveller connected to the objective unity of the whole group. Pre-modern empires connected up the various parts through sending out state officials to far-flung corners of the territory. Similarly, political movements sent speakers out to the constituencies and organized mobile demonstrations, like the Hunger Marches of the 1930s, which arrived at a fixed central point in a large city from several directions.

Simmel also notes that settled groups may resent mobile groups. An example of this would be the prejudice that communities of 'gypsies' or travellers often have to face. All the advantages seem to lie with settled populations since they can be mobile whenever the occasion demands, while travellers or nomads cannot share the benefits of settlement.

CRITICAL DEVELOPMENTS

Simmel developed the idea of social space in a number of essays on the metropolis, the stranger, the adventure, the Alpine journey, the sociology of the senses, and the bridge and the door. A strong case has been made that Durkheim (1903), despite criticizing Simmel for his 'indeterminacy', developed his concept of social morphology – territory, population density and boundaries – in part through a close yet critical review of Simmel's writing on social space (Jaworski, 1994). Here, as so often, Simmel's fragmentary, theoretical approach to social space held little appeal for more scientifically-minded sociologists and geographers.

Simmel's own analogy between geometry and sociation is somewhat misleading. A more static sense of social geometry came to be identified with quantitative studies of social network analysis and in the measurement of social space known as 'sociometry'. The concept of 'social distance' was taken up by the Chicago School in the 1920s and quantified by Emory Bogardus's (1959) social distance scale. Such literal measurement was far removed from Simmel's concept of social distance (Levine et al., 1994). More faithfully, Pitrim Sorokin recognized Simmel's original contribution to sociological space in his book *Social Mobility* (1927).

Following Simmel's method, the German social theorists Siegfried Kracauer and Walter Benjamin possessed a more dynamic sense of the social spaces of modernity. Also closer to Simmel's own approach to space is the spatially-sensitized social theory like that of Henri Lefebvre's *The Production of Space* (1991) and Gaston Bachelard's *The Poetics of Space* (1994) although Simmel's social geometry did not seem to influence either directly.

RELATED CONCEPTS

Civil Society; Ideal-Types; Metropolis; Modernity; Social Forms and Sociation; Social Morphology

FURTHER READING

David Frisby's little book *Georg Simmel* (2002) summarizes the main contours of Simmel's social space concisely. Simmel's own rather long version of 'The sociology of space' can be found in *Simmel on Culture* (1997). In his introductory text, *Space and Social Theory* (2007), Andrzej Zieleniec provides a highly accessible outline of Simmel's reasoning.

Suicide

Suicide is commonly understood to be among the most personal decisions that an individual is capable of making. In his famous study *Suicide* (1952), Durkheim seeks to prove that society is as much, or more, the underlying cause of suicide as any inner psychological state. Suicide is a distorted or exaggerated response to the pressures imposed by some quality or virtue that society hold so dear that individuals are prepared to sacrifice themselves on its altar (1952: 240). The rapid increase in suicide in nineteenth-century Europe by up to 400 per cent led Durkheim (1952: 36, 37) to call suicide 'the ransom-money of civilization' arising from 'the general contemporary maladjustment' of modern society. Through the suicidal actions of unconnected individuals, Durkheim (1952: 324) contends, modern society pays its bill only in instalments.

Organized into three books, *Suicide* proceeds methodically in the manner of a scientific demonstration. Durkheim appeals to the available statistical data in order to make reliable comparisons and draw conclusions. This systematic method of data collection, analysis and presentation helped to give the book its fame.

SOCIOLOGICAL DEFINITION

Because of the indefinite and ambiguous meaning of suicide, Durkheim starts with a precise definition. Suicide is a knowing, voluntary death:

> the term suicide is applied to all cases of death which resulting directly or indirectly from a positive or negative act of the victim himself, which he knows will produce this result. (Durkheim, 1952: 44).

It may be the result of positive action, such as jumping from an upper window, or of negative inaction, such as a hunger strike.

In order for Durkheim to prove that suicide is indeed sociological he is required to show that it is not a random occurrence affecting disparate individuals but that it evinces a stable pattern across society. Durkheim (1952: 51) counter-intuitively asserts that: 'Each society is predisposed to contribute a definite quota of voluntary deaths.' Sociology, not individualist psychology, is essential for understanding the social characteristics of suicide-prone communities.

ARGUMENT BY ELIMINATION

Durkheim eliminates non-sociological explanations of suicide. First, the common assumption that suicide is caused by mental illness, 'insane suicide' is excluded by Durkheim's definition because it is not the result of self-conscious motives. Moreover, the empirical relationship between insanity and suicide varies considerably: Scotland had a relatively high level of insanity but a very low rate of suicide while Saxony showed a low level of insanity but a high rate of suicide.

Second, Durkheim similarly dismisses the idea that suicide is closely related to alcoholism. Mental illness and suicide are, therefore, not even weakly correlated but only 'accidentally' related, if at all. Third, he summarily eliminates 'race' as creating a genetic predisposition to suicide. Indeed, 'race' itself is dismissed as an incoherent concept 'due to crossing in every direction, each of the existing varieties of our species comes from very different origins ... no one can say with accuracy where [races] begin and end' (Durkheim, 1952: 83). Fourth, cold, dark weather is often associated with dark moods and suicide. However, more suicides occur in the summer months and at temperate degrees of latitude (50–55 degrees), perhaps because this is when social life is most intensively public, especially in urban areas.

The final non-social cause attributed to suicide that Durkheim examines is 'imitation'. This is the popular idea that behaviour, especially deviant behaviour, is copied from the example of others, an idea associated with Durkheim's rival, Gabriel Tarde. Durkheim argues that mass suicides are often the result of a 'moral epidemic' borne of a common institutional environment, rather than a 'moral contagion' of copycat suicides by separate individuals responding to suicide reports in the newspaper. Durkheim's critique of imitation casts considerable doubt on the adequacy of contemporary explanations of deviant conduct as the result of media-driven copycat behaviour.

EGOISTIC SUICIDE

Having dispensed with rival accounts, Durkheim constructs his social types of suicide. These types vary with social integration and moral regulation. He first constructs 'egoistic suicide' which varies inversely with group integration. Unable to withstand the slightest shock, individual egoism becomes ready prey to suicide. As a response to social disintegration, modern individualism detaches the individual from the group, breaks the moral and customary ties that bind the individual to the collective, and throws the individual back on to their own self-sufficient resources, which have no other purpose than mere survival.

> If we agree to call this state egoism, in which the individual ego asserts itself to excess in the face of the social ego and at its expense, we may call egoistic the special type of suicide springing from excessive individualism. (Durkheim, 1952: 209)

Well-integrated social institutions moderate and temper egoistic individualism; the weakly integrated social institutions of modern society make 'personal troubles' a largely private affair.

In Europe Catholic countries show a much lower rate of suicide than Protestant ones. Protestants place a far greater emphasis on the rational interpretation of the Bible by individual conscience while Catholics adhere to the collective unity of faith as rendered by hierarchical church authorities. By enlarging individual judgement Protestant society is less compact and unified than Catholic or Jewish societies. More generally, as independent conscience and rational learning replace collective and customary prejudices, popular education becomes an index for suicide. Suicide is more common among more highly educated groups, especially men in the liberal professions and wealthier classes.

Conversely, marriage as an institution reduces suicide. Even more important than the 'conjugal group' of husband and wife is the 'family group' with children. Suicide is less likely for a widowed man with children than for a married man without children. Married women without children are even more likely to commit suicide than unmarried women. Large families function as small-scale, integrated societies. Even the unity found in great political upheavals seems to reduce suicide, though the reverse is usually assumed. Revolution or a state of war will generate internal unity and are therefore typically accompanied by a decrease in suicides.

In all these cases, suicide is inversely related to the degree of social integration and internal unity. For Durkheim (1952: 213) social life is 'the masterpiece of existence'. But as social life becomes privatized, resistance to suicide is weakened among individuals. Owing nothing to society, troubled individuals have no external obligation to preserve their own life; owing nothing to the individual, 'society' is indifferent about how individuals exercise their private rights and liberties, including what they decide to do with their one final possession, their own life.

ALTRUISTIC SUICIDE

If egoistic suicide relates to *weak* integration, what Durkheim calls 'altruistic suicide' is related to an *excessive* integration into social norms. It is *altruistic* because life is willingly surrendered to something exterior to the individual, the moral community. Durkheim refines the concept further as '*obligatory* altruistic suicide' where it is performed as a social duty. Some suicides are committed for the benefit of the social group as '*optional* altruistic suicide'. In some societies people will kill themselves for apparently trivial reasons, over some slight offence, disappointment, jealousy, or a real or imagined disrespect. A heroic, honourable suicide brings social esteem even though it is not explicitly commanded as a duty.

Socially valued habits of self-abnegation make it easier to renounce the value of life. An extreme version of this is '*acute* altruistic suicide' where the sheer ecstasy of self-destruction is socially esteemed. Fanatical faith in a 'beautiful perspective beyond this life' can only take hold in a 'lower society' where the individual really counts for nothing (Durkheim, 1952: 225). Durkheim gives examples of acute altruistic suicide in the mystical religions of India and Japan. Suicide is not a right but a duty in such societies; women kill themselves on their husband's death, old or sick men take their own lives, or servants kill themselves on their chief's death. In each case, the weight of social obligation demands self-destruction. Anything else is deemed dishonourable and a threat to social subordination.

A puzzling case of altruistic suicide occurs among soldiers. They are healthy and, most importantly, subject to soldierly camaraderie and military social integration. Yet their suicide rate is higher for their age cohort than for the population in general. Especially vulnerable is the soldier who most completely identifies with the altruistic military values of the army as a compact society and becomes wholly subsumed by its habits of mind and practical dispositions.

ANOMIC SUICIDE

Underlying anomic suicide is the human need for self-regulation in an 'organic equilibrium' between 'means' and 'needs'. Humans, unlike animals, have no fixed limit to their needs. Human needs readily surpass the means to fulfil them. When human goals lack regulation, this insatiable nature becomes dangerous. This condition Durkheim terms *anomie*. Insatiable desires become for Durkheim a 'torment', a 'bottomless abyss', a 'sign of morbidity'. Only the integrative force of moral regulation constrains anomic tendencies. Abrupt disturbances in the 'collective order' of society, demanding a sudden re-adjustment to a new situation, may trigger a rise in suicides.

In modern conditions where religion has ceased to function as an integrative mechanism of regulation 'economic materialism' is liberated from any moral restraint. People more easily surrender to 'the morbid desire for the infinite which everywhere accompanies anomie' (Durkheim, 1952: 271). Economic 'means' become the 'supreme end of individuals and societies alike'. Indeed, any appeal to a moral restraint of the seemingly limitless possibilities of the world market 'seems like a sort of sacrilege'.

Social transition, economic crisis, or technological transformation creates a 'morbid effervescence'. The integrative power of moral regulation is overthrown temporarily. In these exceptional conditions a free rein is given to passions, appetites and ambitions. Previous limits imposed by tradition lose their force precisely at the moment when they seem to be most needed.

One popular image is of bankers jumping from skyscraper windows during financial crises. Such a correlation is confirmed by Durkheim's analysis of suicide with nineteenth-century economic crises. But this is not due to the sudden poverty felt by rich speculators. Anomic suicides increase alongside growing affluence. On the other hand, the wretched lives of very poor peasants coincide with very low levels of suicide, as in nineteenth-century Ireland.

It is not only economic anomie that correlates with increases in the suicide rate. Durkheim also identifies 'domestic anomie' in suicides correlated to the rate of divorce. The matrimonial regulation of the late nineteenth century narrowed the horizon of sexual possibility to a single partner. Perpetual uncertainty makes unmarried life a deeply dissatisfied and anomic one. With divorce matrimonial regulation becomes 'a weakened simulacrum', less able to restrain (male) desire. Reflecting the moral categories of his own time, Durkheim (1952: 272) claimed that women's desires do not need to be channelled by marriage since they are naturally restrained by 'the needs of the organism'. Durkheim, the great theorist of social facts and moral regulation, here lapses into a pre-social account of women's immunity from 'conjugal anomie'.

FATALISTIC SUICIDE

A further form of suicide – 'fatalistic suicide' – is mentioned by Durkheim. It is introduced in a single footnote and is not elaborated or analysed elsewhere. It is fatalistic because suicide derives from severely oppressive discipline and the excessive moral and physical despotism experienced by childless married women, young husbands and slaves. Durkheim (1952: 276, n.25) simply dismisses fatalistic suicide without further ado: 'it has so little contemporary importance and examples are so hard to find aside from the cases just mentioned that it seems useless to dwell on it'.

Durkheim's account of fatalistic suicide seems to have been a bit of an afterthought. In fact, fatalism might account for female suicide in the context of excessive regulation within marriage. Indeed, the abuse of matrimonial and parental authority 'as a *cruel substitute* for all the submissiveness and dependency people in bourgeois society acquiesce in, willingly or unwillingly' is central to Marx's (1999: 54) little-known article on suicide.

Fatalistic suicide lends symmetry to Durkheim's system. Egoistic suicide (excessive individuality) and altruistic suicide (weak individuality) represent extremes of social *integration*; fatalistic suicide (excessive discipline) and anomic suicide (weak discipline) are the extreme ends of moral *regulation*.

CRITICAL DEVELOPMENTS

In his enthusiasm to show that his study of suicide might establish sociology as a systematic science Durkheim made a lasting impact. It also helped establish anomie as a central concept in sociology. However, many limitations have been identified in the overall approach as well as in the detailed findings. Durkheim too hastily dismissed 'non-sociological' suicide variables such as mental health by his restricted definition of suicide and his 'argument by elimination'. This approach has two defects (Lukes, 1992: 31–33): first, there may be a range of other explanations that Durkheim does not consider; and, second, 'extra-sociological' factors may not be wholly incompatible with sociological ones.

In appealing to the most general social facts no account is given of the specific circumstances or psychological motivations behind actual suicide cases, as Durkheim's follower Maurice Halbwachs recognized in his own study of suicide. Durkheim's reliance on the official statistics for suicide meant that biases in data collection compounded the biases in his data analysis. Suicide was recorded differently from country to country according to the local common-sense definition of the situation, although Durkheim seemed well aware of the inadequacies of suicide statistics (Thompson, 2002: 118).

Durkheim reduces every measurable effect (suicide) to a single cause (integration or regulation). It is not always clear that integration and regulation are distinct causes of suicide. Egoistic and anomic suicides may be the result of weak social integration and weak moral regulation respectively, but integration and regulation may be so closely related as different aspects of the same condition that it hardly makes sense to rigidly demarcate them. For Durkheim, society fails to prevent suicide; for Marx, capitalist society causes it (Plaut, 1999).

RELATED CONCEPTS

Anomie; Conscience Collective; Division of Labour in Society (Durkheim); Mechanical and Organic Solidarity; Normal and Pathological; Social Facts

FURTHER READING

Durkheim's book *Suicide* (1952) remains a highly rewarding study. Concise summaries are given in Thompson (2002), Jones (1986), Giddens (1978) and Parkin (1992). A more detailed examination can be found in *Durkheim's Suicide: A Century of Research and Debate*, edited by W.S.F. Pickering and Geoffrey Walford (2000).

suicide

In his major study *The Elementary Forms of Religious Life,* Durkheim (2001) wanted to understand how moral authority produces social solidarity by examining what he thought was its simplest or most elementary form: 'totemism'. A totem is 'a symbol, a material expression of something else' (2001: 154). On the totem can be inscribed as any emblem or blazon considered sacred, usually animals or plants. Totemism is the name given to the visible sacred object that social groups worship. It is the tangible expression of 'god' and, at the same time, the symbol of a particular society. It is a moral force given material form.

TOTEMISM AND SOCIETY

For Durkheim, totemism is the original form of all subsequent religious life and, by extension, collective life in general. Social life is only made possible by a vast organization of collective representations. The collective only becomes self-conscious of its own existence by fixing on some material object. Objects and society facilitate each other. The totem both expresses collective life and helps to create it (Durkheim, 2001: 175). The totem's 'real essence' is that it is only the material form taken by an immaterial substance or unseen energy of a permanent, anonymous and impersonal social force (2001: 140–41). Totemism outlives individuals and lends the social group a sense of eternal existence.

Totemism could not merely superimpose onto reality an unreal world of monstrous aberrations and 'inexplicable hallucinations'. The scared object – the totem – is merely a focal point for collective identity and social structure. Religious exaltation is real exaltation about the moral authority of society. Totems are misrecognized only to the extent that the symbol seems to be an autonomous force. In reality, the god of the clan is really the clan itself, 'but transfigured and imagined in the physical form of the plant or animal species that serve as totems' (2001: 154).

ABORIGINAL TOTEMISM

Against the prejudices of his day, Durkheim assumed that aboriginal tribes were capable of logical thought, coherent representations and the systematic classification of similarities and differences. The clan is envisaged as the simplest social group. At the level of the substratum,

key concepts in classical social theory

Durkheim (2001: 81) shows how various clans combine to form 'phratries' and tribes. He assumes that aboriginal clans stood 'as close as possible to the origins of evolution'. The totem is the simplest tangible image of the intangible solidarity of the simplest social unit.

A particular material object or animal becomes the clan totem and gives the clan its name. Totemic clan names establish kinship bonds between people even if they are separated by geographic space.

> It is its flag; it is the sign by which each clan distinguishes itself from others, the visible mark of its personality, a mark that embodies everything that belongs to the clan in any way: men, animals, and things. (2001: 154)

The objects that serve as totems tend to be general species of plant or animal. The practice of taking totemic names helps to organize the clan. Depending on the type of clan, the totem can be passed on to the child through the mother, or the father, or a mythic ancestor. In some tribes individuals have a personal totem. Elsewhere, sexual totems divide women and men into antagonistic societies.

The totem is not only a name; it is also an emblem, a badge of clan identity. As visual representations of familiar objects, animals and plants, emblems may have been more important than names. As society becomes more settled in fixed dwellings the totem is carved and painted onto doorposts, walls, canoes, weapons, tools and tombs, and even on bodily inscriptions. By imprinting a distinctive mark on the body, tattoos are the most direct means of communicating collective belonging. Masks, decorations, costumes and headdresses resemble or mimic the totem. In such ways, the clan celebrates itself by taking on the appearance of the totem.

SACRED EMBLEMS

The totem distinguishes the holy world from the profane world. Sacred objects, or *churingas*, are collected by the clan and used in ceremonies. *Churingas* are oval-shaped pieces of wood or polished stone engraved with a representation of the totem. The object is sanctified and differentiated from profane things purely by the engraved image of the totem. Indeed, respect for the emblematic image may exceed that of the profane animal represented.

> Since the profane role of plants and animals is usually to serve as food, the sacred character of the totemic plant or animal is acknowledged in the prohibition against eating it. (Durkheim, 2001: 101)

totemism

As individual parts each *churinga* represents the whole in the same way that individual flags are emblematic of the whole nation (Marvin and Ingle, 1999). Profane people – women and uninitiated young men – are kept at a distance from the *churinga*. The place where it is stored becomes a sanctuary from worldly troubles. The fate of individuals and the collective rests on the protection of the *churinga* from profane contamination.

Represented by a material sign rather than a literal likeness, meaning is objectified. In Australia the engraved images do not reproduce a life-like image of the totemic animal, as in American totemism, but take the more abstract form of geometric designs, curved lines, circles, spirals and dots. After all, the typical totemic animal or plant – lizard, caterpillar, rat, frog, turkey, peach tree and so on – cannot themselves produce ecstatic religious feelings.

TOTEMIC FLAGS

Durkheim describes the transfer of feelings aroused by the totem as a 'contagion'. The sign takes the place of the object, as when the flag functions as a totem and stands in for the entire nation in modern society:

> The sign is loved, feared and respected; the sign is the object of gratitude and sacrifice. The soldier who dies for his flag, dies for his country; but in his mind the flag comes first. It can even prompt action directly. The country will not be lost if a solitary flag remains in the hands of the enemy, and the soldier gets himself killed trying to recapture it. We forget that the flag is only a sign, that it has no intrinsic value but serves only to recall the reality it represents; we treat it as if it were that reality. (Durkheim, 2001: 165)

A collective belief in the totem (or flag) is constructed because society seems to have autonomy over and above individuals who must submit to its demands. In the name of collective values, all sorts of hardships and sacrifices are endured because of the genuine respect felt for society's image of itself.

At its root, totemism expresses a joyous confidence that the gods are with us rather than the fear and terror of an external power set against us. Jealous and vengeful gods appear relatively late in totemism. Individuals believe that the gods favour them, elevating their sense of self:

> Because he is in moral harmony with his contemporaries, he has more confidence, courage, and audacity – like the believer who thinks he feels the eyes of his god turned benevolently toward him. Thus our moral being is perpetually sustained. (2001: 159)

This moral conscience is repeated and reinforced through numerous individual instances of the totem (or flag), all the while obscuring its roots in society.

TOTEMIC THOUGHT

Out of totemism's dual nature – moral and material – developed the most diverse practices – law, morality, art, science, technology, industry. Totemic emblems and names classify disparate things on the assumption that they share a common essence. By overruling the profane world of sensory experience and placing it under the impersonal concept of the totem, totemism gave rise to science and philosophy. The material object itself may be relatively trivial but the ideas that surround it are not (Durkheim, 2001: 174).

CRITICAL DEVELOPMENTS

Perhaps the most famous development of the concept of totemism was offered by Sigmund Freud's *Totem and Taboo* (1913), published just one year after Durkheim's book. While the great German modernist Thomas Mann called *Totem and Taboo* 'a literary masterpiece' (in Freud, 1985: 47), many others have since criticized its arguments severely. Like Durkheim, Freud wished to excavate primordial collective representations in order to unearth their hidden meaning for the present. Freud stressed the sexual origins of totemism far beyond anything entertained by Durkheim.

Freud is also aware of conflict in tribal society, which Durkheim tends to submerge. For Freud totemic prohibitions represent a repressed unconscious fear of and ambivalence toward authority rather than moral solidarity. In Freud's (in)famous Oedipus Complex male children compete ambivalently for the affection of their mother alongside respect and admiration for the father figure. Durkheim and Freud construct primordial social and psychological patterns that are continually re-asserted in human history. In modernity, this results in anomie and the neurotic personality.

Durkheim and Freud's male-centred perspective has long been criticized by feminists. They projected their own European society back onto primordial myths. Totemism fell out of favour as a concept along with its evolutionary assumptions. Its methodological basis was challenged by Weber (1978: 434) and in the ethnographic record by anthropologists such as Claude Levi-Strauss, who saw it as a self-serving illusion (Jones, 2005). Totemism shows how a seemingly universal concept reflected the intellectual interests of a very specific social milieu and historical context.

RELATED CONCEPTS

Collective Effervescence; Collective Representations; Conscience Collective; Ideology; Mechanical and Organic Solidarity; Sacred and Profane; Social Facts

FURTHER READING

The discussion of totemism in Emile Durkheim's *The Elementary Forms of Religious Life* (2001) is often striking and vivid. In his book *The Secret of the Totem* (2005) Robert Alun Jones focuses critically on the concept of totemism. Carolyn Marvin and David W. Ingle in *Blood Sacrifice and the Nation* (1999) examine totemism in the pre-9/11 'civil religion' of American nationalism.

Value Freedom

Max Weber wrestled constantly with the problem of 'value-freedom'. This refers to how social science might control various types of bias and distortion that value-judgements introduce into the objective understanding of social action. Weber defined 'value-judgement' as 'referring to the "practical" evaluations of a phenomenon which is capable of being influenced by our actions as worthy of either condemnation or approval' (Runciman, 1978: 69). On the one hand, scientific analysis cannot logically validate value-judgements and, on the other hand, subjective value-judgements cannot ground science.

Weber supported a rigid separation of 'values' from 'facts'. Science deals with claims about the truth of empirical facts, not with the evaluation of normative ideals. Sociologists should restrict themselves to a logical explication of the facts. Ultimate values are not themselves facts. Rather 'the individual's fundamental value-judgement can be, not taken as a "fact", but made the object of a scientific critique' (1978: 79).

FACTS AND VALUES

Statements of fact are entirely appropriate to the 'sea of cool, dispassion-
ate analysis' of what 'is' or what is likely to follow from a certain course
of social action. Such statements are logically demonstrable, as in ideal-
type analytical constructions, or empirically observable data. Statements
of value, in contrast, deal subjectively with the desirable ends of what
'ought' to be the case arguments, often stirred by passions. There is no
single morally correct position say about 'justice' or 'equality' for the
social scientist to impartially discover. Ethical questions cannot be
resolved empirically. All that the logic of scientific analysis can do is to
set out the consequences of following different 'means' to achieve a predetermined 'end'.

Sociology's claim to be an objective interpretative science rests on
'value freedom' or 'value neutrality'. Weber's point was that while sociology depended on 'interpretative explanations' the purely empirical sciences should not enter into disputes about ethical preferences or
'ultimate values'. A sociology of art, for example, would not concern
itself with questions of aesthetic judgement but would restrict itself to
clarifying empirical matters of its material, social and psychological conditions. Even though the sociologist of art must have a capacity to understand artistic activity and also have a feeling for aesthetic judgement, this
in itself 'tells us nothing at all about the logical character of historical
work' (Runciman, 1978: 98).

Ethical values are closer to religious conviction than science. Empirical
sociology can offer guidance in three ways: means, side-effects and value
conflict:

> All that an empirical discipline with the means at its disposal can show is
> (i) the unavoidable means; (ii) the unavoidable side-effects; (iii) the result-
> ing conflict of several possible value-judgements with each other in their
> practical consequences. (Runciman, 1978: 85).

For Weber empirical science is concerned with how the game is
played, what its 'means' mean, rather than being oriented towards the
final result, the desired 'end'. In setting out means, side-effects and
value conflict, empirical sociology merely charts alternative courses of
action but refuses to make a choice between them. Sociology should
strive to understand value-judgements and what they really mean without approving or rejecting them. Awareness of the meaning of ultimate
values, their truth content, is a fundamental 'presupposition' of empirical
sociology.

VALUE RELEVANCE

Weber castigated social scientists who adopted value judgements that corresponded to the dominant mores of the times, such as an uncritical 'loyalty to the state' at a time when the state censored free discussion in German universities. Yet this did not mean that there was no relationship at all between values and facts. As Weber (1949: 60) put it, 'An attitude of moral indifference has no connection with scientific "objectivity".' Social science must always have what Weber called 'value relevance'. By this he meant that the 'ultimate values' of a social scientist will guide their choice of research problem and the methods used to investigate it:

> 'value-relevance' refers merely to the philosophical interpretation of that specifically scientific interest which governs the selection and formulation of the object of an empirical enquiry. (Runciman, 1978: 87)

Indeed, Weber supported the idea of employing anarchists as legal scholars precisely because their 'value relevance' led them to question underlying assumptions about the foundation of the state and so help objective knowledge to develop further. As Weber (Runciman, 1978: 75) put it, 'the most radical doubt is the father of knowledge'.

Social scientists need to clarify their own values. Weber accepts that social scientists will dispute his strictures on the fact-value distinction. In such cases, it is incumbent on sociologists to make their own values explicit, especially where they are moving from scientific statements of fact and logic to introducing value-laden assumptions as part of their explanation. In presenting his 1913 paper 'Value-judgements in Social Science' (Runciman, 1978) for the Association for Social Policy, Weber lost the debate and stormed out of the meeting. So much for cool, objective rationality!

Weber outlined exactly how he thought the logical investigation of value-judgements should proceed. First, analysis begins with the particular value judgement and examines its possible meanings. This produces internally coherent value-axioms. Second, necessary 'consequences' are deduced logically from the value-axioms. Then, third, consequences are interpreted empirically in terms of means and side-effects. This allows values to be examined in practice and revised if they conflict radically with empirical reality. Such analysis, Weber argued, 'bears lasting fruit in empirical work, in that it supplies basic questions for investigation' (Runciman, 1978: 87).

SCIENCE AS A VOCATION

Weber felt that there was little place in sociology for emotive language, illogical arguments or political slogans. He rejected a populist approach to teaching, refusing to act 'the prophet' or 'the demagogue' or elicit student sympathy through personal anecdotes and 'confessions' in the lecture hall. Social scientists need to banish personal value judgements and political commitments from their professional practice. In his lecture 'Science as a Vocation' Weber argued:

> One can only demand of the teacher that he have the intellectual integrity to see that it is one thing to state facts, to determine mathematical or logical relations or the internal structure of cultural values, while it is another thing to answer questions of the *value* of culture and its individual contents and the question of how one should act in the cultural community and in political associations ... If he asks further why he should not deal with both types of problems in the lecture-room, the answer is: because the prophet and the demagogue do not belong on the academic platform. (1946: 146)

When science becomes a 'vocation' scientific values are adopted with passion even though these values cannot be scientifically validated. Its intrinsic value must either be accepted or rejected but cannot be logically deduced. But he qualifies this endorsement of science as an 'absolute value' with a hatred of 'intellectualism as the worst devil'. Weber urged that only through the deepest immersion in scientific values can 'the devil' finally be overcome:

> It means that if one wishes to settle with this devil, one must not take flight before him as so many like to do nowadays. First of all, one has to see the devil's ways to the end in order to realize his power and his limitations. (1946: 152)

Weber's rejects any 'naïve optimism' that science will lead to happiness and the good life. In fact Weber recognized that science led to increasing rationalization, abstract intellectualism and 'the disenchantment of the world'. In these conditions the only choice that can be made is either to affirm or reject the value of science.

PUBLIC SOCIOLOGY

Weber never advocated a politically or morally disengaged form of sociology. He participated fully in the turbulent public intellectual and political life of his society. He was a committed German nationalist and described himself as 'a class conscious bourgeois'. But each activity must take place in its own appropriate arena. Political matters of state or cultural policy may be debated openly in the press, in meetings and in essays. Scientific matters of fact must be pursued methodically within a community of scholars. Indeed, while it is in the nature of political debate to suppress facts that are 'inconvenient', science does the exact opposite and seeks out 'inconvenient facts' as a test of objective knowledge.

Weber calls for self-restraint on the part of the sociologist in the public arena. They must expect to receive no privileged platform based on their background of technical expertise in knowledge production. The empirical sciences can only advise politicians that there are, first, certain conceivable positions to be taken on any practical problem and, second, set out the facts that need to be taken into account in choosing between 'ultimate values'. Weber gives the example of science's limited role in understanding the consequences of a General Strike for militant syndicalists:

> Once the syndicalist view has been reduced in this way to as rational and consistent a form as possible, and once the empirical conditions of its realization, its chances of success and empirically predictable practical consequences have been stated, the task of value-free science, at any rate in relation to it, is complete. (Runciman, 1978: 90)

Syndicalists will pursue the logic of their own militant value structure and disregard the 'empirically predictable consequences' that a General Strike will merely give their enemies the opportunity to crush them violently.

CRITICAL DEVELOPMENTS

As many of Weber's critics have noted it is difficult, if not impossible, to leave values outside the door when we enter the hallowed room of facts. Weber (Runciman, 1978: 76) admitted to 'as much as anyone else, continually offending' against his own strictures. Even where values are explicitly acknowledged they might still distort social knowledge in unanticipated ways. An example of this is the way that gender-specific assumptions informed certain strains of otherwise radical theory until they were challenged by feminist sociologists in the 1970s.

Marxist critics like Kieran Allen (2004) argue that Weber's insistence on abstaining from any critique of dominant values was very convenient for ruling elites. Weber himself recognized that appeals to 'value-freedom' are often a 'pose' adopted by powerful interest groups. Anderson (1992) detects a certain incoherence in Weber's splitting of the 'intoxicating' passions behind 'value relevance' from the iron discipline needed for 'value free' social science, which led Weber to support his own national state in the carnage of the First World War.

Radical critics of value neutrality argue that it could become an excuse for professional timidity and anodyne commentary. Alvin Gouldner (1973) called this 'the Minotaur' in sociology, a half-man, half-beast dualism of uncritical professional narrowness combined with a dependency relationship on powerful interests. This was far from Weber's own sense of objective, value-free social science:

> Weber's own view of the relation between values and social science, and some current today are scarcely identical. If Weber insisted on the need to maintain scientific objectivity, he also warned that it was altogether different from moral indifference. (Gouldner, 1973: 6)

RELATED CONCEPTS

Historical Materialism; Ideal-Types; Ideology; Positivism; Social Action; Social Facts; *Verstehen*

FURTHER READING

Weber's lecture 'Value-judgements in social science' is translated in Runciman (1978). 'Science as a vocation' can be found in the Gerth and Mills' (1946) collection. For overviews of the debate about value freedom see Hans Henrik Brun's *Science, Values and Politics in Max Weber's Methodology* (2007) and Sven Eliaeson's *Max Weber's Methodologies: Interpretation and Critique* (2002).

Verstehen

Verstehen is usually translated from German to mean 'interpretive understanding'. In many ways, *verstehen* can be seen as an alternative to the positivist approach to the scientific study of fixed, causal laws (Outhwaite, 1975). Max Weber's interpretative sociology insisted that social science needed to be able to account for what is truly distinctive about human societies: purposeful, meaningful action by rational individuals. This goal forms part of the German philosophical tradition known as 'hermeneutics'. While positivism attempts to 'explain' objective nature *verstehen* 'understands' the subjective meanings of culture.

UNDERSTANDING

Understanding is of two kinds: observational and explanatory. First, direct observation of a given action allows the subjective meaning that it holds for actors to be understood rationally by a third party. A rational understanding of ideas, for instance, emerges whenever any numerate interpreter sees the proposition '2 × 2 = 4'. A rational understanding of emotions like anger is conveyed directly by contorted facial expressions or agitated movements. A rational understanding of action is explicable in observing a door opening, wood being cut or an animal being hunted, or any other overt action.

Second, and crucially, beyond immediate observation science aims for what Weber calls 'explanatory understanding'. This requires that an action be placed within a wider context of meaning explicable in terms of an individual's motivation. Motives can be rational or irrational, planned or 'spontaneous', intellectual or emotional. Where direct observation asks the question *what* is going on, explanatory understanding asks the question *why*. Why does the actor write 2 × 2 = 4 at this particular time and place? It makes a difference if the motive is a scientific calculation or teaching multiplication to a classroom of children. Or, why is wood being chopped: for a wage, as part of a home improvement or simply to let off steam? Why is an animal being hunted: for food, for pestilence control, or as part of an aristocratic ritual?

MEANING AND CONTEXT

An explanatory interpretation of meaning has three possibilities.

1 The 'actually intended meaning for concrete individual action'.
2 A statistically 'average intended meaning' of mass sociological phenomena.
3 The 'appropriate' meaning attributed by an ideal-type of social action.

Weber views the ideal attribution of meaning as the strongest form of explanatory understanding. Ideal-type social action tells an 'as if' story of strict rationality that is unlikely to be found in reality. What it gains in 'clarity and certainty' for science it loses as a 'causally valid interpretation'. As such, it remains limited to a 'peculiarly plausible hypothesis'. Hypothetical interpretation can only be verified by comparing large numbers of historical or contemporary examples.

Interpretative sociology is aware of the 'motivational context' that informs intended action. Analysis usually begins from the 'outcomes' of social action. In the absence of comparative evidence, however, sociologists adopt the 'dangerous and uncertain procedure' of logically deducing a 'chain of motivation' as part of an 'imaginary experiment' (Weber, 1978: 10). Logical deductions from ideal concepts must face the facts for empirical verification, just as the facts of experience need to be organized by conceptual clarification.

Verstehen does not seek to explain every type of behaviour. It is confined as a methodological tool by Weber to the development and clarification of formal concepts to account for, rather than a substantive analysis of, the social action of individuals.

> In all cases, rational or irrational, sociological analysis abstracts from reality and at the same time helps us to understand it, in that it shows with what degree of approximation a concrete historical phenomenon can be subsumed under one or more of the concepts. (1978: 20)

Verstehen is sometimes erroneously dismissed as demanding the impossible task of determining the inner motivations of individuals. Interpretation cannot include extra-rational action, for example 'mystical' experiences or insanity. *Verstehen* is not concerned with recreating or imagining the exact psychological state of historical actors' minds at any moment but only the specifically *social* context of meaningful action. As Gerth and Mills (1946: 55) put it, 'Not Julius Caesar, but Caesarism; not Calvin, but Calvinism is Weber's concern'.

ADEQUACY OF MEANING AND CAUSES

Another common fallacy is that Weber succumbed to a subjective, intuitive kind of interpretive sociology. On the contrary, Weber wanted to combine interpretative understanding and causal explanation. Sociological generalization distinguishes '*adequacy of meaning*' from '*causal adequacy*'. 'Adequacy of meaning' interprets a motive from 'a [typical] complex of subjective meanings which seems to the actor himself or to the observer as adequate ground for the conduct in question' (Weber, 1978: 12). This is distinguished from 'causal adequacy' which predicts with numerical accuracy the probability of an action from an already established generalization. If statistical probability has been determined precisely but lacks 'adequacy of meaning', the data remain sociologically empty and 'incomprehensible'. Conversely, in the absence of causal adequacy it is impossible to estimate accurately the probability that action will take its regular course.

Numerous attempts were made to assimilate *verstehen* into sociological theory (Outhwaite, 1975). Clarification of Weber's basic concept of *verstehen* was, for instance, a central concern of Alfred Schütz's (1970) phenomenology of the social world. *Verstehen* has also been subject to severe criticism and dispute. Some of the difficulties reflect ambiguities in Weber's usage of the term, as well as translation problems. Although Weber emphasized the context-dependent, culturally intended sense of an action rather than imputing inner motives to psychological individuals, it isn't always clear that he maintains the distinction between 'intention', 'motive', 'purpose' and 'sense'.

Neither is the distinction between *verstehen* as observation and *verstehen* as explanation particularly coherent (Parkin, 2002: 22–6). The idea of context-free observation makes little sense. Understanding always depends on some wider context within which meaning is made comprehensible: 'what' always requires 'why'. Second, if interpretation depends on cultural familiarity and assumptions about rational conduct, then the problem of cultural relativism would make it well nigh impossible to understand radically different cultures other than those immersed in secular Western 'rationalism'. Third, it is simply impossible to demonstrate once and for all that the claimed scientific interpretation of individual motive and meaning really is the 'correct' one. Fourth, actors themselves may be mistaken about their own motives because the context includes misleading or false ideas.

Undoubtedly, grave difficulties confront the concept of *verstehen*. However, a more generous reading would recognize that Weber talks not about empirical reality as such but rather ideal-types and 'marginal' or 'borderline' cases. *Verstehen* is a point of departure for analysis, not its final result. Weber saw interpretation as an iterative process or a 'heuristic', working back and forward between an 'adequacy of meaning' of conceptual clarification and 'causal adequacy' as demonstrated by empirical data. Neither does *verstehen* require empathy at an individual level. As Weber (1978: 5) memorably put it, 'one need not have been Caesar to understand Caesar'.

RELATED CONCEPTS

Ideal-Types; Positivism; Rationality and Rationalization; Social Action; Social Facts; Social Forms and Sociation; Value Freedom

FURTHER READING

Weber discusses *verstehen* at the start of *Economy and Society* (1978), reproduced in Sam Whimster's reader *The Essential Weber* (2004). Frank Parkin's *Max Weber* (2002) gives a succinct summary of the concept. Long overdue to be back in print, William Outhwaite's *Understanding Social Life* (1975) remains an excellent accessible introduction to *verstehen*.

verstehen

bibliography

Abercrombie, N., Hill, S. and Turner, B.S. (1980) *The Dominant Ideology Thesis*. London: Allen & Unwin.

Abrams, P. (1968) *The Origins of British Sociology, 1834–1914*. Chicago, IL: Chicago University Press.

Adorno, T.W. (1976) *The Positivist Dispute in Germany*. London: Heinemann.

Adorno, T.W. (2000) *Introduction to Sociology*. Stanford, CA: Stanford University Press.

Aglietta, M. (1979) *A Theory of Capitalist Regulation: The US Experience*. London: Verso.

Allen, K. (2004) *Max Weber: A Critical Introduction*. London: Pluto Press.

Allen, N.J. (2000) *Categories and Classifications: Maussian Reflections on the Social*. New York and Oxford: Berghahn.

Althusser, L. (2008) *On Ideology*. London: Verso (new edition).

Andersen, H. and Kaspersen, L.B. (eds) (2000) *Classical and Modern Social Theory*. Oxford: Blackwell.

Anderson, P. (1992) 'Max Weber and Ernest Gellner: Science, politics, enchantment', *A Zone of Engagement*. London: Verso.

Andrews, H.F. (1993) 'Durkheim and social morphology', in S.P. Turner (ed.), *Emile Durkheim: Sociologist and Moralist*. London: Routledge. pp. 111–135.

Applerouth, S. and Edles, L.D. (2009) *Sociological Theory in the Classical Era*. Thousand Oaks, CA: Pine Forge Press.

Arrighi, G. (2007) *Adam Smith in Beijing: Lineages of the Twenty-First Century*. London: Verso.

Arthur, C. (1992) *Marx's Capital: A Student's Edition*. London: Lawrence & Wishart.

Axelos, K. (1976) *Alienation, Praxis, and Technē in the Thought of Karl Marx*. Austin, TX: University of Texas Press.

Baali, F. (1988) *Society, State, and Urbanism: Ibn Khaldun's Sociological Thought*. New York: State University of New York Press.

Bachelard, G. (1994) *The Poetics of Space*. Boston, MA: Beacon Press.

Barker, C. (1999) 'Empowerment and Resistance: "Collective effervescence" and other accounts', in Bagguley, P. and Hearn, J. (eds), *Transforming Politics: Power and Resistance*. London: Macmillan. pp. 11–31.

Bauman, Z. (1989) *Modernity and the Holocaust*. Cambridge Polity Press.

Beamish, R. (1992) *Marx, Method and the Division of Labor*. Urbana and Chicago, IL: University of Illinois Press.

Bendix, R. (1992) *Max Weber: An Intellectual Portrait*, Berkeley, CA: University of California Press.

Benjamin, W. (1940) 'On the concept of history', in *Walter Benjamin: Selected Writings, Volume 4, 1938–1940*. Cambridge, MA: The Belknap Press of Harvard University Press. pp. 389–400.

Berman, M. (1983) *All That is Solid Melts Into Air: The Experience of Modernity*. London: Verso.

Billig, M. (1991) *Ideology and Opinions: Studies in Rhetorical Psychology*. London: Sage.

Blumenberg, W. (1998) *Karl Marx: An Illustrated History*. London: Verso.

Bogardus, E. (1959) *Social Distance*. Yellow Springs, OH: Antioch Press.

Bourdieu, P. (1984) *Distinction: A Social Critique of the Judgement of Taste*. London: Routledge.

Bourdieu, P., Chamboredon, J-C., Passeron, J-C., and Krais, B. (1991) *The Craft of Sociology: Epistemological Preliminaries*. Berlin: Walter de Gruyter.

Bratton, J., Denham, D. and Deutschmann, L. (2009) *Capitalism and Classical Social Theory*. Toronto: University of Toronto Press.

Braverman, H. (1974) *Labor and Monopoly Capitalism: The Degradation of Work in the Twentieth Century*. New York: Monthly Review Press.

Brenner, R. (1977) 'The origins of capitalist development: A critique of neo-Smithian Marxism', *New Left Review*, 104: 25–92.

Brewer, J.D. (1989) 'Conjectural history, sociology and social change in eighteenth-century Scotland: Adam Ferguson and the division of labour', in D. McCrone, S. Kendrick and P. Straw (eds), *The Making of Scotland: Nation, Culture and Social Change*. Edinburgh: Edinburgh University Press/British Sociological Association, pp. 13–30.

Brewer, J.D. (2007) 'Putting Adam Ferguson in his place', *British Journal of Sociology*, 58 (1): 105–122.

Brubaker, R. (1984) *The Limits of Rationality: An Essay on the Social and Moral Thought of Max Weber*. London: George Allen & Unwin.

Brun, H.H. (2007) *Science, Values and Politics in Max Weber's Methodology*. Aldershot: Ashgate.

Buchan, J. (1998) *Frozen Desire: An Inquiry into the Meaning of Money*. London: Picador.

Buchan, J. (2006) *Adam Smith and the Pursuit of Perfect Liberty*. London: Profile Books.

Bukharin, N. (1921) *Historical Materialism: A System of Sociology*. Ann Arbor, MI: University of Michigan Press (1969).

Cahnman, W.J. (1973) *Ferdinand Tönnies: A New Evaluation*. Leiden: E.J. Brill.

Calhoun, C., Gertis, J., Moody, J., Pfaff, S. and Virk, I. (eds) (2007) *Classical Sociological Theory*. Malden, MA: Blackwell (second edition).

Callinicos, A. (1989) *Against Postmodernism: A Marxist Critique*. Cambridge: Polity Press.

Callinicos, A. (2004) *Making History: Agency, Structure and Change in Social Theory*. Lieden: Brill.

Callinicos, A. (2007) *Social Theory: A Historical Introduction*. Cambridge: Polity Press (second edition).

Carter, M. (2003) *Fashion Classics from Carlyle to Barthes*. Oxford: Berg.

Carver, T. (2003) *Engels: A Very Short Introduction*. Oxford: Oxford University Press.

Chalcraft, D. and Harrington, A. (2001) *The Protestant Ethic Debate: Max Weber's Replies to His Critics, 1907–1910*. Liverpool: Liverpool University Press.

Childe, V.G. (1964) *What Happened in History*. Harmondsworth: Penguin.

Cladis, M.S. (2001) 'Introduction', Emile Durkheim, *The Elementary Forms of Religious Life*. Oxford: Oxford University Press.

Comte, A. (1998) *Auguste Comte and Positivism: The Essential Writings*. G. Lenzer, (ed.), New Brunswick, NJ: Transaction.

Corning, P.A. (1982) 'Durkheim and Spencer', *British Journal of Sociology*, 33 (3): 359–382.

Craib, I. (1997) *Classical Social Theory: An Introduction to the Thought of Marx, Weber, Durkheim and Simmel*, Oxford: Oxford University Press.

Crompton, R. (2008) *Class and Stratification*. Cambridge: Polity Press (third edition).

Davis, M. (2006) *Planet of Slums*. London: Verso.

Dobb, M. (1946) *Studies in the Development of Capitalism*. New York: International Publishers (1963).

Du Gay, P. (2000) *In Praise of Bureaucracy: Weber, Organization, Ethics*. London: Sage.

Durkheim, E. (1895) '*The Rules of Sociological Method*', in Lukes (1982). pp. 31-163.

Durkheim, E. (1897) 'Marxism and sociology: The materialist conception of history', in Lukes (1982). pp. 167–74.

Durkheim, E. (1899) 'Social morphology', in Lukes (1982). pp. 241–42.

Durkheim, E. (1903) 'Sociology and the Social Sciences', in Lukes (1982). pp. 175–208.

Durkheim, E. (1908) 'The method of sociology', in Lukes (1982). pp. 245–47.

Durkheim, E. (1909) 'Sociology and the social sciences', in K. Thompson (ed.), (2004) *Readings From Emile Durkheim*. London: Routledge. pp. 11–17.

Durkheim, E. (1933[1893]) *The Division of Labour in Society*. New York: Free Press (1964).

Durkheim, E. (1952[1897]) *Suicide: A Study in Sociology*. London: Routledge & Kegan Paul (1970).

Durkheim, E. (1974) 'Individual and collective representations', *Sociology and Philosophy*. New York: Free Press. pp. 1–34.

Durkheim, E. (1978) 'Review of Ferdinand Tönnies *Gemeinschaft und Gesellschaft*', in M. Traugott (ed.), *Emile Durkheim on Institutional Analysis*. Chicago, IL: University of Chicago Press. pp. 115–22.

Durkheim, E. (1983) *Pragmatism and Sociology*. Cambridge: Cambridge University Press.

Durkheim, E. (2001[1912]) *The Elementary Forms of Religious Life*. Oxford: Oxford University Press.

Durkheim, E. and Fauconnet, E. (1903) 'Sociology and the social sciences', in Lukes (1982). pp. 175–208.

Durkheim, E. and Mauss, M. (1963) *Primitive Classification*. Chicago, IL: University of Chicago Press.

Eagleton, T. (2007) *Ideology: An Introduction*. London: Verso.

Eldridge, J.E.T. (ed.), (1971) *Max Weber: The Interpretation of Social Reality*. London: Michael Joseph.

Eliaeson, S. (2002) *Max Weber's Methodologies: Interpretation and Critique*. Cambridge: Polity Press.

Elster, J. (1985) *Making Sense of Marx*. Cambridge: Cambridge University Press.

Emirbayer, M. (1996) 'Useful Durkheim', *Sociological Theory*, 14 (2): 109–130.

Emirbayer, M. (ed.), (2003) *Émile Durkheim: Sociologist of Modernity*. Oxford: Blackwell.

Engels, F. (1844) *The Condition of the Working Class in England*. London: Penguin (1987).

key concepts in
classical social theory

Engels, F. (1884) 'Origins of the family, private property and the state', in Tucker (1978). pp. 734–59.

Engels, F. (1890) 'To Joseph Bloch', in Tucker (1978). pp. 760–65.

Engels, F. (1893) 'Letter to Franz Mehring, 14 July 1893', in Tucker (1978). pp. 765–77.

Evans-Pritchard, E.E. (1965) *Theories of Primitive Religion*. Oxford: Clarendon.

Ferguson, A. (1980) *An Essay on the History of Civil Society*. New Brunswick, NJ: Transaction.

Fine, B. (2002) *The World of Consumption: The Material and Cultural Revisited*. London Routledge.

Fine, R. (1997) 'Civil society theory, enlightenment and critique', *Democratization*, 4 (1): 7–28.

Finley, M.I. (1983) 'The ancient city: From Fustel de Coulanges to Max Weber and beyond', *Economy and Society in Ancient Greece*. Harmondsworth: Penguin. pp. 3–23.

Fish, J.S. (2005) *Defending the Durkheimian Tradition: Religion, Emotion and Morality*. Aldershot: Ashgate.

Foucault, M. (2008) *The Birth of Biopolitics: Lectures at the College de France, 1978–79*. Basingstoke: Palgrave Macmillan.

Freud, S. (1985[1913]) 'Totem and Taboo (1913)', in *The Pelican Freud Library, Volume 13: The Origins of Religion*. Harmondsworth: Penguin. pp. 43–224.

Frisby, D. (1985) *Fragments of Modernity: Theories of Modernity in the Work of Simmel, Kracauer, and Benjamin*. Cambridge: Polity Press.

Frisby, D. (1992a) *Sociological Impressionism: A Reassessment of Georg Simmel's Social Theory*. London and New York: Routledge (second edition).

Frisby, D. (1992b) *Simmel and Since: Essays on Georg Simmel's Social Theory*. London and New York: Routledge.

Frisby, D. (2001) *Cityscapes of Modernity: Critical Explorations*. Cambridge: Polity Press.

Frisby, D. (2002) *George Simmel*. London and New York: Routledge (revised edition).

Frisby, D. and Sayer, D. (1986) *Society*. Chichester and London: Ellis Horwood and Tavistock.

Gane, M. (1988) *On Durkheim's 'Rules of Sociological Method'*. London: Routledge.

Gane, M. (ed.) (1992) *The Radical Sociology of Durkheim and Mauss*. London: Routledge.

Gerth, H.H. and Wright Mills, C. (eds) (1946) *From Max Weber: Essays in Sociology*. New York: Oxford University Press.

Giddens, A. (1971) *Capitalism and Modern Social Theory: An Analysis of the Writings of Marx, Durkheim and Weber*. Cambridge: Cambridge University Press.

Giddens, A. (1972) *Emile Durkheim: Selected Writings*. Cambridge: Cambridge University Press.

Giddens, A. (1978) *Durkheim*. Glasgow: Fontana.

Gouldner, A.W. (1973) 'Anti-Minotaur: The myth of value-free sociology', *For Sociology: Renewal and Critique in Sociology Today*. New York: Basic Books. pp. 3–26.

Gramsci, A. (1971) *Selections From The Prison Notebooks of Antonio Gramsci*. London: Lawrence and Wishart.

Gubby, J (1997) 'A Marxist critique of Weberian class analyses', *Sociology*, 31 (1): 73–89.

Habermas, J. (1984) *The Theory of Communicative Action, Volume One: Reason and the Rationalization of Society*. Cambridge: Polity Press.

Habermas, J. (1987) *The Theory of Communicative Action, Volume Two: The Critique of Functionalist Reason*. Cambridge: Polity Press.

Hagens, T.G. (2006) '*Conscience collective* or false consciousness? Adorno's critique of Durkheim's sociology of morals', *Journal of Classical Sociology*, 6 (2): 215–237.

Halbwachs, M. (1960) *Population and Society: Introduction to Social Morphology*. New York: Free Press.

Halbwachs, M. (1992) *On Collective Memory*. Chicago, IL: University of Chicago Press.

Halfpenny, P. (2001) Positivism in the twentieth century', in G. Ritzer and B. Smart (eds), *The Handbook of Social Theory*. London: Sage. pp. 371–85.

Hanley, R.P. (2009) 'Social science and human flourishing: The Scottish enlightenment and today', *Journal of Scottish Philosophy*, 7: 29–46.

Hardt, M. and Negri, A. (2000) *Empire*. Cambridge, MA: Harvard University Press.

Harman, C. (2008) *A People's History of the World*. London: Verso.

Harman, C. (2009) *Zombie Capitalism: Global Crisis and the Relevance of Marx*. London: Bookmarks.

Harvey, D. (2005) *A Brief History of Neoliberalism*. Oxford: Oxford University Press.

Harvey, D. (2006) *The Limits to Capital*. London: Verso (new edition).

Hawkins, M. (2004) 'Why begin with Aristotle? Durkheim on solidarity and social morphology', *Durkheimian Studies*, 10: 21–37.

Heilbron, J. (1995) *The Rise of Social Theory*. Cambridge: Polity Press.

Herberle, R. (1948) 'The sociology of Georg Simmel: The forms of social interaction', in H.E. Barnes (ed.), *An Introduction to the History of Sociology*. Chicago, IL: University of Chicago Press. pp. 269–93.

Hill, L. (2006) *The Passionate Society: The Social, Political and Moral Thought of Adam Ferguson*. Dordrecht: Springer.

Hill, L. (2008) 'Adam Smith, Adam Ferguson and Karl Marx on the division of labour', *Journal of Classical Sociology*, 7 (3): 339–366.

Hilton, R. (ed.) (1978) *The Transition From Feudalism to Capitalism*. London: Verso.

Hirst, P.Q. (1973) 'Morphology and pathology: Biological analogies and metaphors in Durkheim's *The Rules of Sociological Method*', *Economy and Society*, 2 (1): 1–34.

Hirst, P.Q. (1975) *Durkheim, Bernard and Epistemology*. London: Routledge & Kegan Paul.

Hobsbawm, E. and Ranger, T. (eds) (1983) *The Invention of Tradition*. Cambridge: Cambridge University Press.

Holmwood, J. (1996) *Founding Sociology: Talcott Parsons and the Idea of General Theory*. London: Longman.

Hughes, J., Martin, P. and Sharrock, W.W. (1995) *Understanding Classical Sociology: Marx, Weber, Durkheim*. London: Sage.

Hunt, T. (2009) *The Frock-Coated Communist: The Revolutionary Life of Friedrich Engels*. London: Allen Lane.

Jakubowski, F. (1990) *Ideology and Superstructure in Historical Materialism*. London: Pluto Press.

Jaworski, G.D. (1994) 'Simmel and the *Année*', in D. Frisby (ed.), *Georg Simmel: Critical Assessments, Volume 1.* London: Routledge. pp. 199–208.

Jaworski, G.D. (1997) *Georg Simmel and the American Prospect*, Albany, NY: State University of New York.

Jones, R.A. (1986) *Emile Durkheim: An Introduction to Four Major Works.* Beverly Hills, CA: Sage.

Jones, R.A. (2005) *The Secret of the Totem: Religion and Society from McLennan to Freud.* New York: Columbia University Press.

Karady, V. (1981) 'The prehistory of present-day French sociology (1917–1957)', in C.C. Lemert (ed.), *French Sociology: Rupture and Renewal Since 1968.* New York: Columbia University Press. pp. 33–47.

Kasler, D. (1988) *Max Weber: An Introduction to His Life and Work.* Cambridge: Polity Press.

Kolakowski, L. (1972) *Positivist Philosophy: From Hume to the Vienna Circle.* Harmondsworth: Penguin.

Kracauer, S. (1995) 'Georg Simmel', in T.Y. Levin (ed.), *The Mass Ornament: Weimar Essays.* Cambridge, MA: Harvard University Press. pp. 225–257.

Leck, R.M. (2000) *Georg Simmel and Avant-Garde Sociology: The Birth of Modernity, 1880–1920.* New York: Humanity Books.

Lefebvre, H. (1972) *The Sociology of Marx.* Harmondsworth: Penguin.

Lefebvre, H. (1991) *The Production of Space.* Oxford: Blackwell.

Lefebvre, H. (2009) *Dialectical Materialism.* Minneapolis, MN: University of Minnesota Press.

Lenoir, R. (2001) 'From Maurice Halbwachs to Pierre Bourdieu: Social nature or naturalized social construction', *International Journal of Contemporary Sociology*, 38 (1): 41–53.

Levine, D.N. (1971) 'Introduction', in D.N. Levine (ed.), *Georg Simmel: On Individuality and Social Forms, Selected Writings.* Chicago, IL and London: University of Chicago Press. pp. ix–lxv.

Levine, D.N. (1985) *The Flight From Ambiguity: Essays in Social and Cultural Theory.* Chicago, IL and London: University of Chicago Press.

Levine, D.N. (1997) 'Simmel reappraised: Old images, new scholarship', in C. Camic (ed.), *Reclaiming the Sociological Classics: The State of the Scholarship*, Malden, MA: Blackwell. pp. 173–207.

Levine, D.N. (2005) 'The continuing challenge of Max Weber's theory of rational action', in C. Camic, P.S. Gorski and D.M. Trubek (eds), *Max Weber's Economy and Society: A Critical Companion.* Stanford, CA: Stanford University Press. pp. 101–25.

Levine, D.N., Carter, E.B. and Miller Gorman, E. (1994) 'Simmel's influence on American sociology', in D. Frisby (ed.), *Georg Simmel: Critical Assessments, Volume III.* London: Routledge. pp. 227–272.

Limoges, C. (1994) 'Milne-Edwards, Darwin, Durkheim and the division of labour: A case study in reciprocal conceptual exchanges between the social and the natural sciences', *Boston Studies in the Philosophy of Science*, 150: 317–343.

Lukacs, G. (1923) *History and Class Consciousness: Studies in Marxist Dialectics.* London: Merlin (1971).

Lukacs, G. (1991) 'Georg Simmel', *Theory, Culture & Society*, 8: 145–150.

Lukes, S. (ed.), (1982) *Emile Durkheim: The Rules of Sociological Method, and Selected Texts on Sociology and its Method*. Houndsmills: Macmillan.

Lukes, S. (1992) *Emile Durkheim: His Life and Work: A Historical and Critical Study*. London: Penguin.

Luxemburg, R. (1913[2003]) *The Accumulation of Capital*. London: Routledge.

MacIntyre, A. (1986) 'Positivism, sociology and practical reasoning: Notes on Durkheim's *Suicide*', in A. Donagan, A.N. Perovich and M.V. Wedin (eds), *Human Nature and Natural Knowledge: Essays Presented to Marjorie Grene on the Occasion of her Seventy-fifth Birthday*. Dordrecht: Reidel. pp. 87–104.

MacRae, D.G. (1969) 'Adam Ferguson (1723–1816)', in T. Raison (ed.), *The Founding Fathers of Social Science*. Harmondsworth: Penguin/New Society. pp. 17–26.

Maffesoli, M. (1996) *The Time of the Tribes*. London: Sage.

Mannheim. K. (1929) *Ideology and Utopia: An Introduction to the Sociology of Knowledge*. New York: Harcourt, Brace & World (1936).

Manning, B. (1991) *The English People and the English Revolution*. London: Bookmarks.

Marcuse, H. (1941) *Reason and Revolution: Hegel and the Rise of Social Theory*. London: Routledge & Kegan Paul.

Marshall, G. (1980) *Presbyteries and Profits: Calvinism and the Development of Capitalism in Scotland, 1560–1707*. Oxford: Clarendon Press.

Marvin, C. and David W. Ingle (1999) *Blood Sacrifice and the Nation: Totem Rituals and the American Flag*. Cambridge: Cambridge University Press.

Marx, K. (1843) 'Contribution to the Critique of Hegel's *Philosophy of Right: Introduction*', in Tucker (1978). pp. 53–65.

Marx, K. (1844) 'Economic and philosophical manuscripts', in D. McLellan (ed.), *Karl Marx: Selected Writings*. Oxford: Oxford University Press (2000). pp. 75–112.

Marx, K. (1845) 'Alienation and social classes (from *The Holy Family*)', in Tucker (1978). pp. 133–35.

Marx, K. (1847) *The Poverty of Philosophy*. Moscow: Progress Publishers (1975).

Marx, K. (1852) 'The Eighteenth Brumaire of Louis Napoleon', in David Fernbach (ed.), *Surveys From Exile: Political Writings Volume 2*. Harmondsworth and London: Penguin and New Left Review (1973). pp. 143–249.

Marx, K. (1854) 'The knight of noble consciousness', in *Marx and Engels Collected Works, 12:1853–54*. New York: International Publishers. pp. 479–508.

Marx, K. (1859) 'Marx on the history of his opinions', in Tucker (1978). pp. 2–6.

Marx, K. (1959) *Capital: Volume III*. London: Lawrence and Wishart.

Marx, K. (1973[1857–8]) *Grundrisse: Foundations of the Critique of Political Economy (Rough Draft)*. Harmondsworth: Penguin.

Marx, K. (1976[1867]) *Capital: Volume 1: A Critique of Political Economy*. Harmondsworth: Penguin.

Marx, K. (1999) 'Peuchet on suicide', in E.A. Plaut and K. Anderson (eds), *Marx on Suicide*. Evanston, IL.: Northwestern University Press. pp. 43–75.

Marx, K. and Engels, F. (1845–6) '*The German Ideology*: Part 1', in Tucker (1978) pp. 146–200.

Marx, K. and Engels, F. (1998[1848]) *The Communist Manifesto: A Modern Edition*. London and New York: Verso.

Massey, D. (1984) *Spatial Divisions of Labour: Social Structures and the Geography of Production*. London: Macmillan.

Mauss, M. (1927) 'Sociology: Its divisions and their relative weightings', in M. Mauss (2005) *The Nature of Sociology*. New York and Oxford: Durkheim Press/Berghahn Books, pp. 31–89.

Mauss, M. with H. Beuchat (1979) *Seasonal Variations of the Eskimo: A Study in Social Morphology*. London: Routledge & Kegan Paul.

McIntosh, I. (1997) *Classical Sociological Theory*. Edinburgh: Edinburgh University Press.

McLellan D. (1997) *Marx*. Glasgow: Fontana.

McLellan D. (2006) *Karl Marx: A Biography*. London: Palgrave Macmillan (fourth revised edition).

Meek, R.L. (1967) 'The Scottish contribution to Marxist sociology', in *Economics and Ideology and Other Essays*. London: Chapman and Hall. pp. 34–50.

Mellor, P.A. (2004) *Religion, Realism and Social Theory: Making Sense of Society*. London: Sage.

Merton, R. (1968) *Social Theory and Social Structure*. New York: Free Press.

Meštrović, S.G. (1993) *Émile Durkheim and the Reformation of Sociology*. Lanham, MD: Rowan & Littlefield.

Meszaros, I. (2005) *The Power of Ideology*. London: Zed Books.

Mitzman, A. (1985) *The Iron Cage: An Historical Interpretation of Max Weber*. New Brunswick, NJ: Transaction.

Mitzman, A. (1987) *Sociology and Estrangement: Three Sociologists of Imperial Germany*. New Brunswick, NJ: Transaction.

Mooers, C. (1991) *The Making of Bourgeois Europe: Absolutism, Revolution, and the Rise of Capitalism In England, France and Germany*. London: Verso.

Morrison, K. (2006) *Marx, Durkheim, Weber: Formations of Modern Thought*. London: Sage (second edition).

Neilson, D.A. (1999) *Three Faces of God: Society, Religion and the Categories of Totality in the Philosophy of Emile Durkheim*. Albany, NY: State University of New York.

Nisbet, R.A. (1993) *The Sociological Tradition*. New Brunswick, NJ: Transaction.

Olaveson, T. (2004) '"Connectedness" and the rave experience: Rave as new religious movement?', in G. St. John (ed.), *Rave Culture and Religion*. London: Routledge. pp. 85–106.

Orwell, George (2008[1947]) *1984*. London: Penguin.

Outhwaite, W. (1975) *Understanding Social Life: The Method Called Verstehen*. London: George Allen & Unwin.

Outhwaite, W. (2006) *The Future of Society*. Oxford: Blackwell.

Parkin, F. (1979) *The Marxist Theory of Class: A Bourgeois Critique*. London: Tavistock.

Parkin, F. (1992) *Durkheim*. Oxford and New York: Oxford University Press.

Parkin, F. (2002) *Max Weber*. London and New York: Routledge.

Parsons, T. (1949) *The Structure of Social Action*. New York: Free Press.

Perrin, R. (1995) 'Émile Durkheim's *Division of Labour* and the Shadow of Herbert Spencer', *The Sociological Quarterly*, 36 (4): 791–808.

bibliography

Pickering, M. (1993) *Auguste Comte: An Intellectual Biography, Volume 1.* Cambridge: Cambridge University Press.

Pickering, W.S.F. (1984) *Durkheim's Sociology of Religion: Themes and Theories.* London: Routledge & Kegan Paul.

Pickering, W.S.F. (ed.) (2000) *Durkheim and Representations.* London: Routledge.

Pickering, W.S.F. and Walford, G. (eds) (2000) *Durkheim's Suicide: A Century of Research and Debate.* London: Routledge.

Pines, C.L. (1993) *Ideology and False Consciousness: Marx and his Historical Progenitor.* Albany, NY: State University of New York Press.

Plaut, E.A. (1999) 'Marx on suicide in the context of other views of other views of suicide and of his life', in E.A. Plaut and K. Anderson (eds), *Marx on Suicide.* Evanston, IL: Northwestern University Press. pp. 29–40.

Poggi, G. (1993) *Money and the Modern Mind: George Simmel's Philosophy of Money.* Berkeley, CA: University of California Press.

Radkau, J. (2009) *Max Weber: A Biography.* Cambridge: Polity Press.

Ray, L.J. (1999) *Theorizing Classical Sociology.* Buckingham: Open University Press.

Remender, P.A. (1973) 'Social facts and symbolic interaction: A search for the key emergent in Durkheim's sociological analysis', *Wisconsin Sociologist*, 10 (4): 83–94.

Richards, E. (2000) *The Highland Clearances: People, Landlords and Rural Turmoil.* Edinburgh: Birlinn.

Ritzer, G. and Goodman, D.J. (2007) *Classical Sociological Theory.* New York: McGraw-Hill.

Robertson, R. (1992) *Globalisation: Social Theory and Global Culture.* London: Sage.

Robertson Smith, W. (2002 [1894]) *Religion of the Semites.* Brunswick, NJ.: Transaction.

Rosenberg, N. (1965) 'Adam Smith on the division of labour: Two views or one?', *Economica*, 32 (126): 127–139.

Runciman, W.G. (ed.) (1978) *Weber: Selections in Translation.* Cambridge: Cambridge University Press.

Schütz, A. (1970) *On Phenomenology and Social Relations: Selected Writings.* Chicago, IL: University of Chicago Press.

Scott, J. (2006) *Social Theory: Central Issues in Sociology.* London: Sage.

Shapiro, S. (2008) *How to Read Marx's Capital.* London: Pluto.

Shelton, B.A. and John, B. (1996) 'The division of household labour', *Annual Review of Sociology*, 22: 299–322.

Shilling, C. and Mellor, P.A. (1998) 'Durkheim, morality and modernity: Collective effervescence, Homo Duplex and the sources of moral action', *British Journal of Sociology*, 49 (2): 193–209.

Simmel, G. (1955) *Conflict and the Web of Group-Affiliations.* New York: Free Press.

Simmel, G. (1971) *Georg Simmel: On Individuality and Social Forms, Selected Writings.* D.N. Levine (ed.). Chicago and London: University of Chicago Press.

Simmel, G. (1976) 'The intersection of social spheres', in P.A. Lawrence (ed.), *Georg Simmel: Sociologist and European.* Sunbury: Nelson. pp. 95–110.

Simmel, G. (1900) *The Philosophy of Money.* London: Routledge.

Simmel, G. (1902) 'Tendencies in German life and thought since 1870', in D. Frisby (ed.), *Georg Simmel: Critical Assessments, Volume 1.* (1994). London: Routledge. pp. 5–27.

Simmel, G. (1997) *Simmel on Culture: Selected Writings*. D. Frisby and M. Featherstone (eds). London: Sage.

Simmel, G. (2009[1908]) *Sociology: Inquiries into the Construction of Social Forms*. Leiden: Brill.

Smith, A. (1952 [1776]) *An Inquiry into the Nature and Causes of the Wealth of Nations*. Chicago, IL: Encyclopaedia Britannica/University of Chicago.

Smith, G.W.H. (1994) 'Snapshots "*sub specie aeternitatis*": Simmel, Goffman and formal sociology', in D. Frisby (ed.), *Georg Simmel: Critical Assessments, Volume III*. London: Routledge. pp. 354–383.

Sorokin, P.A. (1927[1998]) *Social Mobility*. London: Routledge Thoemmes.

Spencer, H. (1971) *Structure, Function and Evolution*. London: Michael Joseph.

Spykman, N.J. (1925) *The Social Theory of Georg Simmel*. New Brunswick, NJ: Transaction (2004).

Stedman Jones, S. (2001) *Durkheim Reconsidered*. Cambridge: Polity Press.

Stoetzel, J. (2006) 'Sociology and demography', *Population*, 61: 19–28.

Strikwerda, R.A. (1997) 'An analysis of Alasdair MacIntyre's "Notes on Durkheim's Suicide"', *Durkheimian Studies*, 3: 59–72.

Swedberg, R. (1998) *Max Weber and the Idea of Economic Sociology*. Princeton, NJ: Princeton University Press.

Sweezy, P. (1950) 'A critique', in R. Hilton, (ed.) *The Transition From Feudalism to Capitalism*. London: Verso (1978).

Swingewood, A. (1970) 'Origins of sociology: The case of the Scottish Enlightenment', *British Journal of Sociology*, 21 (2): 164–180.

Therborn, G. (1976) *Science, Class and Society: On the Formation of Sociology and Historical Materialism*. London: NLB.

Therborn, G. (1999) *The Ideology of Power and the Power of Ideology*. London: Verso (new edition).

Thomas, P. (2008) *Marxism and Scientific Socialism: From Engels to Althusser*. London: Routledge.

Thompson, K. (2002) *Emile Durkheim*. London: Routledge (revised edition).

Tiryakian, E.A (2009) *For Durkheim: Essays in Historical and Cultural Sociology*. Aldershot: Ashgate.

Tönnies, F. (2002[1887]) *Community and Society: Gemeinschaft und Gesellschaft*. C.P. Loomis (ed.). Newton Abbot: David & Charles.

Traugott, M. (1984) 'Durkheim and social movements', *European Journal of Sociology*, 25 (2): 319–326.

Tucker, R.C. (ed.) (1978) *The Marx-Engels Reader*. New York: Norton (second edition).

Turner, B.S. (1999) *Classical Sociology*. London: Sage.

Turner, J.H. (1994) 'Marx and Simmel revisited: Reassessing the foundations of conflict theory', in D. Frisby (ed.), *Georg Simmel: Critical Assessments, Volume III*. London: Routledge.

Turner, J.H. (2001) 'The origins of positivism: The contributions of Auguste Comte and Herbert Spencer', in G. Ritzer and B. Smart (eds), *The Handbook of Social Theory*. London: Sage. pp. 30–42.

Varty, J. (1997) 'Civic or commercial? Adam Ferguson's concept of civil society', *Democratization*, 4 (1): 29–48.

Veblen, T. (1994[1899]) *The Theory of the Leisure Class*. New York: Dover.
Volosinov, V.N. (1973) *Marxism and the Philosophy of Language*. Cambridge, MA: Harvard University Press.
Wallerstein, I. (2004) *World-Systems Analysis: An Introduction*. Durham, NC: Duke University Press.
Weber, M. (1930[1905]) *The Protestant Ethic and the Spirit of Capitalism*. London: Unwin University Books.
Weber, M. (1946) 'Science as a vocation', in Gerth and Mills (1946). pp. 129–56.
Weber, M. (1949) *The Methodology of the Social Sciences*. E.A. Shils and H. Finch (eds). New York: Free Press.
Weber, M. (1978) *Economy and Society: An Outline of Interpretive Sociology, Volumes I and II*. Berkeley and Los Angeles, CA: University of California Press.
Weber, M. (2004) 'The "objectivity" of knowledge in Social Science and Social Policy' in Whimster (2004). pp. 359–404.
Weinstein, D. and Weinstein, M.A. (1993) *Postmodern(ized) Simmel*. London: Routledge.
Weiss, D.D. (1976) 'Marx versus Smith on the division of labour', *Monthly Review*, 28 (3): 104–118.
Wheen, F. (2000) *Karl Marx*. London: Fourth Estate.
Wheen, F. (2006) *Marx's Das Kapital: A Biography*. London: Allen & Unwin.
Whimster, S. (ed.) (2004) *The Essential Weber: A Reader*. London: Routledge.
Williams, R. (1980) *Problems in Materialism and Culture: Selected Essays*. London: Verso Editions and NLB.
Wirth, L. (1938) 'Urbanism as a way of life', *The American Journal of Sociology*, XLIV (1): 1–24.
Wolff, K. (ed.) (1950) *The Sociology of Georg Simmel*. New York: The Free Press.
Wood, A.W. (2004) *Karl Marx*. London: Routledge.
Wright, E.O. (1985) *Classes*. London: Verso.
Zeitlin, I.M. (1990) *Ideology and the Development of Sociological Theory*. Englewood Cliffs, NJ: Prentice-Hall (fourth edition).
Zieleniec, A. (2007) *Space and Social Theory*. London: Sage.
Žižek, S. (ed.) (1994) *Mapping Ideology*. London: Verso.

key concepts in classical social theory